the cinema of MICHAEL WINTERBOTTOM

DIRECTORS' CUTS

the cinema of
MICHAEL WINTERBOTTOM

borders, intimacy, terror

Bruce Bennett

 **WALLFLOWER PRESS** LONDON & NEW YORK

A Wallflower Press Book
Published by
Columbia University Press
Publishers Since 1893
New York • Chichester, West Sussex
cup.columbia.edu

A complete CIP record is available from the Library of Congress

ISBN 978-0-231-16736-9 (cloth : alk. paper)
ISBN 978-0-231-16737-6 (pbk. : alk. paper)
ISBN 978-0-231-85053-7 (e-book)

Series design by Rob Bowden Design

Cover image of Michael Winterbottom courtesy of the Kobal Collection

Columbia University Press books are printed on permanent
and durable acid-free paper.
This book is printed on paper with recycled content.
Printed in the United States of America

c 10 9 8 7 6 5 4 3 2 1
p 10 9 8 7 6 5 4 3 2 1

CONTENTS

ACKNOWLEDGEMENTS

Thank you to Clem Blakemore at Revolution Films, and also to Michael Winter-bottom for taking the time to speak to me. Thank you too to Yoram Allon at Wall-flower Press for being flexible and enthusiastic.

At various points in its development, conversations with my good friends Lisa Baraitser, Marc Furstenau, Katarzyna Marciniak, Jules Pidduck, Jackie Stacey and Paul Sutton have been very important in helping me to formulate aspects of the project.

Most valuable of all in completing this book has been the support of my partner, Imogen Tyler. Sections of chapter four are adapted from a piece we co-wrote on Winterbottom and border cinema, but more generally this couldn't have been written without her editorial advice, patience and encouragement.

'I've never met anyone quite like you before' ('Temptation', New Order)

This book is for Imogen.

INTRODUCTION

Whether it is understood primarily as art or commodity, or a complex double articulation of both, cinema is a medium infused with the potential to challenge and reconfigure prevailing 'ways of seeing'; it makes particular (real and imaginary) faces, bodies, communities, spaces and landscapes visible, while leaving others out of focus, obscured or beyond the frame. A film's soundtrack gives voice to certain real or fictional figures while leaving others indiscernible, distorted or mute. Film narratives put linear temporalities into play, through repetitions, elisions, flashbacks, anachronisms and non-chronological plot structures, slowing, accelerating or stopping time. Film narratives can stretch, compress and loop time. The choices made during a film's planning, production and editing with regard to which images we see, and how these images are combined with other images and with sounds are necessarily political decisions that direct both our gaze as it scans the frame, and our consequent interpretation of sequences of images. In this book I explore how a film can either reinforce a dominant 'régime of visibility' or, by focusing on subaltern figures or on border spaces that are typically excluded from view or at the blurred peripheries of our vision, it can contest dominant aesthetic regimes and contribute to the construction of resistant or multiple 'image régimes' (Rancière 2006: 22). Criticism may be understood as similarly political since analysis, interpretation and theory work to make visible certain texts, aesthetic objects, styles, perspectives or meanings. In directing attention towards particular passages, details or motifs of a film, as well as to relevant critical writing and to the social and historical contexts of the film, this book's critical discussion will filter, refract, magnify or illuminate the politics of cinematic images.

This introductory chapter sets out the main critical, conceptual and thematic concerns of this book's analysis of Winterbottom's cinematic oeuvre. I begin by considering three of the key categorical frameworks through which the director's work is often interpreted, and through which its heterogeneity is contained: 'genre', 'national cinema' and 'authorship'. While Winterbottom's films are commonly discussed in relation to these conventional critical frames, my argument is that to do so is, in effect, to miss the ways in which this body of work functions to trouble these generic categorisations, putting them into play. Indeed, in so far as Winterbottom's cinema can be understood as political, in so far as it is engaged with exposing, rupturing or queering prevailing cinematic norms, the politics of 'his' filmmaking praxis stems in part from a concern continually to breach categorical borders in relation to cinema – borders between art and commodity, media borders between film and television, geographical and political borders between regions and nations, imagined borders between communities and classes, gendered borders between men and women, and intimate borders between individuals and bodies. In this respect, the border and its transgression is a recurrent motif in Winterbottom's work and also in my examination of it. This motif brings together formal and thematic properties of the work with a sympathetic and appropriate critical framing in its examination of the political aesthetics of the films.

The three main chapters of the book are thus concerned with the inter-related ways in which Winterbottom's work approaches the question of borders. In chapter two, the treatment of intimacy is discussed through an analysis of *Go Now* (1995), *The Trip* (2010), *Code 46* (2003), *9 Songs* (2004), *Butterfly Kiss* (1995) and *The Killer Inside Me* (2010). Intimacy is the figure through which these films and programmes explore the borders between individuals and the variously violent, intense, moving and erotic transgression of these boundaries. These examples are also concerned with the unbreachability of these borders and the impossibility of intimacy. The third chapter focuses upon the over-determined relationship between nation and cinematic genre in its discussion of *With or Without You* (1999), *Jude* (1996), *The Claim* (2000), *A Cock and Bull Story* (2005) and *24 Hour Party People* (2002). This chapter examines the way in which Winterbottom's films interrogate and trouble the borders between genres and the destabilising effect this has on the conceptual integrity of regional and national borders and of a bounded national culture represented in and constituted by such genres as the heritage or costume film. The fourth chapter is concerned primarily with depictions of the War on Terror in Winterbottom's work and examines the way in which anxieties about national border security in response to economic and political migration and the spectacular terrorist attacks of September 2001 shaped policy and international relations as well as the thematic preoccupations of popular film and television and the press. Through an analysis of *The Shock Doctrine* (2009), *In this World* (2002), *A Mighty Heart* (2007) and *The Road to Guantánamo* (2006), this chapter explores the ways in which Winterbottom's films offer an alternative perspective on the narration of the War on Terror and its ramifications within news media and popular culture, inviting us to consider both the potential and the limitations of politically critical cinema. To some extent the critical themes explored in these three chapters in relation to each group of films might be traced across other films and, by way of illustration, the first chapter examines the way that the thematic, formal and stylistic features explored throughout the book intersect in a single film, through an analysis of *Welcome to Sarajevo* (1997).

Inter-generic cinema

I want to begin by suggesting that one of the characteristic features of Michael Winterbottom's films is a self-conscious and sophisticated attention to the film image as well as to the mediating processes of contemporary culture. Rather than simply adopting and refining the formal and narrative conventions of mainstream film and television, this body of work displays a restless, playfully heterogeneous and experimental audio-visual style in its representation of this world (as well as a variety of fictional and dystopian worlds such as the technologically advanced and socially unequal future depicted in *Code 46*). As one reviewer writes, 'Cinematic realism embraces an abundance of styles and production methods; Michael Winterbottom seems determined to try them all' (Arthur 2006: 71). In working through the formal and technical permutations available to filmmakers, Winterbottom's films make visible the dominant aesthetic conventions of contemporary film and television not from the oppositional perspective of a Godardian 'counter-cinema', but from the financially precarious, semi-independent position of a director working on the margins of mainstream commercial cinema (Wollen 1985). In this book I will argue that this stylistic promiscuity is not gratuitous or empty – although it is sometimes deployed lightly and to ambiguous or comic effect – but that it is a sign that Winterbottom and his collaborators are casting around for modes of expression that are adequate and appropriate to the themes explored in the films. I suggest that Winterbottom's work demonstrates a consistent concern with the political potential of popular film and, to a lesser but nonetheless significant extent, television. This concern has perhaps been most evident in the recent sequence of films that have depicted the consequences of the global War on Terror conducted by the US and its allies: *In This World, The Road to Guantánamo* and *A Mighty Heart*. However, a political sensibility and a strong social commitment runs throughout his work from his earliest TV dramas, such as *Love Lies Bleeding* (1993), which follows a convicted killer/political prisoner seeking revenge for his girlfriend's murder while on 24-hour home leave from the Maze prison outside Belfast in Northern Ireland. With their focus upon characters caught at the uncomfortable borders between social classes, nations, regions, cultures, and bodies, or in the heterotopic spaces of prisons and internment camps, the majority of Winterbottom's films and TV dramas depict spaces, landscapes, relationships and individuals that are largely peripheral to mainstream cinema and television. In this respect his work follows in a certain tradition of (British) realist cinema which turned the camera lens towards working-class communities and experience, but what makes the films of Michael Winterbottom a valuable and challenging focus for thinking through the relationship between politics and contemporary cinema, is the distinctive ways in which they are preoccupied with transnational régimes of visibility.

Indeed, while his work traverses the generic territory associated with British cinema, individual films correspond only loosely to the types of film that have come to represent (however inaccurately) archetypes of British filmmaking. Instead, Winterbottom's films frequently cross the boundaries between apparently distinct or incompatible genres, breaching the systems of expectation that they comprise. Winterbottom has directed several costume dramas, for example, producing three adaptations of novels by Thomas Hardy, *Jude, The Claim* and *Trishna* (2011), as well as *A Cock and Bull Story*, a *film à clef* treatment of Lawrence Sterne's novel, *The Life and Opinions of Tristram Shandy, Gentleman* (1759–67), and the films can be read as interrogations of the restricted conventions of this emblematic field of national cinema. Claire Monk has argued that *Jude* can be understood as a 'post-heritage' film, refusing the ideologically and formally conservative formations of many literary adaptations of the 1980s and 1990s through its dramatisation of what Julianne Pidduck terms the 'hard labour of class mobility' in its characters' progression through the narrative (Monk 1995, Pidduck 2004). *The Claim* is a reframing of *The Mayor of Casterbridge* (1886) that relocates the narrative from Wessex to the American frontier, citing such revisionist New Hollywood westerns as *McCabe and Mrs Miller* (Robert Altman, 1971) and *Heaven's Gate* (Michael Cimino, 1980) in its plotting and *mise-en-scène*. Situating the action at a literal and metaphorical distance from the setting of the novel enables the film to tell the story of immigrant experience, of European settlers trying to establish a home for themselves in a hostile environment in which almost all relationships and decisions are negotiated or weighed in financial terms. *A Cock and Bull Story* meanwhile reproduces the complex, self-reflexive, meta-narrative structure of the source novel, embedding filmed sequences from the novel within an account of a film crew's chaotic attempt to make the film of Sterne's book.

Interviewed during the production of *Genova* (2008), Winterbottom described that film as situated 'between genres', and this idea of a film as an interstitial inter-generic text that traces the borders between categories and juxtaposes incompatible or unexpected elements is helpful for understanding the heterogeneous form of his films more generally (Farndale 2007). A number of his films are difficult to locate in generic terms, borrowing elements from different types of film with *9 Songs* perhaps the most radical example in its matter-of-fact collision of explicitly sexual art cinema with the concert documentary (although, there is a logic to this abutment of classes of film since both genres similarly offer spectators the thrill of vicarious participation through the appearance of documentary authenticity).

I Want You (1998), meanwhile, is shot like an American neo-*noir* film from the 1980s or early 1990s with chiaroscuro lighting, non-naturalistic colour filters and a vivid colour scheme dominated by saturated reds, yellows, blues and greens. Spaces and characters are colour-coded and many shots are almost monochromatic. The film opens with a bound body dragged across a beach at night and dumped into the sea and this is followed by a montage in which we see Martin (played by the American actor Alessandro Nivola) hitching a lift and arriving on the empty outskirts of a rather desolate town. Over the course of the film we learn that he has returned to this town, Haven, after serving eight years of a prison sentence for murdering the father of his under-age lover, hairdresser Helen. He longs to resume their relationship, but is hesitant and torn (partly because his parole conditions require him not to contact her) while she is reluctant to meet him and is currently in an unhappy relationship with the local radio DJ. It is revealed at the end of the film that in fact it was Helen who murdered her own father when he discovered the two lovers, and that Martin took the blame to protect her. Schematically, this story of fatal love, violence and Oedipal desires, a *femme fatale* and a love-struck dupe in the context of a small town corresponds well to the framework of the neo-*noir* film. As if to emphasise this generic affinity, one self-reflexive scene shows Martin and others watching the similarly stylised neo-noir thriller *Romeo is Bleeding* (Peter Medak, 1993)[1] on TV, and there is also a brief excerpt of dialogue from *Red Rock West* (John Dahl, 1992). However, there are some significant deviations from the generic model. The story takes place in a wintry English seaside town and the superimposition of this American narrative template which belongs in California or a dusty small town in the Mid-West, onto an English coastal town produces a sense of dislocation that corresponds to a central thematic concern with displacement or estrangement.

One of the film's key characters is Honda, a voluntarily mute orphan from former Yugoslavia who lives with his older sister, Smokey, in a wooden fisherman's shack on the beach. His status is left unclear, although the fact that he does not appear to attend school may indicate that he is an illegal immigrant, and his origin is only revealed obliquely through a brief glimpse of a letter addressed to Yugoslavia that he keeps in a suitcase along with old family photographs and a scrap of Yugoslavian newspaper. Like sound recordists Harry Caul in *The Conversation* (Francis Ford Coppola, 1974) or Jack Terry in *Blow Out* (Brian De Palma, 1981) he is a voyeur or spy, documentarist or filmmaker, surreptitiously recording erotic and violent encounters around the town with his tape recorder and long-range directional microphone. A motif associated with Honda is the unfocused image suggesting that he has a confused, distorted or alienated relationship with his surroundings, one that is managed by mediation. Scenes in which Honda is recording often have a shot/reverse shot or eyeline-match structure, cutting between images of Honda listening, and shots of the action he is observing, which are frequently visually and aurally distorted. The visual disintegration of the image – which is blurred, sometimes abstract, sometimes oscillating, sometimes employing close-up shots of a video monitor – simulates the electronically mediated sound Honda hears in his headphones and that we hear on the soundtrack. The teenage boy is a key character in so far as the film appears to depict events from his perspective using these point-of-view shots, internal flashbacks, and the (non-diegetic) voice-over in the film's opening scene which is presumably delivered by him, although we never *see* him speak and never again hear him. In his watchful silence he remains a critical presence and as a surrogate spectator, offers us a point of identification at once within and outside the narrative. Although they interact with Martin and Helen, the couple at the centre of the drama, Honda and Smokey remain more or less incidental to the conventional *noir* narrative. Nevertheless, they function to defamiliarise the film; they are a diverting intrusion into the flow of the narrative through, for example, the intermittent scenes in which Smokey has sex with several partners or sings in the club with her band, through Honda's collision with Helen as she crashes into him while cycling along the promenade in the opening scene, or through the climactic scene in which Honda smashes a bottle on Martin's head interrupting his rape of Helen.

In this respect a generic clash enables the film to articulate something quite different from the fetishistic, solipsistic, hermetically self-referential and reassuringly fictional reworking of American genre cinema that can be found in some recent *noir* films. Instead, the film employs this stylistic disjunction to render an aspect of contemporary immigrant experience – alienated, marginalised (consigned to the border-zone of the beach), experiencing difficulty in communication, situated at a voyeuristic distance. In this respect the film is a counterpart to Winterbottom's previous feature film, *Welcome to Sarajevo*, which also concerned a child from former Yugoslavia albeit one adopted by a British family and welcomed into a secure middle-class household, rather than living as an outsider on the marginal space of the seashore. Although we learn little about Honda and his sister they nevertheless provide a point of anchorage or identification. In other words, the generic incongruity is not arbitrary or gratuitous and not a matter of incompetence, indecision, or compromise induced by conflict between commercial prudence and self-conscious experimentalism. It is carried through to the film's visual style which employs systematic graphic discontinuities such as a pattern of cutting between shots with different colour casts, following a yellow shot with green, then red, then blue shots.

Of course, the narrative marginalisation of these characters means that the film's treatment of immigrant experience in contemporary Britain remains indirect and suggestive. This is not to suggest that *I Want You* fails adequately to address contemporary concerns with the plight of asylum-seekers, refugees and illegal immigrants in Britain. As a melodramatic thriller the film's literal and affective focus lies elsewhere – and indeed other more or less contemporary films like *Last Resort* (Pawel Pawlikowski, 2000),[2] as well as Winterbottom's own *In This World* explore this issue more directly and emotively – although it is notable that *I Want You* constitutes a rapid and early cinematic response to the issue of immigration that has become much more prominent and divisive due to the disastrous fallout from the War on Terror. It is indicative of the journalistic tendency that runs through Winterbottom's work. However, my argument here is that the film's strategy is representative of a broader tendency in Winterbottom's work, which is to work with a popular form such as the neo-*noir* film or the historical costume drama, while modifying and extending the form, pulling at threads and unravelling some sections, discarding integral components or splicing together elements in unlikely or intriguing combinations. This approach results in films that have the structural quality of patchwork with ideas and images juxtaposed and organised in a provisional assemblage rather than in tightly linear fashion following a causal progression.

In breaching conventional genre boundaries through such strategies as displacement (of story and characters from one location to another), *I Want You* makes visible such boundaries, foregrounding and, arguably, interrogating them as a means of representing or formally embodying the experience of dislocation or displacement (and uncertainty/danger) experienced by certain characters.

Marketing inter-generic films

The tendency of Winterbottom's work to upset generic systems of expectation has undoubtedly also made the distribution and marketing of the films difficult. The dynamic trailer for *Code 46*, for instance, suggests that the film is a futuristic, erotic Hollywood detective thriller in the manner of *Blade Runner* (Ridley Scott, 1982) and the dramatic voice-over, delivered in deep, masculine tones and American accent explains: 'Now … an investigator with a unique gift … is about to forget everything he knows … to save the woman he loves.' The 'unique gift' of extraordinary insight or perceptiveness, is actually an effect of an 'empathy virus' the corporate investigator has been infected with to help him do his job, and it is this virus that appears to lead him to behave erratically and to fall in love with the woman he is investigating. Again, there is a schematic *film noir* narrative underlying the film, and the screenwriter Frank Cottrell Boyce has also suggested that the film originated with Winterbottom's idea for an adaptation of Sophocles' *Oedipus Rex* with its theme of determinism or inescapable destiny. However, the trailer's condensation of the film disregards the characters' ambivalence and lack of agency as well as the film's oneiric mood and pace, in order to recast it as a tense action film.[3]

The no longer extant promotional website for *A Cock and Bull Story*, on the other hand, made a virtue of that film's undecidable 'narrative image', to use John Ellis's term (or perhaps its narrative image of undecidability), by making the problematic marketability of the film its central theme (Ellis 1990: 24). The complex website, which mimics the infinitely regressive structures of the film and source novel, looks like a computer desktop with a recycling bin, email inbox and document folders and is described therein as a 'Metasite'. It also includes a link to the 'real' site that resembles a more conventional promotional website on which can be viewed a trailer, plot synopsis, and various files available for downloading. The email messages stored in the inbox on the Metasite recount discussions about the organisation and content of the website and the production and release schedule of the film and DVD. Some of the emails have attachments that include the film's production notes or an MP3 file

The promotional website for *A Cock and Bull Story*

of an interview with Winterbottom. One of the deleted emails ironically records the rejection of an intern's suggestion that 'the Web site should be a really fun Web site about making a Web site for a postmodern movie about making a movie based on the first postmodern novel', while the recycling bin on the desktop contains nine rejected designs for the one-sheet poster, each of which ascribes a slightly different generic character to the film (the funniest of which has the candid tagline: 'It's Difficult to Explain').

Cinema, nations and borders

In the early 1960s, French critic and director François Truffaut conducted several interviews with Alfred Hitchcock that were transcribed and later compiled and published as 'The Definitive Study' on Hitchcock. During a discussion of the early stages of Hitchcock's career, before he was employed by Hollywood producer David O. Selznick, Truffaut asks Hitchcock, 'Well, to put it quite bluntly, isn't there a certain incompatibility between the terms, "cinema" and "Britain"?' (Truffaut 1986: 170). Enquiring after the reasons why Hitchcock worked mainly for American film studios from 1940 onwards, Truffaut speculates that Britain is a particularly unsuitable context for a filmmaker:

> This may sound far-fetched, but I get the feeling that there are national characteristics – among them the English countryside, the subdued way of life, the stolid routine – that are anti-dramatic in a sense. The weather itself is anticinematic. Even British humor – that very understatement on which so many of the good crime comedies are hinged – is somehow a deterrent to strong emotion. (Ibid.)

He concludes that, apart from Hitchcock, with regard to international cinema the only other historically significant British filmmaker was Charlie Chaplin. Hitchcock agrees (predictably enough) with Truffaut's assessment, and recalls the comparative insularity of British culture, although he ascribes the anti-cinematic culture of Britain to a strong class system, suggesting that before 1925, 'No well-bred English person would be seen going into a cinema; it simply wasn't done' (Hitchcock in Truffaut 1986: 171). Until the 1920s, he states, cinema was 'held in contempt by the intellectuals' (ibid.). Surprisingly, Truffaut's mildly provocative question, which was presumably calculated to prompt Hitchcock to respond with some reflections on British culture and the cinema, continues to provoke an indignant defence of British cinema and its unfairly overlooked strengths. Almost always taken out of context, or misquoted and rephrased as if it were a statement, Truffaut's question is typically treated as a dismissive value judgement upon British films by defensive British academics, journalists and filmmakers. For example, a recent article on British cinema opens with a quotation from director Stephen Frears (director of the Academy Award-winning transnational co-production, *The Queen* (2006)) speaking in a documentary about British cinema entitled 'Typically British':

The great French filmmaker, François Truffaut, once famously said that there was a certain incompatibility between the words British and Cinema. Well, bollocks to Truffaut. (Lovell 2001: 200)

In this inaccurate paraphrasing of Truffaut, Frears reframes Truffaut's comment not as a tentatively provocative question about an unstable national cinema culture made in the course of a conversation, but as a flatly dismissive statement about the value of British films by a Frenchman. Frears suggests that Truffaut's disparaging comments about British cinema are motivated by national rivalry and professional competitiveness and his comically abusive response to this presumed slight invokes the nationalism that is almost always associated with discourses of national (cultural) identity. This epigraph appears in an essay by Alan Lovell concerned with the perception of British cinema both within and outside the country, and this article concludes with an impassioned defence of the importance or worth of British films:

Arguments can be made that comparable cinemas like the French or Italian have, over their whole history, been superior to the British cinema but the differences are only relative ones. British cinema isn't a special case. There isn't some fundamental British cinematic deficiency which needs to be accounted for. Bollocks to Truffaut, indeed! (Lovell 2001: 204)

However, the idea of films produced and circulated within an 'anti-cinematic' culture is intriguing and warrants further consideration. For a classicist like Truffaut, of course, 'cinema' is implicitly defined with reference to Hollywood melodrama and is constituted by strong emotion, high-key lighting (or bright Californian sunlight), narrative integrity and strong causality, formal unity, superficial naturalism, and expressive, foregrounded *mise-en-scène*. Obviously, such a model of cinema is neither definitive nor necessarily desirable, and thus we need not see the incompatibility of 'Britain' or 'Britishness' with such a concept of cinema as a failure, or even a point to contest. Instead we might see it as an acknowledgement of the heterogeneity of global cinema, and – insofar as it is helpful to generalise in this way – we might, for instance, think of British cinema as a field of tensions and incongruence, riven with political/cultural/aesthetic fault lines. As represented by Winterbottom's films, this is a cinema of borders. Indeed, we might argue that those British films that explore such incoherence are far more fascinating and challenging than those that aspire to formal, narrative and ideological unities. Taken literally, Truffaut's passing remark might serve as the basis for conceptualising a British 'cinema of incompatibility' that does not depend on limited, unitary categories, but rather puts these categories into play. On the face of it Truffaut's caricature of the typicalities of British culture – subjugation and impassivity, emotional repression, understated comedy, overcast climate and over-present, over-determined landscape – is echoed in many of Winterbottom's films, prompting journalist Geraldine Bedell to write, 'If I had to put together a Michael Winterbottom retrospective, I'd call it "Struggle Actually"' (Bedell 2004).[5] *Wonderland* (1999), for example, is described by Charlotte Brunsdon as epitomising 'the melodrama of everyday life' in its depiction of cheerless life in contemporary London, while *I Want You*, is set in the vacant, desolate spaces of an out-of-season seaside town on the south coast, and *Butterfly Kiss*, Winterbottom's first theatrical release, is a road movie that narrates the murderous progress of a serial killer and her lover along the A-roads and motorways of north west England, climaxing with one drowning the other compassionately in the shallows of Morecambe Bay (Brunsdon 2004: 61).

More generally, the notion of an 'incompatible cinema' whose constituent elements remain incongruent and in tension, is richly suggestive. Rather than describing an aesthetically homogeneous and commercially stable national cinema intrinsic to the country's imaginary and material cultural heritage and that serves to embody and assert an instrumental national identity, it suggests instead a financially precarious and heterogeneous constellation of films and filmmakers and circuits of distribution. The films produced in Truffaut's anti-cinematic Britain emerge within a mercurial and insubstantial commercial and industrial infrastructure and might (partly as a direct consequence of these conditions of production) be characterised by non-linear narratives or a profusion of meta-narratives, and scattered or episodic story-telling structures that defy resolution. They might explore formal experimentation and anti-realism, visual and graphic, spatial and temporal discontinuities and disjunctive relationships between sound and image. These are films that are concerned with anxiety and uncertainty, repression and misrecognition, with divisions and irreconcilable emotional and ideological conflicts, peripherality and the marginal. They are films that elicit ambiguous responses from viewers and that show us figures traversing and becoming stranded in unfamiliar, alienating and disorienting spaces and landscapes.

As will be discussed later, the critical concept of national cinema is immensely problematic with discourses of national cinema often bound up with defensive, nationalistic claims. One of the key points of interest of Winterbottom's films is their complicated relationship to what might be termed British cinema and their implicit insistence that conventional categories of British film are inadequate as an interpretive framework or useful account of the context in which he works. So, situating them within a dispersed field of incompatible cinema allows us to approach questions of meaning and effect from a productive alternative perspective.

Authorship

There is a certain tendency of film criticism and historiography to identify selected film directors as autonomous creative artists with a superior sensibility for whom a film is a means of personal expression. The director is represented as a forceful and almost inevitably masculine individual, often working in a frequently hostile or unsupportive context, whose work is marked by a signature style, intellectual complexity or thematic bias. As André Bazin observes, when adopted as a codified critical policy, as was the case at *Cahiers du Cinéma*, the film journal he co-founded and edited through the 1950s, 'the *politique des auteurs* consists, in short, of choosing the personal factor in artistic creation as a standard of reference, and then assuming that it continues and even progresses from one film to the next' (Bazin 1985: 255). In these terms, the director's biography serves as an interpretive key to the film text, which in turn may be read as an encrypted and obliquely metaphorical autobiographical statement. This concept of the film director as originary *auteur* is politically and technically problematic[6] and among the limitations of an author-centred approach to film criticism is the risk of 'suspending' the films from their economic, social and historical contexts. Winterbottom himself has dismissed the critical over-valuation of the director as *auteur* as a misrepresentation of the collaborative filmmaking process:

> I find that attitude ludicrous because filmmaking is either an industrial or a collaborative process, whichever way you want to describe it. So to have this bourgeois, liberal-romantic idea of the creator seems to me like the ultimate perversion. (Winterbottom in Gilbey 2004: 31)

Among other things, what is excluded from and effaced by such accounts is the collective labour of many people, their knowledge and experience, and the complexity of the creative processes that go into making a film; the industrial infrastructures from which even an *avant-garde* film must emerge, and the systems of distribution by which films are broadcast and circulated tend to be marginalised or disregarded.

It is necessary to stress that there are several Michael Winterbottoms under discussion here. First of all there is an individual who has been centrally involved in various capacities in the production of a set of films and television programmes. Born in March, 1961, in Blackburn, a large post-industrial town in the north of England, he was educated at the local grammar school, from where he won a place to study English Literature as an undergraduate at Oxford University, and then took a postgraduate course at film school in Bristol. From there he got a job in television as an assistant editor before working as a researcher on a documentary by director Lindsay Anderson on British cinema. On the basis of this experience he was able to direct several television films and documentaries of varying lengths.[7] With Andrew Eaton, who produced *Family* (Michael Winterbottom, 1994), he set up the production company Revolution Films in 1994, which has produced most of his subsequent films as well as work by other directors.

A second Michael Winterbottom, the publicly visible figure, is generated through the circuits of publicity and marketing. Winterbottom is an articulate and voluble interviewee and his frequent participation in TV, newspaper and magazine interviews constructs a public persona for the director. This assemblage is complicated or multiplied by the proliferation of fictional representations of the director in circulation in and around Winterbottom's work, despite the director's protestations that his work is not directly self-referential.[8] These include the taciturn, laconic Mark, who is directing the adaptation of Lawrence Sterne's novel in *A Cock and Bull Story*, the director, Mark Morrison in the novel *Descent* (2004), by Winterbottom's ex-wife Sabrina Broadbent, as well as the multiple, more or less fictional, more or less self-referential story-tellers scattered across the films that perhaps also function as projections or representations of aspects of Winterbottom's character or operations: among these are the journalists Tony Wilson (*24 Hour Party People*), Michael Henderson (*Welcome to Sarajevo*), and Mariane Pearl (*A Mighty Heart*), Tristram Shandy the unreliable self-mythologizing narrator, Paul Raymond the self-promotional pornographer and entrepreneur (*The Look of Love*, 2013), Honda the secretive sound recordist (*I Want You*), Jude the artisan, Matt the glaciologist (*9 Songs*), Lou Ford the serial killer (*The Killer Inside Me*), Miriam, the infatuated partner of a serial killer (*Butterfly Kiss*), and William Geld the emotionally compromised detective in *Code 46* (played by Tim Robbins who happens to bear a striking resemblance to the director).

In discussing Winterbottom's cinema, this volume is not concerned with identifying or perversely reintroducing a 'bourgeois, liberal-romantic' idea at the source of the films. Instead it is primarily concerned with identifying and tracing a set of distinctive stylistic and thematic characteristics that run through this body of work for which 'Michael Winterbottom' is the sign. 'Winterbottom' is in this respect an author-function in Michel Foucault's terms, a conjectural, partial figure produced by or inferred from these films and related texts (Foucault 1977). In this respect the construct derived from the films also serves to represent the work of a great many people (and of course it does not preclude other ways of framing the work that may be equally productive or accurate). As Peter Wollen argues in a critical re-evaluation of *auteur* analysis in relation to the emphasis placed upon the text in structuralist theory:

> *Auteur* analysis does not consist of tracing a film to its origins, to its creative source. It consists of tracing a structure (not a message) within the work, which can then *post factum* be ascribed to an individual, the director, on empirical grounds ... Fuller or Hawks or Hitchcock, the directors, are quite separate from 'Fuller' or 'Hawks' or 'Hitchcock', the structures named after them, and should not be methodologically confused ... the situation in the cinema, where the director's primary task is one of coordination and rationalisation, is very different from that in the other arts, where there is a much more direct relationship between artist and work. It is in this sense that it is possible to speak of a film *auteur* as an unconscious catalyst (Wollen 1992: 602)

It is arguable that no matter how direct the relationship between the artist and the work, and whatever the scale of the artistic or creative production, the artist remains an unconscious catalyst. Following Roland Barthes's 1968 essay, 'The Death of the Author', we might argue that in cinema just as in literature, 'a text is made of multiple writings, drawn from many cultures and entering into mutual relations of dialogue, parody, contestation, but there is one place where this multiplicity is focused and that place is the reader, not, as was hitherto said, the author' (Barthes 1977: 148). For Barthes, 'the text is a tissue of quotations drawn from the innumerable centres of culture', and this concept of a layered, complexly allusive text describes well the structure of Winterbottom's films, as if they take this intertextuality as a central aesthetic principle (ibid.).

In any case, this discussion of Winterbottom's work retains the distinction between Winterbottom and 'Winterbottom' indicated by Wollen above, and so is not concerned with mapping the films onto the biographical profile or psychic composition of Michael Winterbottom. The book's approach is also modulated to recognise that 'Winterbottom' is the composite sign of multiple authors. This is not to say that every member of the filmmaking team has an equivalent creative role, and nor is it to indicate that the conventional hierarchies of film production have been abandoned or deliberately challenged in the production of these films (in spite of the name of Winterbottom's production company, 'Revolution'). Indeed, there remain very few examples of the sort of radically politicised collective filmmaking practice employed by, say, Newcastle-upon-Tyne's Amber Films. However, as Berys Gaut observes in a discussion of the critical fetishism of the *auteur*, 'there is no aspect of the finished film which can be attributed solely to the director's activity by virtue of his directorial role. The director is someone who supervises others. When we survey artistically significant aspects of the film … we see the results of others' actions, actions supervised by the director and not attributable to him alone' (Gaut 1997: 136).

The frequency with which Winterbottom has worked with certain actors, composers, screenwriters, technicians and crew members (such as Trevor Waite, editor of eleven of his films and Marcel Zyskind, cinematographer on ten), is a clear indication of the importance in this work of collaboration or collective labour. It means that these films must be understood, to some extent at least, as jointly or collectively authored texts that cannot be 'explained' as Winterbottom's own. Beyond the scale of personal filmmaking, collaboration is a practical necessity of film production, and presumably the primary attraction for Winterbottom and Eaton of working repeatedly with certain individuals is predictability and ease; maintaining a working relationship from one project to the next allows for the development of an understanding among collaborators and efficient communication. As the director comments in a TV documentary on the production of *A Cock and Bull Story*, 'We all know each other. We all know how we work, so at times of stress you at least know that there's a relationship to fall back on.'[9] Perhaps as a result of this familiarity, it seems that Winterbottom's directorial touch is relatively light and he explains, 'I never really give any directions to any actors. I just hope they get on with it and do their stuff. I wouldn't presume to tell them how to act because that's their job.'[10] This is confirmed by Steve Coogan, who observes of his method, 'There's very little said. You know, he comes up and says, "Maybe try that a bit quicker or slower". He says very little but you kind of understand what he wants. I don't know. It's almost by osmosis.'[11] One effect of this minimal direction, as Shirley Henderson observes, is the sense for an actor that, 'Whatever you do is not wrong. He never makes you feel what you've done is not good or it's bad. It's just something that you've offered up and let's try something else now.'[12] Henderson's sense that the performers are invited to offer up material collaboratively is encouraged by the reliance upon improvisation during shooting. As Coogan recounts, 'the thing with Michael's films is, because so much of it is improvised, in so much of it you can just carry on. He doesn't call, "cut", quite often for a long time, and his middle name is "one more"'.[13] This final comment is a reference to the frequency with which the director asks the cast and crew to repeat scenes. This is not so much because he has a precise sense of how, say, a particular line should be delivered, but, on the contrary, because he is concerned with generating plenty of coverage, which will give the editors as much flexibility as possible during the assembly of the film in post-production. As Winterbottom explains:

> There's a script for the scenes, which is maybe seven or eight lines, so the idea is that we do various versions of that idea. In this way if you're shooting ten minutes or fifteen minutes or twenty minutes for a scene which is only four lines of dialogue, obviously you have a lot of choice about content later, so you're delaying some of the decision until the cutting room.[14]

As Berys Gaut notes, one of the reasons why the concept of the *auteur* has taken hold so powerfully within discourses on cinema is that 'The dominant paradigm for understanding films has been a literary one' (Gaut 1997: 167). French critic Alexandre Astruc's influential 1948 concept of the *caméra-stylo* (camera-pen) as wielded by the director is the most stylishly condensed example of this equation of filmmaking with expressive writing (Astruc 1968). Appropriately, given the importance of music in Winterbottom's work, Gaut suggests that a comparison with musical performance is a better means of understanding the interactions of filmmakers during production than a comparison with novel-writing: 'The multiple authorship theory of films encourages us to look at films in the same way as we do jazz: as a product of many individuals, whose work is inflected in a complex manner by their interactions with their colleagues. A film is no more the product of a single individual than is the music of an improvising jazz group' (Gaut 1997: 166–7).

While this analogy offers a means of conceptualising the creative complexity of authorship underlying film production that is disregarded by the traditional elevation of the *auteur*, it nevertheless remains an idealised conception of authorship that abstracts the process of production from any specific commercial or historical context. With the emphasis upon improvisation it also conflates performance with production in a way that fails to recognise the significance of the distinct phases of pre- and post-production. It replaces one romantic model of creative labour with another which often functions as a sign of creative 'freedom'. The idea of improvised jazz as a field of unbridled experimentation rather than, say, the conservative reproduction of generic conventions, is a cliché that, as it happens, is challenged in *24 Hour Party People* where Tony Wilson explains impatiently to his friend Alan Erasmus that, 'Jazz is the last refuge of the untalented. Jazz musicians enjoy themselves far more than anyone listening to them. It's like theatre. It's what you do when you can't get a gig. It's one down from *Celebrity Squares*.'

Warren Buckland's account of Steven Spielberg's authorial role offers another way of conceptualising the role of the contemporary director that is helpful in understanding Winterbottom's practice. Theorists such as Andrew Sarris, who elaborated the director-oriented criticism of the *politique des auteurs* into the connoisseurial '*auteur* theory', celebrated above all those directors who worked within the tightly regulated Hollywood studio system. The rationalised production system in which the director had very little independence, was typically unable to select projects, collaborators, cast and crew and was generally excluded from post-production, meant that the only opportunity for the director to personalise the film was in the process of direction. Thus, a director's signature style and thematic preoccupations emerge in tension with the hostile, repressive commercial system within which s/he works. It is in the *mise-en-scène* of the film – the only areas of production that the director can control directly on the set – rather than the dialogue, story structure or subject matter that the director's signature becomes perceptible as what Sarris terms vaguely 'an élan of the soul' (Sarris 1992: 587). Since the 'divorcement' of the major studios and the outlawing of block booking in the late 1940s led to a gradual change in the nature of Hollywood film production with power shifting away from the producer to the director, it is clear that this concept of authorship describes a historically specific set of power relations. Moreover, while different countries developed studio systems modelled on the Hollywood majors in the early twentieth century, this concept of authorship also describes a nationally specific filmmaking infrastructure. Buckland regards Spielberg as an *auteur* but since Spielberg began making films well after the studio system had disintegrated, this means that conventional theories of authorship are of limited use since they understand the director's role as restricted to 'internal authorship' (Buckland 2006: 14). In order for a contemporary director to develop a distinctive body of work, Buckland suggests, s/he must be involved more generally in other areas of the film's production such as financing and marketing. Rather than working antagonistically or mischievously against the system s/he must learn to work with it:

> Mastery of the filmmaking process is necessary but no longer a sufficient criterion for authorship status: the director also needs to control external factors such as production, money, and the deal-making process. The director needs to become a power-broker, a talent worker (which involves mastery of management skills), and must also create a brand image in order to gain positional advantage over the competition.
>
> In the age of mass production, internal authorship – mastery over the creative process – is no longer sufficient in the creation of authorship. External control – that is, control of the immediate organizational and economic environment – is also necessary. (Ibid.)

Obviously, Winterbottom is engaged with film production on a much smaller scale than Spielberg, but it is at least as important for a director walking the margin between independent and mainstream cinema to control the 'external factors' that make filmmaking possible in the age of digital reproduction, as it is for a filmmaker managing blockbuster productions financed and distributed by major media conglomerates. In this respect, the traditional binary opposition between the classical auteur and the Romantic auteur described by Buckland is insufficient: 'the classical auteur, a skilled craft worker who has mastered – and indeed represents – "the tradition"; and the Romantic auteur: a lone, creative genius who works intuitively and mysteriously outside of all traditions' (Buckland 2006: 13). The prolific output of films and television programmes is a measure of the success of Winterbottom, Andrew Eaton and their collaborators in controlling the 'external factors' of financially insecure independent film production such as funding, distribution and marketing. Buckland proposes that 'Spielberg is an auteur because he occupies key positions in the industry (producer, director, studio co-owner, franchise licensee); he is therefore attempting to vertically reintegrate the stages of filmmaking' (Buckland 2006: 15). While Winterbottom is not in a position to attempt vertical integration in this way, nevertheless, Buckland's concept of the auteur who controls 'external' as well as 'internal factors' of filmmaking is a useful way of understanding the director's role.

As Buckland observes, one important aspect of the director's role in the contemporary commercial landscape of film production, is the development of 'a brand image'. This is developed through the self-conscious establishment of an authorial style, and also through the promotional and critical intertextual material that accompanies and is generated by the release of a film such as press kits, interviews and newspaper and magazine reviews. The director's persona is a means of 'product differentiation' which may be quite deliberately generated by filmmakers and, in the context of independent cinema, this may also take on a particular significance as a guide to audiences in how to read a film in the absence of familiar generic markers – *Code 46*, for example, might appear unsatisfactory or incoherent when approached as a science fiction film, but viewed as a 'Michael Winterbottom' film that addresses issues of intimacy, globalisation and economics, race, border-crossing and displacement, the formal organisation of the film, in which visual and narrative elements of *film noir* collide with the images and thematics of science fiction cinema as well as elements of politicised social realist film, is less unpredictable and confusing. The development of an authorial brand identity has a similar function in low-budget independent cinema as it does in relation to more commercially visible cinema, but is perhaps more important in independent cinema given the financial precariousness of such films. As David Bordwell suggests in an examination of the conventions of what he terms 'art cinema narration', 'the consistency of an authorial signature across an oeuvre constitutes an economically exploitable trademark' (Bordwell 2003: 47). 'International art cinema' is understood here to refer to experimental European narrative cinema from the 1950s to the 1970s and Bordwell cites Bergman, Buñuel, Fassbinder, Fellini, Pasolini, Ken Russell and Truffaut among exemplary directors. It is a tradition that Bordwell terms, 'the cinema of ambiguity', and Winterbottom's 'cinema of incompatibility' returns to and builds on the excesses, playfulness and experimentation of those directors' films in more or less direct ways (such as the appropriation of the score from *8½* (Federico Fellini, 1963) in *A Cock and Bull Story*). Art cinema narration is characterised by a 'marked self-consciousness' that implies the presence of narrator by contrast with classical cinema's aesthetic of transparency that suppresses the signs of narration (Bordwell 2003: 43). Art cinema displays a 'general tendency to flaunt narrational procedures' and 'when these flauntings are repeated systematically, convention asks us to unify them as proceeding from an "author"' (Bordwell 2003: 45). Thus, the author is deduced from the formal organisation of the film as the original decision-maker.

Incidentally, Winterbottom is a willing and articulate interviewee who seems relatively comfortable when speaking on screen or on radio. When interviewed he talks very quickly, often breaking off mid-sentence to switch topics and follow another line of thought, his speech patterns echoing the condensed, fragmented structure of the films. The impression is that his responses are spontaneous rather than dreary repetitions of the same pre-prepared lines but my experience of meeting the director suggests also that he approaches interviews as a routine aspect of his professional activities.

When I interviewed Winterbottom I arrived at the open-plan office of Revolution Films in Clerkenwell, London, at the arranged time and then waited for twenty or thirty minutes on the sofa by the kitchen while Winterbottom continued editing a sequence of film on a computer, presumably a sequence from *The Shock Doctrine*. When he had finished he introduced himself and we walked around the corner to the local pub, 'The Slaughtered Lamb' (which, aptly enough, shares its name with the pub in *American Werewolf in London* (John Landis, 1981)), as he said he'd prefer not to conduct the interview in front of the staff in the office most of whom were working at two banks of computers. Of course, at 6pm on a Thursday evening this central London pub quickly filled up with people and so the recording I made of the conversation is intermittently drowned out by the background hubbub of loud music and shouted conversations. He was generous with his time – we spoke for around 90 minutes until a phone call from his daughter brought the meeting to an end – and bought several drinks. Although he challenged the terms of some of my questions before going on to answer them, and expressed little interest in academic engagement with his work, he was not hostile and my impression of the discussion was that, although he is clearly a practised interviewee, it was a relatively casual encounter. He seemed open and unguarded and, occasionally, disarmingly indiscreet. However, an interview with Winterbottom by a journalist from *The Times*, in advance of the UK screening of *The Shock Doctrine* describes a very similar encounter in the same venue. The article ends with the barmaid turning the music up to deafening volume: 'Winterbottom laughs and mutters, as I catch only when I play the tape back: "Good luck transcribing this"' (O'Connell 2010: 134). It is a small detail but it suggests that even a minor interview is approached strategically, the *mise-en-scène* staged so as to put the interviewer at a disadvantage and give the director control over proceedings. This is not to suggest a cynicism or inauthenticity on Winterbottom's part, but rather to acknowledge the competence with which the filmmaker manages an interview as an inevitable component of the business of making films.

Thus, like Tristram Shandy, the 'Michael Winterbottom' discussed in this book is an unstable, compound, conjectural figure that is reconfigured with the release of each new film and television programme. As a result the life and opinions of the individual are of limited use in helping us to understand his films, and, as is appropriate for a director so critical of *auteur*-ism, although he is a willing interviewee, he remains notably reluctant to discuss his personal history; O'Connell recounts in his article, for instance, that 'only when the conversation turns personal does Winterbottom seize up' (O'Connell 2010: 133). Recognising that he is white, male, British, and middle-class may nevertheless shed light on some aspects of the films, or confirm certain interpretations. It is, at least, a helpful reminder of the inevitably restricted ideological perspective adopted or reproduced by films that emerged from a specific material and historical context and were produced through specific working practices and knowledges in British television and small-budget independent cinema in Europe. Framed in this way, for example, Winterbottom's films correspond to the category of 'second cinema' outlined by Argentinian film directors, Octavio Getino and Fernando Solanas in their polemical 1969 manifesto for 'a cinema outside and against the System … a cinema of liberation: the *third cinema*' (Getino & Solanas 1976: 52). The second cinema, which they suggest, might also be termed 'author's cinema' or 'expression cinema', emerged in response to the ideologically reactionary, commercially and culturally dominant American cinema, the function of which is 'to satisfy, in the first place, the cultural and surplus value needs *of a specific ideology, of a specific world-view: that of US financial capital*' (Getino & Solanas 1976: 51). Getino and Solanas suggest that, while second cinema represented a progressive move towards 'cultural decolonisation', it remained restricted by commercial aspirations:

> the proposal of developing a mechanism of industrial production parallel to that of the System but which would be distributed by the system according to its norms, the struggle to better the laws protecting the cinema and replacing 'bad officials' by 'less bad', etc., is a search lacking in viable prospects, unless you consider viable the prospect of becoming institutionalized as 'the youthful, angry wing of society' – that is, of neocolonialized or capitalist society. (Getino & Solanas 1976: 52)

For these writers, inspired by the work of Frantz Fanon, a truly revolutionary or oppositional third cinema would be a militant guerrilla 'cinema of the masses' that 'provokes with each showing, as in a revolutionary military incursion, a liberated space, *a decolonized territory*' (Getino & Solanas 1976: 61). Measured against this hypothetical deterritorialising radical cinema, second cinema clearly comprises compromise and capitulation. However, I would suggest that the interest and political potentiality of Winterbottom's films is revealed in its awkward relationship to the category of author's cinema – they trouble, if sometimes only modestly, the concept of the depoliticised arthouse auteur's film, in their variety, their transnational production contexts, and in their insistent preoccupation with contemporary global politics. In this respect, the value of locating Winterbottom's films within the tradition of an 'author's cinema' – the second cinema – is to stress its (problematic and problematising) political potential, rather than to place it within an aestheticised, ahistorical frame.

The transnational character of Winterbottom's films is evident in their focus upon place and space. Allied with this fascination with space is a particular importance placed upon cities and the ways that individual characters negotiate and inhabit these spaces. The various cities within Winterbottom's films, some of them over-familiar cinematic locations, take on a distinct and sometimes melancholic or minatory register.[15] Films like *Wonderland*, which traces a network of family and erotic relations across London, are concerned not with a topographically accurate account of the city so much as a psychogeographically rich account.[16] In traversing urban spaces, characters experience these cities affectively and idiosyncratically, wherein Shanghai is a futuristic dreamscape for Maria Gonzales in *Code 46*, the eponymous Italian city is a haunted, uncanny space in *Genova*, echoing the melancholic Venice of *Don't Look Now* (Nicolas Roeg, 1973), while in *24 Hour Party People*, late twentieth-century Manchester is experienced by Tony Wilson as a crucible of intense creativity that is the equal of Renaissance Florence and revolutionary Paris.

Shooting on location is a regular practice in Winterbottom's work, and is a crucial component of the transnational character of the films. For example, shooting *Welcome to Sarajevo* involved employing locals who had lived through the war as extras and crew, a common practice for politicised filmmakers but also driven here by practical contingencies. Among the local employees were members of the Sarajevan SaGa film production company, which also provided technical support. SaGa (Sarajevo Group of Authors), which was established before the war, continued to produce documentaries during the conflict including the ironically titled portmanteau feature film, *MGM Sarajevo: Man, God, Monster* (Ismet Arnautalic, Mirsad Idrizovic, Ademir Kenovic, Pjer Zalica, 1994), which includes documentation of Susan Sontag's 1993 production of *Waiting for Godot* in the city and which the filmmakers describe as representing a new cinematic aesthetic: 'Sarajevo super-realism'.[17]

Cinematic Tourism, TV and Border-Crossing

Welcome to Sarajevo is one of three films directed by Winterbottom in which the protagonist is a journalist (although we might add *The Shock Doctrine* as a fourth). The war correspondent in particular exemplifies the journalist's identity as a privileged border-crosser able to move across national and regional boundaries and in and out of war zones (from outside to inside and back again) with relative ease. The mobility of the war correspondent demonstrates by contrast, the inequality of mobility in the contemporary world, which is dramatically exaggerated in the city under siege in this film. Whereas most of the inhabitants are trapped in this exceptional space that has become a shooting gallery in which even a wedding party is a target for snipers, the reporters, like the politicians in the stock footage, are well-resourced, comparatively free to come and go, and are placed at one remove from the events taking place around them (as if the gaze of the camera erects a protective shield around them).

As is the case with many films that take television and news media as their object, the film dramatises the incomparibility of the journalist's ethical concerns with the commercial and ideological interests of the corporation he works for, which in this case broadcasts what his cameraman Gregg (James Nesbitt) dismissively terms, '"news as entertainment" bollocks'.

The stock television footage scattered throughout the film anchors the film in historical reality but also shapes the film's characteristic 'documentary realist' aesthetic. Television remains a significant medium throughout Winterbottom's career as an institutional source of financing – *Welcome to Sarajevo* was co-funded by the UK company Channel Four – a screening platform, subject matter (and archival footage), and aesthetic, stylistic and intellectual model – with its heterogeneous organisational principles of 'flow' and 'segmentation'.[18]

In this way, *Welcome to Sarajevo* highlights Winterbottom's continuing tendency to work across the institutional/aesthetic media border, as well as geographical and political borders. Like many other filmmakers internationally, television companies provided him with technical training and professional experience after leaving formal education, although Winterbottom says that he had comparatively limited responsibility for some of the early TV work, such as *Under the Sun* (1994), a feature-length drama about Ellie and Linda, two young women from Manchester travelling to Africa via Spain. He observes, for instance, of his earliest experience in television 'in any area, especially when you're starting working in TV, there's some things that you kind of feel involved with, and some things that are the equivalent of going to work in a pub to make some cash. You have to make some distinction between what you want to do and what you have to do at times'.[19] In spite of this disavowal of authorial responsibility, there *are* parallels – if we choose to look for them – between this drama, which was developed from a story by Winterbottom and Susan Campbell, and later work by the director; after Linda and Ellie go their separate ways, Ellie encounters the free-spirited, dynamic and self-destructive Tina who prefigures Eunice in *Butterfly Kiss*. An intellectually pretentious, capricious and rebellious tomboy transposed from a *nouvelle vague* film, she improvises on the saxophone, quotes Nietzsche and declares at one point, 'Clothes construct and limit me. I hate them'. The soundtrack also foregrounds some of the contemporary pop music from Manchester that recurs on several soundtracks and is the subject of *24 Hour Party People*. However, an analytical preoccupation with an emergent authorial signature reveals little about the film that would not otherwise be obvious with its broad thematic interest in the transformative experience of travel, marginal and eccentric characters, and narratives oriented around the perspective of women. The fact that the film was produced early on in Winterbottom's career might suggest that any coherent authorial style or approach has yet to become visible, although equally we might argue that, if a consistent characteristic of Winterbottom's work is a readiness to experiment with a range of representational approaches, rather than the solidification of a particular set of stylistic tropes, then this film with its loose narrative structure, punctuated by voice-overs reading Ellie's postcards home, corresponds directly to exploratory patterns that can be tracked across his work.

Independence

While working within the institutional and conventional framework of British television imposes certain constraints that are undoubtedly frustrating from a filmmaker's perspective,[20] it seems that Winterbottom has been able to operate in British TV with relative autonomy, establishing a pattern of independence that is a central principle of his practice. Whereas he might have been expected to capitalise upon his success to undertake more logistically and formally extravagant film projects with bigger budgets – a familiar career narrative for independent filmmakers – one of his skills, in collaboration with his producer Andrew Eaton, has been to negotiate a path through television and the independent film industry that affords him considerable independence. As a result of this retention of creative control, working with 'A-list' Hollywood stars such as Woody Harrelson, Tim Robbins and Angelina Jolie, or a Hollywood production company like Plan B Productions owned by Brad Pitt and Jennifer Aniston, has not resulted in films that are radically different in terms of structure, style or thematics from the films that feature unknown actors.

The experience of his first few years in television is described by the director as resembling being in a 'little bubble where it doesn't matter, you can do what you like'.[21] Winterbottom began working in TV just at the point when the two main UK broadcasting organizations, the commercial ITV (Independent Television) network and the state-owned BBC (British Broadcasting Corporation), were under growing pressure from the government to increase the proportion of programmes purchased from independent production companies rather than commissioned 'in-house' in order to introduce greater commercial competition. In the late 1980s, however, before the increasing commercialisation of British TV began to set in, there were still opportunities within these corporations to work in a relatively non-commercial mode. Of the two documentaries on Ingmar Bergman that he produced for Thames TV (the London-based division of ITV) in the late 1980s (*Ingmar Bergman: Magic Lantern*, 1988 and *Ingmar Bergman: The Director*, 1989) Winterbottom relates that 'I really had a lot of freedom. Basically the only constraint was Bergman said at the beginning I'll have to see the films and then tell you whether I give you approval afterwards'.[22] In this respect, Winterbottom's initial professional experience provided him with a model for a flexible, independent mode of working (while Bergman similarly provided him with an example of a heterogeneous and prolific independent practice).

Television, however, continues to offer a space for innovation with practical approaches to filmmaking that would be impossible within the short-term financial cycles of film production. This is exemplified by *Everyday* (2012), a project funded by British TV company Channel 4 and which began shooting in 2007 (Dawtrey 2007). The drama tells the story of a young man serving a five-year prison sentence and his relationship with his wife and four children, and it was filmed a few weeks at a time over five years in order to capture the effect of age on the actors. The story written by Winterbottom and regular collaborator Laurence Coriat (who wrote the screenplays for *Wonderland* and *Genova*), was developed as the production progressed, but what is immediately striking about this project is the central conceit of extending the duration of a film shoot to match the duration of the story. This has an additional practical advantage insofar as it allows the possibility for two films to be in production simultaneously, but at the same time it slows down the process of filmmaking dramatically, opening it up to contemplation and reflection. It offers the opportunity to watch actors age – especially children – and it may be that such a protracted production process will shape the film that is produced. For example, Winterbottom observed in 2008, 'you realise by filming it … what five years is. It's like we're filming this forever and we're still not half-way through yet'.[23] It is an example of filmmakers exploiting the formal flexibility and funding arrangements of the medium in order to devise a restrictive but generative, rule-based approach to film production.

While there are a few instances wherein feature films have been shot over several years, usually for financial reasons – David Lynch's *Eraserhead* (1977) took five years,

for example, and Orson Welles' *Othello* (1952) three due to intermittent funding –
by most accounts feature film production tends to be frantic and stressful and films
must be shot as quickly as possible in order to avoid costly over-runs. The model for
a deliberately protracted approach to shooting comes instead from television, where
guaranteed funding streams allow longer term planning, and such documentaries as
Michael Apted's documentary project, *7–56 Up*, which has been produced at seven-
year intervals since 1964. Like several other of Winterbottom's TV dramas including
the series, *Family*, and *The Trip*, the film was released theatrically outside the UK so
that, as films cross international (market) boundaries, their media identity blurs.

Conversely, however, producing work for television broadcast rather than theatrical
release can mean access to larger budgets than an independent filmmaker can secure
to make a film for theatrical release, as well as rapid access to larger audiences, and a
peculiarly intimate mode of address, by comparison with cinema's more public scale
and context. In some cases, as with the campaigning film, *The Road to Guantánamo*,
this can mean that TV is a more appropriate medium than film. It may also be that,
in a looser sense, the broad public service remit of British television that influenced
the commercial network, ITV, as well as being integral to the charter of the BBC, has
had a bearing on Winterbottom's approach to commercially disinterested and socially
engaged work.

The televisual aesthetic and intimate address

There is also a recognisable 'televisual aesthetic' that extends from Winterbottom's TV
dramas to the feature films made for theatrical release, in their embrace of a documentary style, for example, and the eschewal of 'cinematic' spectacle. This encompasses a
visual preoccupation with the *mise-en-scène* of 'ordinary' and domestic spaces, interiors
of houses, cafés, pubs and concert halls, public transport carriages, road networks
and the unexotic (if made-strange) British landscape. To describe his films as distinc-
tively televisual is in some respects an unhelpful and anachronistic claim when much
contemporary cinema is produced for viewing on a range of screen sizes and shapes. In
this sense, cinema more generally is becoming increasingly televisual. There is a notable
convergence or a blurring of the boundaries between the aesthetic regimes of film and
television that is partly facilitated by developments in affordable TV technology such
as multi-channel surround sound systems and large, high-definition screens, but is
also an inevitable consequence of the recognition that TV is the primary viewing platform for almost all commercial films.[24] John Ellis suggests, on the other hand, that an
ambiguous narrative principle is in fact also a fundamental characteristic of (British)
television itself, extending across all types of television programme:

> a model that is capable of inflection by fictional or non- fictional concerns. This
> explains the ease that TV has long since had of producing programmes that are
> ambiguous in their status: the documentary-drama, or the drama-documen-
> tary, forms that seem to have existed in the late 1950s at least, on the BBC.
> The divisions between fiction and non-fiction exist at another level to that of

narration; they are chiefly concerned with the origin of material used in the programme. (Ellis 1990: 145–6)

In spite of this general referential ambiguity, Ellis suggests, there remains a distinct 'regime of representation' that is particular to broadcast TV and which assumes and constructs distinct spectatorial relations. A key quality is that of immediacy:

> The TV image has the effect of immediacy. It is as though the TV image is a 'live' image, transmitted and received in the same moment that it is produced … the notion that broadcast TV is live still haunts the medium; even more so does the sense of immediacy of the image. The immediacy of the broadcast TV image does not just lie in the presumption that it is live, it lies more in the relations that the image sets up for itself. Immediacy is the effect of the directness of the TV image, the way in which it constitutes itself and its viewers as held in a relationship of co-present intimacy. (Ellis 1990: 132)

This effect of immediacy or intimate co-presence – what Parker Tyler described as the television's 'centripetal' relation to the viewer, 'drawing the world into his domestic space' (Krämer 1998: 294) – is generated through such means as tight, disciplinary scheduling, a thematic, normative insistence upon the family, and a range of formal devices such as open-ended narratives, direct address, 'tight' framing and staging conventions that reduce the amount of visual detail in a shot. The features of the 'presentational aesthetic' summarised by Warren Buckland describe well the characteristic formal conventions of Winterbottom's films as well as the television dramas:

> due to the small size of its screen and its lack of resolution, television has little use for complex, deep focus shots. Instead it is dominated by close-ups (showing single objects in isolation), rapid cutting (since the close-up requires less time for its content to be exhausted), a highly mobile camera (for the same reason as rapid cutting), and a shallow lateral space, partly created by the use of telephoto lenses. (Buckland 1998: 169–70)

For British audiences, or viewers familiar with contemporary British television comedy and drama, this intimate address or co-presence of the film image is amplified by the recurrence of performers familiar from British television. Filmed performances by actors like Christopher Eccleston, John Simm, Rob Brydon, Steve Coogan, Stephen Fry, Dylan Moran, Dervla Kirwan, Samantha Morton, Doon Mackichan, Simon Pegg, David Walliams, Mark Williams and Benedict Wong carry a certain intertextual resonance as viewers inevitably read these roles in relation to the television roles through which they are generally better known. This is arguably distinct from the intertextual play of references that characterise the star performances of actors who work primarily on film. Whereas the personae of film stars are associated with a spectacular and glamorous auratic distance, TV actors and comedians, however famous, embody the mundane, ubiquitous character of the medium.

Notes

1   A film that also happens to have taken its title from a song.

2   See Bardan 2008 for a comparative analysis of *Last Resort* and Winterbottom's *Wonderland*.

3   The film's box office performance suggests this may have been an unsuccessful marketing strategy; budgeted at $7.5m, the film's worldwide gross was $285,585. (http://www.boxofficemojo.com/movies/?id=code46.htm).

4   http://www.tristramshandymovie.com

5   Bedell here parodies the title of the commercially successful romantic comedy, *Love Actually* (Richard Curtis, 2003), which grossed $247m.

6   See Stam, 2000, pp. 83–92 for a helpful overview of *auteur* theory.

7   See Ciment and Tobin 1996, (in French) for Winterbottom's account of his early career.

8   For example, Winterbottom dismisses his producer Andrew Eaton's comment that the script for *Genova* has many echoes of Winterbottom's life as 'Rubbish' (Johnston 2009).

9   *South Bank Show: A Cock and Bull Story*, Archie Powell, 2005, UK ITV. Tx. 23/10/05

10   Ibid.

11   Ibid.

12   Ibid.

13   Ibid.

14   Ibid.

15   See, for example, Charlotte Brunsdon's discussion of the depiction of London in *Wonderland* (Brunsdon 2004).

16   Hence, for example, Andrew Dix's description of the London depicted in *Wonderland* as both transnational and 'sticky', mobile and inert: 'While a seemingly autonomous landscape, this portion of South London is, in Atar Brah's phrase, "diaspora space"' (Dix 2009 : 4).

17   http://www.sagafilm.com/saga2010/MGM_Sarajevo_eng.html

18   See Williams 1975 for a discussion of televisual flow and Ellis 1990, for a discussion of segmentation.

19   From author's interview transcript (4/12/08).

20   For example, Ken Loach declared in a public address at the 2010 London Film Festival that, due to bureaucratic expansion, 'Television has now become the enemy of creativity. Television kills creativity' (Brown 2010).

21   From author's interview transcript (4/12/08).

22   Ibid.

23   Ibid.

24   As David Bordwell and Kristin Thompson note, this has informed film production technically so that 'widescreen films are often shot with eventual television presentation in mind [...] Many cinematographers try to compose their shots for both widescreen and video' (Bordwell & Thompson 1993: 207).

CHAPTER ONE

Welcome to Sarajevo: television, 'documentary fiction' and border-crossing

An analysis of *Welcome to Sarajevo* illustrates the value of an approach that employs the author as an interpretive filter in order to generate certain readings. One of Winterbottom's best known works, and the third of his films made for theatrical release, it serves as a useful introduction to the director's body of work since it foregrounds several narrative themes and motifs that are explored repeatedly in other films and TV dramas, displays stylistic and structural patterns that are visible across a number of other films, and employs strategies of storytelling, spectatorial address and empathic engagement that are employed elsewhere. Concerned with a contemporary geo-political crisis, the film is not an empty exercise in formal innovation, but is an attempt to find an appropriately provocative and troubling narrative vehicle for a disturbing and complex sequence of events. It exemplifies the social commitment that underpins many of Winterbottom's film and television projects and, co-produced and distributed by the major independent film company Miramax and featuring a Hollywood star, the high-profile film is also an example of the way in which the director's work straddles a boundary between mainstream visibility and art cinema obscurity. The film is, thus, an indicator of the way that Winterbottom's output is marked by a repetitive tendency, as if, from one film to the next, the director and his collaborators are worrying away at the problem of how best to realise certain concepts or aspirations, and how best to represent certain fictional and historical events, while recognising (but simultaneously disavowing) the impossibility of a comprehensive and successful treatment. The director returns repeatedly to certain genres, such as *film noir* (in *I Want You*, *Code 46*, *The Killer Inside Me*) and the heritage film, adaptations of certain authors, most notably Thomas Hardy (*Jude*, *The Claim*, *Trishna*), and certain themes such as the plight of child refugees. It is as if the lines from Samuel Beckett's novella, *Worstward Ho* (1983) are the maxim for a practice that consists of filmic essays: 'Try again. Fail again. Fail better.' In this sense, failure is intrinsic to the creative process. It is a positive force that drives the filmmakers to produce more work, rather than a dismissive, silencing evaluation of their work as unrefined, unconventional, or unengaging. It is in their failures as well as for their successful elements that the films are interesting and reward attention.

Failure runs across Winterbottom's work on a number of parallel levels, from the narrative failures and fracturing of *A Mighty Heart*, *9 Songs* and *A Cock and Bull Story*, to the failures of family unity and romantic relations that recur repeatedly within the narratives. Indeed, as well as constituting failure in certain respects as discussed below, *Welcome to Sarajevo* is also a film *about* failure – the failure of diplomacy, the failure of Western Europe and liberal democracy, NATO and the UN, the failure of TV news, the failure of charity organisations, the failure of compassion, the failure of cosmopolitanism, the failure of nationalism. Underlying this reflection on failure is an optimistic and romantic assertion of the function of art as a field that holds open the possibility of a more enlightened, emancipated way of being – which is suggested, for example, by the film's conclusion with a musical performance – and also an assertion of the security of the middle-class nuclear family.

The story centres on a British television journalist, Michael Henderson, reporting from Sarajevo, the capital of Bosnia-Herzegovina, during the Bosnian war that ran from 1992–95 in the aftermath of the break-up of Yugoslavia. While reporting on the siege of Sarajevo by Bosnian Serb forces, during which the city's inhabitants were shelled and fired on by snipers stationed in the surrounding hills, Henderson becomes preoccupied with the perilous situation of a local orphanage. The plight of the children living there becomes the focus of his reports, and he makes contact with an American charity worker who has arranged for a bus to transport some of the children out of the city. Having befriended one of the children, Emira, and promised her earlier that he would get her out of Sarajevo, he colludes with the charity worker to smuggle Emira out of the city to visit him in London on the false premise that he is a relation, since the children are being evacuated temporarily on the understanding that they will stay with family members. The children leave Sarajevo by bus, accompanied by Henderson and his cameraman, to the Croatian port of Split, where they board a ferry. Henderson then returns home with Emira, but sometime later he is contacted by his producer, still in Sarajevo, who tells him that she has been approached by Emira's uncle to say that the girl's mother is still alive and that she wants Emira back. Henderson returns to the city which is still under siege, and makes contact with friends and colleagues. After meeting Emira's uncle, who explains that the family made her mother give the baby up, Henderson visits Emira's mother who tells Henderson unexpectedly that she is giving Emira to him. He takes her to the ITN news office in the city where she watches video footage of Emira and speaks to her on the phone. Henderson then attends the 'Koncert Za Mir' ('concert for peace') on a hill overlooking the city at which the friend of Henderson's driver and interpreter, who was killed shortly before, gives a cello recital.

Documentary/fiction

A *film à clef* scripted by regular collaborator Frank Cottrell Boyce, *Welcome to Sarajevo* is adapted from *Natasha's Story* (1994), ITN correspondent, Michael Nicholson's memoir of his experience of reporting from Sarajevo and adopting and raising Natasha, the girl he smuggled out of the country. The film is thus a reconstruction of historical events, mediated through Nicholson's autobiographical account, with creative embellishments, condensations and fictional substitutes for some of the individuals discussed in Nicholson's book. Michael Henderson (Stephen Dillane) represents Nicholson, for example, Emira (Emira Nušević) stands for Natasha, and Jacket (Igor Dzambazov) replaces Vedran Smailović, the cellist who famously performed at funerals and other events during the siege.

This documentary/fiction composite, articulated in what Mercedes Maroto Camino describes as 'a semi-documentary style', is a characteristic of much of Winterbottom's work, but is employed here in a particularly striking fashion to dramatic and ironic effect (Camino 2005: 119). This style is visible from the first scene which opens with stock video footage of Serb soldiers celebrating the occupation of Vukovar in Croatia in November 1991, after a bloody and largely unreported siege. This is followed by shots of the streets of the devastated city inhabited by Serb soldiers and civilian refugees, which are accompanied by a martial song in Bosnian and the sound of distant gunfire. Over this footage, a voice is heard stating, 'Today the city of Vukovar has fallen' and there is a cut to a shot of Michael Henderson, addressing the camera while in the background a line of refugees walks in front of a bombed-out building. 'It is now no more than a heap of rubble', continues Henderson. 'In the past two months the Serbs have pounded it with more than two million shells. These survivors are heading for Bosnia hoping to escape the war, but tonight we must face the possibility that this is only the beginning.' The informed spectator might understand that the battle of Vukovar was a beginning of sorts for a complex conflict that extended into Bosnia and continued beyond the release date of the film, but this is also a self-referential announcement of the beginning of the film and of a particular narrative route that is plotted through this context. The shot of Henderson has the same visual quality as the stock footage – it is placed within a televisual 4:3 frame that identifies it as distinct from the meta-narrative (cinematic) frame. In this way, the film effects a seamless transition from genuine documentary footage to staged footage, and the documentary material serves a number of functions in the film. First of all, it anchors the film in objective historical reality, connoting authenticity, or constituting visual evidence that what we are shown actually happened. The most viscerally shocking instance of this occurs in a sequence in which the international reporters race from their base in the Holiday Inn to the scene of a notorious 'bread queue massacre' in which civilians in a bread line were injured or killed by a mortar shell. The news crews round a corner and are stopped in a freeze frame before a cut to stock video footage of the massacre that shows dead, wounded and mutilated bodies strewn along the street, some of them lying in pools of blood. This gruesome footage is intercut with film of the reporters moving through a reconstruction of the scene, filming and taking photographs. Inserted in this scene

The bread queue massacre – the documentary authenticity of stock footage

(further imbricating the stock footage with the restaged footage) is also some video footage of the reconstruction, which was shot by the video-cameraman who shot the original news footage.

Elsewhere actuality footage functions as an ironic counterpoint to the immediate reality of the situation presented by the narrative. The stock footage of diplomats, politicians and military leaders in press conferences or entering and leaving buildings, is often deployed to demonstrate the distance between television and public relations representations of the war for external audiences, and the reality documented by the film. The title sequence, for instance, appears to be a montage of faded promotional images of Sarajevo from the time of the 1984 Winter Olympics, showing the city as a sunny, bustling, dynamic place. Set to a jaunty, nostalgic song by Van Morrison, 'The Way Young Lovers Do', this touristic view of Sarajevo demonstrates the extent of the devastation of this cosmopolitan city, and its brutal reduction is emphasised later when Henderson's driver and interpreter, Risto, is buried in the Olympic stadium which was repurposed as a cemetery during the siege.

Despite the grim content, the stock footage, which is characterised by faded colour, visual static, low resolution (especially in the case of night-vision shots), scan lines and *moiré* patterns, also offers a certain visual pleasure. It draws attention to the composition of the film as a heterogeneous material construction, and demonstrates the reliance upon discontinuous montage, rather than conventional, causally structured linearity and continuity editing, which characterises much of Winterbottom's work. In this respect the film exemplifies the way that Winterbottom's cinema maintains a distance from cinematic realism while exploring various modes of realist representation. The montage of different types of footage refuses the illusion of transparency of realist cinema by making its material components visible. At the same time, these

The title sequence – the ironic nostalgia of stock footage

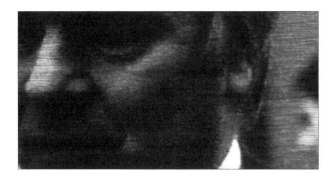

Visual heterogeneity –
extreme close-up of a
CRT television screen
(showing David Owen)

elements retain a distinctive affective potential as signs of reality, however mediated this reality is.

The decision to shoot much of the film on location gives the non-documentary material a greater sense of authenticity. Most of the film was shot in Sarajevo, only a few months after the war ended in December 1995 (the director visited the city in January 1996 and the film's premiere in Cannes was in May 1997), and so the ruined buildings and shrapnel-damaged streets and roads, and makeshift grave markers are a very visible backdrop to the action. In its search for scenographic realism, the film belongs, as Mercedes Maroto Camino observes, 'to a particular tradition of filming the aftermath of war just after its cessation, which was inaugurated by Roberto Rossellini's *Rome, Open City* in 1945' (Camino 2005: 119). Winterbottom explains that this resulted in a hazardous shoot since, 'there were mines in the verges …, so you couldn't go off concrete in case there were still mines to be discovered. We had to have people cleaning areas we were filming on to make sure there were no unexploded bombs or mortars or land mines.'[1] Whether or not these circumstances are directly responsible for the pervasive sense of danger characterising the scenes set in and around Sarajevo, nevertheless, in telling Henderson's story, the film seems equally concerned with mapping the characters' movements across and out of the topography of this damaged city. As the title announces, quoting ironic graffiti glimpsed on a building, the film places the viewer in the city, in a way that news coverage fails to.

This decision to shoot the film in post-war Sarajevo, despite the hazards, is an indicator both of the importance of location in Winterbottom's films, and of the particular importance of cities. Many of the films under discussion here are concerned with

Authenticity of *mise-en-scène* – Henderson, Carson and Flynn in Sarajevo

characters' navigation of specific landscapes from the Iranian desert to Californian mountain ranges, and from the Antarctic to the British countryside and coastal areas. One of the pleasures offered by Winterbottom's films is thus the sensation of movement through space that is fundamental to the medium, although the characters' travel is rarely experienced as easy movement. Mobility is frequently hindered or rerouted by borders and obstructions. In this respect, the film highlights a consistent thematic focus upon the violent instability of boundaries that is already present in earlier work and concerns the configuration of gendered, ethnic, cultural and social borders, as well as regional and national limits. Completely isolated within territory dominated by Bosnian Serb forces, the city of Sarajevo constituted a border-zone in the most direct way, with the boundaries of the city corresponding to regional or national boundaries as well as battle lines. The film is, thus, an example of what Hamid Naficy describes as a 'border film' due to this concern with questions of migration and passage across borders (against a background of the violent redrawing of borders). Among the characteristic features of border films identified by Naficy are plots that deal with travelling and border-crossing and feature 'border subjects' in films that are 'shot on location in the borderlands', that cross 'generic and narrative boundaries' and refer to 'the problems of ethnic or national identity' (Naficy 2001: 239).

Television, reportage and mediation

Among the border-crossers foregrounded in *Welcome to Sarajevo* are the television journalists who offer us a point of identification and ethical reflection on the war. The orientation of this war story around the experiences of a war correspondent means that a number of issues around representation and intervention, which are raised repeatedly elsewhere by the director are here brought to the fore. Most directly, the figure of the journalist raises questions about the ethical responsibility to act and intervene insofar as impartiality or objectivity is commonly understood as central to journalistic practice. A question about journalistic ethics is posed early in the film when news crews arrive at the spot where a sniper has opened fire on a wedding procession, hitting the bride's mother whose body now lies in the street. While a group of photographers and camera-operators shelter in doorways and behind vehicles, an American reporter, Jordan Flynn (Woody Harrelson) strides calmly across the now empty street, framed like the hero of a classic 1930s western, ignoring gunshots, to help a priest carry the dead woman's body into the church.

Discussing Flynn's behaviour later, Gregg offers, 'I suppose he was only trying to help', to which Henderson retorts, 'We're not here to help we're here to report.' Shortly afterwards, over drinks in the bar of the Holiday Inn where the journalists are staying, a disgusted freelance journalist tells Flynn, 'It wasn't about Sarajevo, it was about you.' Flynn defends his action explaining, 'Oddly enough, back home no-one's heard of Sarajevo, but they've all heard of me.' These exchanges describe the axes of responsibility placed upon the professional observers. Journalism is framed here as a choice between impersonal distance and compassionate intervention on the one hand, and a choice between objective representation and subjective self-referentiality on the other.

Flynn braving sniper fire
to help a fatally injured
woman

This is a choice that becomes progressively troubled as Henderson's initial espousal of objectivity becomes increasingly intolerable in the face of the unfolding catastrophe and the censorious, commercially dictated editorial priorities that shape television news. By implication similar questions about the humanitarian effect and intentionality of representations, and the relationship between helping and reporting, might be posed in relation to the film itself. This ironically self-referential scene demonstrates a self-critical tendency that characterises much of Winterbottom's work. In casting a Hollywood star in a minor role (in terms of screen time), the filmmakers are presumably fully conscious of the visibility that a celebrity performer brings to their project, and so Flynn's response is, equally, a knowing comment upon Harrelson's casting and the film's pragmatic promotional strategy. Moreover, as becomes clear as the film progresses, the journalist's accusation applies equally to the film's narrative, which is not about the inhabitants of Sarajevo or the circumstances of the war, so much as it is about the reporter, Henderson.

Indeed, *Welcome to Sarajevo* traces Henderson's growing disillusionment with a professional role that requires him to remain an impartial witness. When his producer, Jane Carson objects to his insistent pursuit of the story of the orphanage, asserting, 'that's not news, that's a campaign', Henderson retorts, 'I don't care what it is, I'm going to get those kids out of there.' Later, drinking coffee in the Holiday Inn with Carson and Gregg, he observes disgustedly, 'We're like vultures.' Thus, over the course of the film his growing cynicism at the complicity, prurience and inefficacy of journalism and diplomacy, and his personal contact with the children at the orphanage, prompts Henderson to reject commercially prudent professional impartiality – passivity – in favour of spontaneous action. Motivated by a sense of individual responsibility – 'She thought that I could help her get out, and I realised that I could, and then there didn't really seem to be any reason not to', he tells his wife – he persuades the head of the orphanage and the American charity worker to smuggle Emira out of Sarajevo along with the orphan evacuees so that he can adopt her. Thus, whereas Flynn and Henderson initially occupy opposing ethical positions in relation to the wedding shooting– passive observation versus active participation/identification – by the film's conclusion, Henderson is aligned more closely with Flynn. This shift is paralleled by the development of Flynn's character during the film. He is presented at first as a glamorous, macho caricature of a war reporter familiar from films such as *The Year of Living Dangerously* (Peter Weir, 1982), *The Killing Fields* (Roland Joffé, 1984) or

Salvador (Oliver Stone, 1986) – gregarious, flirtatious and hard-drinking. However, this caricature is subsequently challenged when, after visiting the Serb-run concentration camp in Trnopolje, he asks Henderson to drive him to the family of one of the prisoners where he hands them a photograph of their son. It is revealed in the conversation with the parents that Flynn has learnt Bosnian and so he represents a model for a compassionate journalistic ethics marked by identification with, rather than distance from, the object of scrutiny. For Henderson, this identification with the people whose situation he is reporting extends to the intimate burden of the adoption of a young Bosnian girl as his daughter.

The figure of the journalist occupies an ambivalent position as a relay or mediator between events and audience, and as Dina Iordanova notes, of the several dozen films made about Sarajevo, this quickly became a conventional trope: 'the films about Sarajevo most commonly narrated the story from the view point of a stranger – a young traveller, an aid worker, a journalist' (Iordanova 2001: 247). As an observer of events from outside, the journalist is effectively an avatar for the film viewer. 'Like ethnographers', Mercedes Maroto Camino suggests, 'war correspondents approach their subject very much like voyeurs who come from a different universe of meaning' (Camino 2005: 116). In drawing this parallel between voyeurism and war reporting, Camino effectively likens the reporter's motivation to the film viewer's desire for titillation and sensation. In this way, Henderson is a point of identification for the viewer, echoing or anticipating our relationship to the screen in his fascinated, emotionally engaged relationship to the horror, ironies and melodramatic unfolding of life in a war-torn city.

Secondly, as a television reporter who is seen several times at an editing suite, Henderson is also effectively an *auteur* who writes, directs, performs in and edits short films. Preoccupied with accuracy, integrity and communication, and railing vainly against the trivialising commodification of the medium, he is an idealistic campaigning filmmaker intent upon moving his audience, prompting them to action. In this respect we might understand the film as a meditation upon cinema in which a certain mode of filmmaking is equated with reportage as a directly political form of communication that has the capacity to effect social change. Henderson moves from making conventionally impartial reports, like that with which the film opens, to more impassioned, personal, and narratively inconclusive reports. In doing so he develops from disinter-

Henderson and Gregg
assembling a report
on the orphanage at
the editing suite

ested reporter into an expressive author. Through Henderson's quietly heroic transformation, the film affirms both a romantic image of the *auteur*-director, and also asserts the close relationship between the roles of journalist and filmmaker, which is a convergence that Winterbottom and his collaborators re-enact in the production of other campaigning films such as *The Road to Guantánamo* and *The Shock Doctrine*.

Thus, in exploring the ethical issues regarding Henderson's role as a reporter, *Welcome to Sarajevo* also reframes these issues in relation to spectatorship and filmmaking. For example, the question faced by Henderson of whether or not to intervene, is relayed on to the viewer of the film who is asked, implicitly, whether she can watch the film without being moved to action. Given that the film is an account of past history, albeit relatively recent, in one sense the question posed remains safely hypothetical, a point of criticism from writers who insist on a literal reading of the film in which the Sarajevo siege has no wider ramifications or parallels. For Dina Iordanova, for instance, 'The film came at a time when it no longer mattered' (Iordanova 2001: 251). However, as Jacques Rancière observed prophetically in 1996, the wider significance of the conflict lies in the foregrounding of ethnicity as the basis on which to draw territorial borders and the concomitant restatement of the moral supremacy of Western neo-liberal capitalism. This framing of the conflict, writes Rancière,

> is not merely a local affair confined to a small end of Europe. No doubt we should remain level-headed about the prophecies announcing the widespread outbreak of ethnic, religious and other types of identity fundamentalism. Yet, so long as 'socialists and liberals' act in concert to identify democratic government with the global law of wealth, partisans of ancestral law and of separating 'ethnicities' will be permitted to present themselves as the sole alternative to the power of wealth. (Rancière 2010: 7)

In this respect, as Rancière suggests, the political questions posed by *Welcome to Sarajevo* resonate well beyond the specificity of the events depicted, raising deeper questions about the role of the West in 'humanitarian conflicts' that re-emerged in dramatic fashion in relation to the humanitarian rhetoric deployed to justify the 'military interventions' of the War on Terror.

Picturing history

Made so soon after the Bosnian war ended, the film grapples with what was then very recent history. It was produced with the speed of a television documentary rather than at the protracted pace of a feature film, and there is perhaps a direct relationship between the speed with which it was made, and the breathless pace of the film. One of the central representational challenges of filming the Bosnian war is that of producing a coherent depiction of a particularly complex conflict – or complex of conflicts – in which regional, national and ethnic boundaries – boundaries both physical and conceptual – were redrawn and fought over as civil war was fought alongside wider conflicts after the dissolution of Yugoslavia in the early 1990s. Thus, for example, the

Croat-Bosniak war, which ran from June 1992 to February 1994, took place within the Bosnian war which ran until 1995 and saw three sides at war with one another: the Republic of Bosnia and Herzegovina, the Croatian Republic of Herzeg-Bosnia (later Croatia), and a coalition of forces including Republika Srpska and the Federal Republic of Yugoslavia. NATO later became involved in bombing the Republika Srpska coalition.

Despite the film's condemnation of superficial television journalism, nothing of the detailed political background to the war is communicated in the film. The soldiers firing on the city remain largely unseen, and there is no discussion of what is at stake in the siege. We are shown fragmentary, confusing glimpses of the broader context with uncaptioned shots of politicians and military leaders, stock footage of Vukovar and the Trnopolje concentration camp, a small convoy of (unidentified) Chetnik irregulars encountered by the evacuees on the road to Split, the casual mass execution of civilians by a Serb soldier with a handgun on the outskirts of the city, a shot of a soldier spraying the name 'Zivko' on a wall, presumably in reference to Bosnian Serb politician Zivko Radisić (although there is no reference to him beyond this graffiti). The only indication of the specific political circumstances of the war occurs when a Chetnik boards the bus and begins removing children with Muslim names. This is the most explicit reference to the racism that drove 'ethnic cleansing' policies and acts of genocide. It is as if the film concedes the impossibility of making sense of the violence for the film's spectators and can only reiterate that war is wretched and irrational – this is epitomised by a scene during the exodus of the orphans when, having camped by the roadside over night, Henderson wakes and walks by himself into a nearby village. He comes upon a scene of devastation – the silent village has been ransacked and the street is strewn with piles of dead animals and executed bodies and an eviscerated corpse hangs from a balcony. These shots are followed by stock footage of Bosnian Serb president Radovan Karadžić (who is on trial for war crimes at the time of writing) explaining, 'we give full guarantees according to Geneva Convention for civilians'. Shots of refugees on foot are then followed by a shot of US president George Bush insisting, 'You can't negotiate with a terrorist', and this is followed in turn by a shot of a smiling Karadžić at a nego-tiating table with British diplomat Lord Carrington. Stock footage of dead bodies, and the graffitied 'Zivko', then appear to confirm that Bush is correct and that negotiation is futile. Since none of the figures or locations in this sequence is identified, the effect is not elucidation of the political context of the war but, on the contrary, an emphasis upon the grotesque and confusing absurdity of political negotiation. Stephen Dillane suggests that 'a lot of what this script is about is the frustration that the journalists themselves felt about not being able to give a clear picture of what was happening' (EPK), and, ironically, the film is confronted by the same problem of spatial and narrative orientation. Discussing the conventional grammar of continuity editing in relation to complex narratives, the director Werner Herzog comments, 'I cannot stand disorientation in movies, and films like *Waterloo* are wonderful examples to learn from: three armies march from three different directions and meet at the battlefield, and you always know who is who, and coming from where' (Cronin 2002: 230–1). By contrast, in abandoning conventional structures of narrative organisation and editing in its account of a city caught between three armies, *Welcome to Sarajevo* makes disorientation a formal and thematic principle. Consequently, in spite of the film's implicit criticism of the simplifications of the television coverage, in its account of the chaotic carnage of the conflict, *Welcome to Sarajevo* risks paraphrasing Prime Minister Neville Chamberlain's description of the stand-off between Germany and Czechoslovakia in 1938 as 'a quarrel in a far-away country between people of whom we know nothing', a comment that was made to justify a policy of non-intervention.[2] The danger here is that the film reproduces a stereotypical account of the Balkans as an irredeemably uncivilised and naturally violent region, a characteristic, as Fredric Jameson writes, of many films about the Balkans both from within and outside former Yugoslavia:

> Such movies seem to offer eyewitness proof that the people in the Balkans are violent by their very nature; they seem to locate a place in which culture and civilisation – the law, civility, the most elementary forms of compassion and cooperation – are the thinnest veneer, at any moment capable of being stripped away to show the anarchy and ferocity underneath. (Jameson 2004: 232)

It is an impression of the region that is also reproduced in the source book as Michael Nicholson attributes the extreme violence of the wars to just such an atavistic racial trait (in a line that could have been lifted from the memoirs of a Victorian adventurer): 'The ferocity of the Balkan peoples has at times been so primitive that anthropologists have likened them to the Amazon's Yanomamo, one of the world's most savage and primitive tribes' (Nicholson 1994: 16). As a result, Patricia Molloy concludes that the film reproduces this preconception: 'Winterbottom sets up an opposition between "us" and "them" in Henderson's desperation to rescue the child from the "uncivilized" Bosnia and introduce her to the civilized world of the "West"' (Molloy 2000: 10).

Intimacy – children, orphans and family

What prompts Henderson to transgress professional impartiality[3] and touristic distance, and to establish an intimate relationship with the place and people that are the subject of his reports, is his encounter with the children living in the Ljubica Iversič orphanage. While a variety of residents of Sarajevo are introduced during the film, particular significance is placed on the figure of the vulnerable young child throughout the film as an exemplification of the injustice, viciousness and incomprehensibility of this war. The pathetic figure of the innocent and lost or displaced child recurs repeatedly in Winterbottom's films with varying significance and narrative prominence from the miserable youngsters in *Jude*, the motherless daughters in *Genova* and the young boy lost and mugged in London at night in *Wonderland*, and the four children deprived of their jailed father in *Everyday*, to the Yugoslavian refugee in *I Want You* and the Afghan refugees of *In This World*. In these different contexts the vulnerable child has a variety of narrative functions, but most obviously it is a particularly affecting figure, a means of direct sentimental engagement with the viewer. As Emma Wilson has observed, 'through his work, Winterbottom engages in a type of *fort/da*

The altar boy in the street confronting Henderson and Gregg

game whereby a child's loss is envisaged, then denied, where the child is lost, and then recovered' (Wilson 2003: 98).

The first significant child in *Welcome to Sarajevo* is a young altar boy participating in the wedding. After documenting the shooting, Gregg and Henderson run down adjoining streets looking for their driver. These shots are intercut with a slow-motion shot of the boy running from the camera, and the two men then come upon him at the bottom of a dead-end street. He stands and shouts at them (in unsubtitled Bosnian) while Gregg films him. When the flustered driver arrives he shouts, 'Go fuck your mother!', at the boy and they drive off. The figure of the altar boy recurs later as Henderson's dream rendered in low resolution hand-held video shots, his robes now blood-stained. The fact that it is an altar boy is perhaps intended to stress the enormity of the violence, through its profanity, however the filmmakers' decision to foreground a Catholic ritual in the context of a predominantly Muslim city is a curious ornamentation of Nicholson's account. While it may be intended to stress the cosmopolitan and tolerant composition of Sarajevo, it also marginalises the Islamophobic hatred and anxiety that was an important motivation behind the siege (and which is a theme that Winterbottom returns to frequently and much more explicitly in subsequent films). This may be strategic too, intended to avoid reproducing the 'Orientalist' othering of Muslim cultural identity that underlies the violence of 'ethnic cleansing' in recognition of the danger that, as Jacques Rancière observed, writing a few months before the film's release:

> whoever says 'Muslim' says 'Oriental', and the partition of Bosnia is a way of introducing into the heart of old Europe an ideal line of division. This line separates the world of Western reason on the march towards a future of common rational prosperity and an "oriental" world doomed, for an indefinite period, to languish in irrational classifications and the obscure identity laws of tribes, religion and poverty. (Rancière 2010: 6)

Intermittent reference is also made to the biblical exodus, with the charity worker telling Henderson that the evacuation of the orphanage will be 'an epic story for you: the exodus'. Earlier, Henderson's companion, Risto, burns a book illustrated with beautiful illuminated manuscripts of the exodus in order to cook in his flat, muttering that 'I could never relate to the exodus.' These asides direct us towards an allegorical

Orphaned girl in the hospital with Henderson

interpretation of the film,[4] hinting that the political complexities of the war obscure a simple morality, and that the rescue of the orphans can be understood as a good deed, a decisive act in the face of moral confusion and liberal indecision. 'What's the problem?', Henderson demands of his producer when she questions his commitment to the story of the orphanage, 'Big guns, little children, evil men. Great television.' Ultimately the film does little to challenge this framing of historical events. The altar boy reappears at the end of the film when Henderson spots him – or his double – running through the streets. In a sequence with an oneiric quality, Henderson attempts to push through the now bustling streets to follow the boy, and eventually finds himself on a hilltop where he is greeted happily by his friends who have gathered to listen to Jacket's cello recital.

The second symbolically significant figure is a little girl who approaches Henderson in the hospital looking for her parents after the shelling of the bread queue. On learning that they are both dead, the crying child wanders out of the hospital by herself, ignoring Henderson's concerned attempts to ask about relatives. Like the altar boy she also reappears in a dream Henderson has before returning from London to Sarajevo, running in slow-motion with a pram laden with firewood and swerving to avoid sniper fire.

The dream is a secondary theme threaded through the film, reiterating a distinction between action and passivity, reality and self-delusion (and, by extension, reality and film). On Henderson's return to Sarajevo, Risto,[5] who has now joined the resistance, remarks, 'I used to think my life and the siege were different things and now I realise there's no life in Sarajevo apart from the siege. The siege is Sarajevo. If you're not part of it you are dreaming. You're asleep.' Elsewhere, in a montage of international politicians intercut with footage from the Trnopolje concentration camp, Lord Owen, the British representative of the EU who worked to negotiate a peace plan, is shown in close-up saying, 'Don't, don't, don't, live under this dream that the West is going to come in and sort this problem out.' This shot is reprised at the end of the film, and the film's final line is Owen's injunction, 'Don't dream dreams.'

The most important child figure is Emira (Emira Nusevič, who lived through the siege) who has been in the orphanage since infancy. It is Henderson's encounter with Emira, and his promise to get her out of Sarajevo that prompts him to disregard Flynn's admonition that 'those orphans are not your responsibility. You're here as a reporter.' Ten-year old Emira is presented as a prematurely aged but nevertheless sweet child who

Emira in the orphanage

smokes and takes parental responsibility for 'Roadrunner', one of the infant orphans, a role that signifies the violence of a war which has stolen her childhood.

Emira's rescue – Henderson's decisive act of intervention (taking on the intimate burden of identification with the plight of the besieged Bosnians) – involves her incorporation into Henderson's family which symbolises attractive (middle-class, English) normality. After a traumatic journey out of Sarajevo and through Croatia, during which the bus is stopped by far-right Serbian Chetniks who search the bus for Muslims and kidnap several children including Roadrunner, Emira's life in London is depicted as wholly positive – a montage of home video footage (which, like the news reports and stock footage, connotes visual evidence) shows her swimming with Henderson, watching fireworks, celebrating Christmas and her birthday, learning English, and playing cricket in the park. Emira is transformed in the process of this Anglicisation to the extent that she has to be instructed by Henderson to use Bosnian when she speaks to her mother on the phone. For Brian Michael Goss, this narrative passage reveals a nationalistic thread within the film, thereby exposing the limits of the film's self-critical capacity:

> *Welcome to Sarajevo* also aggrandizes Britain – history's arch imperialist where imperial bells still chime. Emira's devotion to the English language functions as tribute to Britain as guardian of human rights and as protectorate to the world's vulnerable. (Goss 2009: 217)

What is troubling about this narrative development is precisely the shift away from the complex political topography of the war in Bosnia to the affectively simple terrain of the domestic and the intimate, the racking of focus from Sarajevo to the reporter commenting on it. Winterbottom has commented on the impossibility that this war could be allowed to take place in Europe under the gaze of TV cameras, asking:

> How is it possible now, in Europe, when every day you could see what was happening, that you can let a war happen? And it's as though it's happening on another planet, and it's only happening, really, a couple of hours away.[6]

While this suggests an appropriate strategy might be to emphasise the proximity of Sarajevo, the film ultimately stresses its distance – the hellish otherness of Sarajevo as an irredeemably anomic space suspended in a state of exception during an incomprehensible war. For example, one of Henderson's reports on the orphanage is followed by stock footage of British Prime Minister, John Major speaking in Parliament, as if in direct response to Henderson's report, which is illustrated with images of children's graves: 'If it is possible to treat the children on the spot, near to their families with people around them who speak their language, and in relatively familiar surroundings, then that is obviously the best way.' As Major continues to speak, his image is replaced with a series of shots of children in hospital and Bobby McFerrin's song, 'Don't Worry, Be Happy' (1988) fades up ironically on the soundtrack. The conjunction of sound and image makes it unambiguously clear that Major is at best misguided, and at worst, evil, and that the best way to help the children is to remove them. While Nicholson's memoir gives considerable space over to a (self-justificatory) discussion of the implications of smuggling Natasha into Britain illegally, and the challenges of living with and adopting her, the film has little interest in the potential ambiguities of Henderson's action.

While we might understand Henderson's action as altruistic, it may also be read as the expiation of his guilt at being an impotent voyeur whose reports of atrocities have little obvious function (beyond supplying commercial news channels with spectacular content). Saving Emira offers him a means of redemption as well as offering her relief from her plight. In this sense, the description of *Welcome to Sarajevo* as 'A true story of an extraordinary act of courage' in the film's US teaser trailer, is a generic cliché that inevitably overlooks the film's implicit moral equivocation. Patricia Molloy argues, for instance, that 'the film participates in a discourse of selfhood wherein the self is secured by means of the other. Henderson's "humanity" is measured, tested, against the "inhumanity" of Sarajevo' (Molloy 2000: 7). In other words, in telling the story of Henderson's transformation, his courage, or his biblical role as saviour of the children of Israel, the film adopts a narcissistic frame within which the violence taking place in Sarajevo is reduced to the function of a personal challenge or psychodrama (hence, perhaps, the prominence of dream imagery). Despite Henderson's anxieties about his impotence as a witness and mediator, and his frustration at the incompatibility of commercial news values with his own ethics, the film risks reproducing a superficial, self-congratulatory view of the conflict as inexplicably evil – epitomised by the long-haired Chetnik soldier who snatches several children from the bus, including a baby that he holds triumphantly above his head.

Chetnik soldiers removing
orphans from the convoy

This fearsome figure is the embodiment of what Fredric Jameson terms 'the wild man of the Balkans', a cinematic stereotype that explains the irrational violence of the war (Jameson 2004: 232). Noting the parallel between cinema and tourism (as spectacular mechanisms or practices of movement and othering and temporal and spatial proximity), Patricia Molloy asks,

> what about when the tourist site is the war zone and the film is a depiction of people killing each other in one part of the world and is intended for mass consumption in another part of the world? The question concerning the politics of spectacle is one of ethical responsibility, of how to bear witness to violence against the other without recourse to a violence of representation. (Molloy 2000: 2)

When it is discovered that Emira has a mother, this opens up the possibility for the film to examine the moral complexities of Henderson's position, since the film has affirmed the importance of family with regard to Henderson's. However, when Henderson travels back to Sarajevo to meet Emira's family it confirms that he is correct in his determination not to let her return. Her mother has seen her twice during the past eight years, as Henderson reminds her, while she confesses to having been a 'bad mother'. Moreover, when Henderson puts her on the phone to Emira, the daughter has no interest in talking to her mother and hangs up after a brief exchange. There is clearly no emotional attachment between the girl and her mother and thus, leaving aside the dangers of returning Emira to a warzone, Henderson is vindicated in his illegal adoption of the girl.

Mercedes Maroto Camino suggests that *Welcome to Sarajevo* corresponds to the conservative genre of the western in its preoccupation with masculinity and homosocial groups, wherein 'journalists stand in for cowboys and their cameras for guns' (Camino 2005: 123). While several women appear in key professional roles, the most prominent, dynamic (and apparently fearless) characters are Flynn and Henderson who embody masculinity in different ways as they traverse the frontlines of this war. In this context, Henderson's frustration about his impotence as a reporter can be understood as an anxiety about his performance of masculinity. Fathering a child allows Henderson to re-establish his masculine potency and it is in this narrative trajectory that the film's most conservative tendencies are revealed. In an overview of Winterbottom's films, Goss suggests that a preoccupation with contemporary masculinity in crisis runs through the depiction of male characters in many of the films: 'Given that men have come to recognize the fragility of traditional privileges, Winterbottom's films capture some of the anxiety about what men have to lose' (Goss 2009: 178). This anxiety might be addressed in a number of ways, but as Patricia Molloy argues, in *Welcome to Sarajevo* it is articulated in heteronormative terms so that by the end of the film, characters have been aligned successfully with conventional gender roles. Emira's rescue involves not just evacuation from Sarajevo but becoming feminine, and so her cropped hair is grown out into bunches and her jeans and t-shirt replaced with a dress: 'Henderson's helplessness is satiated, his masculinity restored, his civility secured, with Emira's domestication, which is contingent upon her femi-nization' (Molloy 2000: 7).

Frank Cottrell Boyce explains that after several frustrated attempts at a convention-ally organised screenplay, 'I tried to write a screenplay in which the sequence seemed as random as war, in which the audience would never be quite sure where the next scene was coming from' (Cottrell Boyce 1997: ix–x). He recalls that Winterbottom was enthusiastic about this attempt to convey the contingency and uncertainty of reality and, in particular, the device of including stock footage:

> Michael … liked the mess. He believed he could make a film that worked not by linear narrative momentum, but by the immediacy of the action itself. He took what I did and pushed it further. He removed the helpful chapter head-ings. Taking his cue from the concentration camp suggestion, he peppered the film with real footage. (Cottrell Boyce 1997: x)

In this account, *Welcome to Sarajevo* exemplifies three consistent and distinctive features of Winterbottom's practice. The first is a tendency towards formal experimentation and a rejection of a conventional solution to the central problem of (cinematic) story-telling, that of imposing an artificial, reductive framework upon contingent, formless, fugitive reality – of making meaningless events meaningful. Incoherence and contin-gency is an experience of everyday reality but war is perhaps simply a limit case of such existential uncertainty. In different ways, *Butterfly Kiss*, *9 Songs*, and *A Cock and Bull Story* are also 'as random as war', but the problem of storytelling or narrative adequacy is foregrounded here in a particularly literal way. When, in the professional language of journalism, a news report is a 'story', this means that the film is as concerned with the difficulties of telling and broadcasting stories, as it is with the subject matter of those stories. While Nicholson's book is presented as Natasha's story, the film is oriented more around the storyteller (Nicholson/Henderson) than it is around Natasha/Emira or the war taking place in the background.

The second closely related feature is an emphasis upon 'immediacy' over linearity and classical progression or causality, which is evident at the macro-level of narrative organisation and the micro-level of cinematography and shot relations. As Michael Atkinson observed in an early profile of the director:

> no one could follow the films as models, because they are shot and cut like a heart attack, because their identities are so essentially untrackable, associa-tive, and imbued with the sense of immediate and unstoppable experience. (Winterbottom's shots often approximate the swivel of the head looking over a room or a landscape, and few living directors can so quickly map out in-frame *and* off-frame territory.) (Atkinson 1998: 45)

A third distinctive feature indicated by Cottrell Boyce's account is the importance of collaboration. The screenwriter, who has worked with Winterbottom on six films, continued rewriting during the production of the film and in post-production he and Winterbottom took the script's deviations from linearity further and 'moved material around that we had tried to keep in chronological order in the script' (Cottrell Boyce 1997: xi). Cottrell Boyce reflects that the 'script never felt finished' but, of course, a screenplay is a map or a set of cues for the director and other collaborators, rather than an independent work – the script is only 'finished' in its realisation as a film. And, in any case, the film itself remains unfinished since it represents a single, limited account of a nebulous topic. The screenwriter recalls that when he set about writing the script he was confident that he 'had a thousand great stories' to choose from. The resulting film (as with any film) is one imperfectly told story selected from a myriad others. However, what is notable here is the screenwriter's collaborative involvement throughout the process of production and his roles as a facilitator of the director's decisions. For example, Michael Atkinson observes that Winterbottom's distinctive mode of realism is exemplified by the use of stock footage so that 'often *Welcome to Sarajevo*'s many pre-existing news shots of the Bosnian carnage seem to epitomize Winterbottom's aesthetic' (Atkinson 1998: 47). Cottrell Boyce's account of the production suggests that this signature style (which is not evident in earlier film and television work) emerges partly from the screenplay.

In its presentation of Henderson as a sympathetic protagonist, the film effectively privileges the situated knowledge acquired by Henderson over impartial, objective or external perspectives on events. In a broader sense, the film might then be understood as an argument about the impossibility of representing historical events from an external, neutral perspective. Such accounts can do symbolic violence to the subjects of history, the victims of these events in their reductive focus upon political manoeuvring that disregards the suffering and angst on which political negotiations rest. In this way, an explanation of the conflict that places the narrative details of individual lives under siege within a historical overview also becomes problematic. Within this logic, an appropriate strategy is to convey something of the experience of living under siege, from the mundane difficulties of food shortages and power cuts to the horror of violent and arbitrary death. However, rather than presuming to offer an authentic account of life in Sarajevo, the film depicts life from the privileged perspective of a journalist, living in the Holiday Inn, relatively wealthy and comparatively mobile since he can move around and in and out of the city. His exceptional position, as well as his journalistic desire for authentic experience or close identification with the city's residents, is marked by his refusal to wear the body armour his producer secures for him.

In this way, crucially, the film refuses rather than gratifies a touristic fantasy (which is invoked ironically in the film's title montage sequence) of traversing a warzone. Although the film presents Sarajevo to the viewer from the perspective of an outsider, this perspective remains limited by Henderson's physical estrangement from his environment, his ignorance and his single-mindedness. This narrative perspective disrupts what Urry and Larsen term the 'tourist gaze', a technically and culturally mediated way of seeing that perceives the world in terms of picturesque, consumable images and gratifies a desire 'to take possession of objects and environments, often at a distance' (Urry, Larsen 2011: 158). The promotional images we see in the film's title sequence stress the distance between the pre-war Sarajevo which appears as a space staged for leisure and visual consumption, and the war-torn city which is depicted as spatially disjointed and incoherent and can only be glimpsed rather than gazed contemplatively upon. Indeed, the only conventionally picturesque landscape is briefly visible when the bus carrying the orphans stops by the seashore en route to Split, allowing the children to charge down the beach in the sunshine and play in the sea. It is a brief, joyous, and by implication, normal, interval. The beach is a literally and symbolically marginal space that recurs throughout Winterbottom's work and often signifies or permits a moment of suspension and freedom. In this case however, the scene immediately follows the kidnapping of several children by Chetniks and so is tainted by a lingering sense of threat and impermanence.

The voyeuristic pleasure of moving safely and thrillingly through a dangerous space is obstructed by the foregrounding of the journalist. The delirious, disorienting spectacle of the battleground that is a feature of many contemporary war films, is displaced here by the narrative focus upon Henderson who remains an interested observer of events rather than a participant. Henderson's presence is an implicit acknowledgement that all this film can offer us is a restricted, mediated, account of events that remain in some ways incomprehensible (within the scope of a dramatic film) and beyond narrativisation. Rather than offer a 'clear picture' of the siege of Sarajevo, as Dillane suggests television journalists at the time hoped to do, the film attests to the impossibility of this. The film's final intertitle records that, 'During the war in Bosnia more than a million people lost their homes. 175,000 people were wounded and 275,000 people were killed or went missing; 35,000 children were wounded and 16,000 children were killed or went missing. Emira still lives in England.'

This summarises the film's strategy overall, which is to isolate a detail of this overwhelming event in order to gain some purchase on it, examining the way in which the war is experienced by individuals. More particularly, through the focus on orphans, the film depicts the violence of war as a destructive assault upon the family. This melodramatic scaling of historical events through an examination of their impact upon the private, domestic sphere is the way in which *Welcome to Sarajevo* makes these events intelligible, presenting them within as clear a picture as is possible. The orphan is a sign of the damaged family, which is in turn a sign of the damage done by this conflict, which, in the absence of contextual elaboration is a sign for any conflict. In response to his producer Carson's exasperated insistence that they have 'done' the story of the orphanage, Henderson replies that they have only started the story since the kids are still there. 'As long as the UN are here, I'm going to keep those kids on the screen; every night, different child, same message: "Get me out of here"'. Carson contends that this is not news but a campaign, but what differentiates Henderson's approach from conventional TV journalism is not simply the abandonment of the pretence of neutrality, but also the emphasis upon affect and on an extended narrative. Henderson is a frustrated filmmaker confined to the short form of the prime-time news report.

Conclusion

In a comprehensive study of Balkan cinema, Dina Iordanova suggests that *Welcome to Sarajevo* is the best known film about the siege since it 'is the film which was promoted most vigorously and therefore received most exposure' (Iordanova 2001: 251), but asserts that 'political correctness could not compensate for the artistic shortcomings', with the film failing to win awards at Cannes or the Academy Awards despite 'Miramax's strong marketing muscle' (Iordanova 2001: 249). These artistic shortcomings are not explored in any detail and Iordanova's *ad hominem* attack rests primarily on an accusation of self-interest; responding to a published comment by Cottrell Boyce that he had 'ignored' the war until he was approached to write the script, Iordanova contends that 'It was made by people for whom Sarajevo was not of particular importance. To them, *Sarajevo* was just another project, which, even if marked by artistic accomplishment, would fulfil a certain objective – to stand out as a good listing in the portfolios of its creators' (Iordanova 2001: 251). These conjectured motivations are of questionable relevance to a close analysis of the film, but the assumption that the film was driven by aspiration to critical and commercial success means that, for Iordanova, its modest box-office business and lack of awards demonstrate aesthetic failure. For Iordanova, this aesthetic failure comprises a failure to establish an identificatory relationship with the spectator:

> All that happens and is seen in the film, however, keeps the viewer alienated and relies on a Brechtian type of rational moral judgement rather than on mechanisms of identification and compassion. Compassion and the readiness to identify are presupposed as generated in the course of moral reflection over the story – a risky approach considering the film is targeting a mass audience used to genre conventions that rely on human interest associations, an approach that ultimately fails, accounting for the film's limited appeal (Iordanova 2001: 249).

While the marketing campaign may have targeted a mass audience, it is less clear, given the form of the film, that the filmmakers intended to do so. Adopting the strategy of narrative randomness is guaranteed to interrupt and frustrate generic mechanisms of identification. The film vacillates between alienation and identification, distance and proximity and it is this contradictoriness that has troubled critics writing on the film.[7] As a result, as Patricia Molloy observes, 'Whether *Welcome to Sarajevo* is too "anti-Serb" or not "anti-Serb" enough is, at the risk of oversimplification, contingent upon one's investment in one's location. The *Welcome to Sarajevo* I saw in Toronto would not have been the same *Welcome to Sarajevo* I would have seen in Belgrade' (Molloy 2001: 10).

Molloy suggests that, despite its ambivalence, a failure of *Welcome to Sarajevo* is that: 'What Winterbottom does not do is … provide a counternarrative that would suggest that there is an alternative to a way of thinking about the specificity of Bosnia and our responsibilities "as outsiders" that does not involve an intervention from the West, no matter how seemingly benevolent' (Molloy 2001:10–11). This comment identifies both the point of failure of the film but also its critical potential. In embracing narrative incoherence, the critical position of the film becomes similarly uncertain, hence Iordanova's reading of the film's rhetorical strategy as Brechtian – the spectator is required to search for a critical position by assembling the fragmentary and sometimes contradictory 'mess' of the film's story into a narrative structure. However, it is in the refusal/failure to resolve its material – Nicholson's memoirs, documentary footage, and the generic components of the war film – into a coherent, contextualised, counter-narrative that the film begins to approach an ethical position. This is a war, the film tells us (both implicitly in reference to its own status, and explicitly in relation to television news reports), that remains irreducible to narrative coherence, and in this respect, the film demonstrates an ethical awareness – the problem of narrative adequacy encountered by the screenwriter is an ethical and political one. To reframe this material within the mould of an award-winning or commercially viable film might be to do further symbolic violence to victims of real violence by disregarding the particularity of the conflict; framing the siege in the narrative context of a conventional war film implies that the conflict is predictable and belongs to an endless and inevitable series of similar wars, for example. At the same time, to embrace fully narrative disintegration – a violently radical aesthetics of war, rather than the aestheticised violence of the war film – might deter audiences and so result in a different order of representational failure, reproducing the invisibility of the suffering that the film's journalists are so angered by.

If, as Molloy proposes, 'the key question concerning the politics of spectacle is one of ethical responsibility, of how to bear witness to violence against the other without recourse to a violence of representation', then the narrative dislocations of *Welcome to Sarajevo* constitute one answer (Molloy 2001: 2). It may be true that the film does not advocate an alternative to intervention by the West, but at the same time it is clear that Henderson's intervention is comparatively insignificant and this is emphasised by the fact that the film does not end with the successful adoption of Emira. Instead it continues on to the inconclusive scene in which Henderson listens to Jacket's mournful cello recital at the concert for peace on top of one of the hills overlooking the city. Jacket had previously pledged to play a concert when the UN, which had, with the absurd logic of accountancy or sports commentary, ranked Sarajevo as the thirteenth most dangerous place on earth, upgraded it to pole position. In this sense the recital marks a spectacular failure rather than a redemptive or optimistic gesture towards a peaceful and equitable resolution of the conflict. Close-ups of Jacket's face show him in slow-motion on scratched, flickering film stock, giving the sequence an uncomfortable, perplexing feel, dislocated from the rest of the film. The performance is intercut with shots from the bread queue massacre and shots of protesters and politicians. The scene ends by intercutting home video footage of a smiling Emira with shots of David Owen warning us not to expect the West to come in and 'sort this problem out', thereby acknowledging through this juxtaposition, the limitations of Henderson's action. It makes clear that Emira's adoption is not a solution. Thus the film ends on a note of qualification or contradiction. The intense final shot, which breaks classical realist cinema's principle of indirect address (but which is a motif repeated across Winterbottom's films), is of Jacket returning the camera's gaze with a rueful, knowing and perhaps accusatory smile while playing the final bars of the piece.

Returning the viewer's gaze
– the film's final shot

Notes

1   Electronic press kit, UK DVD release.
2   Chamberlain's full 1938 broadcast is archived here: http://www.bbc.co.uk/archive/ww2outbreak/7904.shtml.
3   This is a convention that may well be a narrative cliché but is nevertheless a conventional expectation of cinematic journalism. As Nicholson observes, 'I was accused of violating a sacrosanct rule of journalism (though I have to admit it was new to me), viz: Never Get Involved' (Nicholson 1994: 79).
4   This framing device is an authorial motif of several of collaborations between Winterbottom and Cottrell Boyce including *Butterfly Kiss*, *24 Hour Party People* and *I Want You*.
5   Goran Višnjić was, in fact, a serving soldier who fought with the Croatian ground army against Croatian Serbs, in an example of the filmmakers' use of locals with direct experience of the war.
6   Electronic press kit, UK DVD release.
7   See Wilkinson 1998 whose account of the film's screening in Belgrade indicates the variety of responses to the film.

CHAPTER TWO

Intimacy

The paradox of cinematic intimacy

HENRY: Name the constituent elements of intimacy.
JUDE: Kissing, caressing, holding, slapping, shouting, talking, waiting, sleeping, crying, listening, hoping, encouraging, forgiving, laughing, relenting.
Surviving Desire (Hal Hartley, 1993)

The promise of intimacy has always been a powerful attraction of cinema from the 1890s onwards. Intimacy has, as it were, an intimate relation to the history, technology and aesthetics of cinema. Cinema promises to bring us thrillingly close to other bodies and spaces and, in so doing, to expose before us the personal, secret, erotic and emotional configurations of individual lives. The public space of the film theatre offers a paradoxical experience of intimacy as we sit more or less immobile in the dark in close proximity to other sensitive bodies that are responding affectively to the sounds and images that flood the cinematic space. One of the distinctive pleasures of this viewing context is the brief, intermittent and perhaps unconscious experience of community or intimate continuity with other aroused individuals who share, and thereby intensify, our experience of a film. A common experience of the particularity of 'cinematic intimacy' is in the way that a film comedy is funnier when watched from within a large audience, or a horror film more disturbing and suspenseful. As the surrealists noted, the phenomenological experience of being in the cinema both resembles and invokes the experience of dreaming – Jean Goudal asserted that 'The cinema … constitutes a conscious hallucination' (Goudal 1991: 96), and Luis Buñuel proposed that the cinema 'is the best instrument to express the world of dreams, of emotions, of instinct. The creative mechanism of cinema images … is among all the means of human expression the one which … best imitates the functioning of the mind in the state of dreams' (Buñuel 1991: 119), This analogy also emphasises the intoxicating sense of closeness or familiarity generated by film, and the accompanying disorientation or desubjectification as the boundary or interface between interior and exterior appears to dissolve as the on-screen images register as projections of the spectator's psyche. A key pleasure of cinematic intimacy, then, is the transgression or dissolution of boundaries between self and other, private and public, inside and outside, screen and reality, cinematic signifier and signified.

Watching a film on a tablet, computer monitor or television in the comparatively private domestic space of the home (which is undoubtedly where the majority of contemporary viewers watch most films) offers a different mode of intimacy as we are alone with a screen or in the company of a small number of friends and/or family members. In this context, the film, a text typically designed for mass distribution, is incorporated into the intimate architecture of the home and the viewer joins an imagined national or international community of home-bound viewers at the same time that she establishes an imagined intimacy with the text.[1]

The promise of intimacy is also a correlative attraction of the technical capacity and formal composition of many of the films we watch in these contexts. The conventions of camera distance and editing, by which narrative space is organised and temporalised in film, can place us in dramatically intense proximity to characters and events through judicious use of the close-up. The close-up or extreme close-up shot appears – particularly when intercut with shots taken from a greater distance – to bring us close to details, faces and bodies. When motivated by a narrative framework, these shots can isolate and bring forward moments of acute emotional or psychological significance. Thus, we can identify across many films – especially those that conform to classical conventions – a formal principle of intimacy. The recent spectacular re-emergence of 3D cinema and television represents a particularly literal and self-conscious but consistent concern with spatial intimacy.

More generally, the expressive codes of film melodrama offer us scenarios in which the imagined interiority of characters is brought to the surface, the *mise-en-scène* becoming an affective extension of the protagonist's psychology. As if they have been turned inside out, these characters' personal, secret and sexual feelings, fantasies and neuroses are made spectacularly visible to the spectator, if not to other characters within the diegesis. More generally still, in various realist modes, film promises to lay bare reality, to expose before us, through an epistemological erotics, the intimate truth beneath the deceptive surface. As Christian Metz puts it, 'The way the cinema, with its wandering framings (wandering like the look, the caress), finds the means to reveal space has something to do with a kind of permanent undressing, a generalized striptease' (Metz 2000: 433). Or, perhaps, cinema's revelatory mechanics is more violent than Metz allows, not just 'undressing', but peeling back the skin of the world to reveal the raw, glistening flesh beneath. The equation of the cinematic gaze with the observation of a strip show speaks volumes about the unequal power relations, misogyny, commodification and violence implicit in the institutions, aesthetics and narrative preoccupations of much cinema.

The attraction of cinematic intimacy has a paradoxical dimension, which is intrinsic to its fascination. Films in many different genres make public what is normally private, and make visible what is typically hidden or unseen. Cinematic intimacy thus has a contradictory structure whose continuing attraction rests on its impossibility. Just as Freud proposed of the uncanny (*das unheimlich*) that it is a term with a range of possible meanings that extend from 'strange' and 'unfamiliar' through to their opposite, '*heimlich*' or 'familiar', so cinematic intimacy connotes both the private and the public, the hidden and the visible. We are brought close to intimate moments and details by a film, but, in becoming publicly visible, intimacy is dissipated and we remain voyeuristically estranged from these moments and encounters. The repetitive practice of film viewing is driven partly by the desire for a fugitive intimacy that is experienced or imagined fleetingly, but is also necessarily foreclosed. We watch films (and engage with other narrative media) repeatedly in order to re-establish the deeply affective relation of intimacy that remains tantalisingly transient, alienating and unsatisfactory. In one respect it is precisely because of our repeated failure to experience immediate intimacy in front of a screen that our desire for it is stimulated, driving us to watch films again and again (and in some cases to watch individual films repeatedly in the hope of repeating and enhancing an initial experience). What we are brought close to is the medium of film, the cinematic apparatus, and the textual and perceptual assemblage of the representation, rather than what is represented therein. Film brings us close to the screen. As Christian Metz observes in his analysis of the perceptual and semiotic processes by which cinema engages the spectator, this displacement of the referent is a special property of cinema: 'More than the other arts, or in a more unique way, the cinema involves us in the imaginary: it drums up all perception, but to switch it immediately over into its absence, which is nonetheless the only signifier present' (Metz 2000: 410) As is demonstrated in *Blow-Up* (Michelangelo Antonioni, 1966), where the fashion photographer Thomas repeatedly enlarges a detail of a photograph in order to identify a murderer he may have inadvertently captured in the background of an image, the closer in he gets, all that is revealed is the increasingly illegible grain of the image, the material composition of the signifier. As Metz explains, absence is intrinsic to the medium:

> the actor, the 'décor', the words one hears are all absent, everything is recorded (as a memory trace which is immediately so, without having been something else before), and this is still true if what is recorded is not a "story" and does not aim for the fictional illusion proper. For it is the signifier itself, and as a whole, that is recorded, that is absence: a little rolled up strip which "contains" vast landscapes, fixed battles, the melting of ice on the river Neva and whole life-times. (Metz 2000: 409)

This absence is just as much a property of the immaterial pixellated digital image stored on a hard drive as it is of the grainy photographic analogue image that has a physical substrate. The promise of cinematic intimacy is, simultaneously, a promise of failure to establish an intimate relation with the objects of scrutiny, and it is this failure, this lack of intimacy that generates desire, the *cinephilia* that impels us repeatedly towards films and screens. Indeed, the voyeuristic relationship to the cinematic image wherein the spectator is positioned as an 'unacknowledged' observer that is constructed through the 'invisibility' of classical realist conventions, or what Bordwell, Staiger and Thompson term, classical cinema's 'excessive obviousness' (1988), is what makes this irreducible separation from the object a structural feature of cinema: 'If it is true of all desire that it depends on the infinite pursuit of its absent object, voyeuristic desire, along with certain forms of sadism, is the only desire whose principle of distance symbolically and spatially, evokes this fundamental rent' (Metz 2000: 421).

The promise of pleasurable cinematic intimacy is redoubled by the correlative thematic preoccupation of many films with documenting close inter-personal relationships between characters, and imaging scenes of emotional and physical intensity. A narrative concern with the intimate lives of characters is both a figure for intimacy – a means of exploring the themes of intimacy and/or of signalling a thematics of intimacy – as well as a means of establishing (or implying) an intimate relationship with the spectator (through disclosure and identification).

The impossibility of intimacy in Winterbottom's films

This chapter will explore several dimensions of cinematic intimacy, which, in various configurations and relations, is a central preoccupation of Winterbottom's films. Some, such as *Welcome to Sarajevo* and *In This World*, attempt to engage us in a deeply affecting and politically provocative fashion with the distressing plight of individual characters who find themselves caught up in situations in which they have limited agency. By contrast, other films, such as *The Road to Guantánamo*, *A Mighty Heart* or *9 Songs*, appear to obstruct such intimate relations, as if in recognition of the intellectual and political limitations of such an affective relation with the spectator, attempting instead to engage us as actively critical spectators. As an attempt to despectacularise or narrativise cinematic sex, for example, *9 Songs* can be read as a critique of pornographic film and video and the alienating commodification of sexualised intimacy.

What I argue in this chapter is that the treatment of intimacy in Winterbottom's films is marked by an acknowledgement of the *impossibility of intimacy* or, more precisely, the way in which intimacy is structured around the impossibility of its fulfilment. Given that the treatment of intimacy in these films is frequently framed with self-reflexive formal devices such as the juxtaposition of generically incompatible or unconventional elements, this thematic preoccupation can thus be understood as both a reflection upon, and an interruption of, circuits of cinematic intimacy, and cinematic representations of intimacy. However, what characterises the thematics of intimacy in the films is the tenuous, provisional quality of intimacy between friends, lovers and family members or, indeed, its absence.

'Intimacy' has various shades of meaning and can refer to what is personal, what is physically close, to objects, texts, garments, body parts that are, or should remain, private and concealed, and to interiority and to emotional and sexual communication. Inter-personal intimacy depends upon the transgression of certain boundaries, processes of self-exposure, and, possibly, the pleasurable, anxious or distressing dissolution of the self. In one respect, inter-personal intimacy is structured around a paradox – which parallels the spectator's desire for an intimate relation with the screen/image/diegesis – which is that the desire for an intimate relation with another remains frustrated and unsatisfied as soon as this relation is established; what was previously private, inaccessible and therefore desired is, by definition, no longer so. Intimacy is always relational: it describes the quality and structure of a relation between two or more beings. Furthermore, intimate relations describe the promise of an *authentic* relationship or encounter with another. The promise of intimacy with another is the promise of access to their internal world of feeling, rather than a superficial relation and/or a simulation or performance of authentic feeling. The promise of cinema, we might argue, is the promise of an intimate encounter, the promise of what Lisa Baraitser describes in another context as 'new experiences, sensations, moods, sensibilities, intensities, kinetics, tingling, janglings, emotions, thoughts, perceptions: new coagulations of embodied and relational modes' (Baraitser 2009: 3). It is also important to stress the negative and violent dimensions of intimacy, since intimate relations are also always power relations. This is just as much the case with spectator relations as it is with relations between individuals; the pleasures (and unpleasures) of film viewing can be understood – particularly in terms of theories of gendered spectatorship – as sadistic or masochistic.[2] In allowing another intimate access to aspects of ourselves, making certain facets of ourselves visible, we make ourselves vulnerable, open to embarrassment, humiliation, and abuse, and thus intimacy opens onto issues of ethical responsibility towards the exposed, visible other.

Mas'Ud Zavarzadeh proposes that relations of intimacy are culturally and historically specific rather than universal. 'Intimacy … like all modes of cultural intelligibility, is a social construct and produced in response to the needs for particular modes of subjectivities necessary for reproducing the dominant relations of production' (Zavarzadeh 1991: 113). Reflecting on the cultural politics of intimacy, Zavarzadeh suggests that the common sense representations of intimacy as spontaneous and 'natural' play a critical role in asserting the possibility of individual freedom and privacy from social power relations. The assumption that intimacy originates within inter-personal interactions, rather than in relation to framing social structures suggests that in the intensity of a romantic, familial or friendly relationships, individuals can be entirely removed from their subjective position within history or society. As Zavarzadeh suggests, 'Intimacy is thus the ultimate sign of their sovereignty as individuals; it signals their freedom' (Zavarzadeh 1991: 114). Conversely, intimate relations only have any significance with regard to relations of what Jacques Lacan termed 'extimity' (see Miller 2008). In this respect, intimacy is comprehensible only as a function of public relation. This is most evident in the cautionary depiction of biopolitical state/corporate power in *Code 46* wherein even the most apparently intimate component of individual identity – the genetic composition of the body – is visible to the state and to medical corporations. However, more generally this means that films which explore intimacy are inevitably concerned not just with the private, a-social, a-historical individual but with the public, social and historical frameworks through which individuals interact and an intimate critical examination of cinematic intimacy is similarly concerned with questions of power and identity. As Zavarzadeh observes, a critical interrogation of intimacy 'is a form of political knowledge of the situatedness and historicity of the relationship as well as of the people involved and regards intimacy as a mode of social collectivity and thus an effect of the social' (Zavarzadeh 1991: 116). Lauren Berlant argues similarly, that we can understand intimacy 'as a public mode of identification and self-development', but since intimacy is a term of such over-familiarity and redundancy, it remains largely unexamined in the many contexts in which the term circulates (Berlant 2000: 5). 'We notice it', Berlant suggests, 'when something about it takes on a charge, so that the intimacy becomes something else, an "issue" – something that requires analytic eloquence' (Berlant 2000: 7). Because intimacy is so intrinsic to the medium, cinema is a context in which intimacy can take on a charge as it is made visible and explicit. Cinema can reveal the properties of public intimacy, which is 'a relation associated with tacit fantasies, tacit rules, and tacit obligations to remain unproblematic', and this chapter explores the ways in which Winterbottom's films expose these fantasies, conventions and constraints (ibid.).

The cinematic encounter, while staged, is nevertheless predicated in some sense on the promise of intimacy. Intimacy is thus a field of promise and encounters, which may be one of the reasons why Winterbottom's films return again and again to this subject: not because it is an unreflective, default choice of subject matter for popular film and television, but in order to tease out different dimensions of intimacy through different configurations of characters and the staging of different intimate scenarios from couples talking, fighting and fucking to women giving birth, and prisoners being tortured. This chapter will explore depictions of masculine intimacy, sexual intimacy, violent intimacy and familial intimacy across a number of Winterbottom's films and TV dramas.

Melodramatic Intimacy

With the exception of the documentary, *The Shock Doctrine*, the narratives of almost all of Winterbottom's films and television productions are oriented around the tensions, intensities, misconstructions and empathy, intimacy and violence of the relationships between couples or family members. The dynamic interaction of friends and lovers, parents, children and siblings provides an armature for the narrative and visual examination of place, landscape and historical change. This is a feature of the melodramatic discourse of much mainstream cinema, which frequently understands and represents the social through the lens of individual experience. This has meant that melodrama has been understood popularly as a conservative narrative mode, unable to address or analyse the structuring contexts of social and sexual inequality that are responsible for the difficulties and miseries experienced by the protagonists, much less to propose solutions. The supposed formal conservatism of melodrama, which is closely associated with generic mainstream film and television (as well as other narrative media), compounds the assumption that melodrama is intrinsically reactionary and ideologically complicit.

However, as many film theorists (and audiences) have observed, film melodrama has a progressive potential in so far as some films emphasise the wretched experiences of the protagonists so completely, that conventional narrative resolution is unconvincing and cursory or over-shadowed by the miseries that have preceded it. The ideologically reassuring function of narrative closure through the re-establishment of the status quo is subverted by the weight placed on the miseries endured by the characters. As Elsaesser explains:

> Even if the form might act to reinforce attitudes of submission, the actual working-out of the scenes could nonetheless present fundamental social evils … [T]here seems a radical ambiguity attached to the melodrama, which holds even more for the film melodrama. Depending on whether the emphasis fell on the odyssey of suffering or the happy ending, on the place and context of a rupture … depending on what dramatic mileage was got out of the heroine's perils before the ending … melodrama would appear to function either subversively or as escapism – categories which are always relative to the given historical and social context. (Elsaesser 1987: 47)

Despite the supposedly escapist function of melodrama, film melodramas can offer a much more challenging critique of contemporary social formations than other genres in their preoccupation with disordered families and dysfunctional intimate relationships: 'Melodrama puts into crisis the discourses within the domain circumscribed by and defined as the legally established social order, the kind of order instituted at the end of westerns and detective films. Melodrama does not suggest a crisis of that order, but a crisis within it, an "in house" rearrangement' (Neale 1987: 22). Melodramas depict not an external threat to the 'legally established social order' but an intrinsic disorder within the social formation described by the film.

One of the most direct ways in which Winterbottom's films investigate intimacy is through the melodramatic frame of the close relationship. In doing so they test the boundaries of this framework and its capacity as a vehicle for exploring issues of sexuality, class, race and international politics, without abandoning or dismantling the form. The relationships depicted in these films and TV programmes are complex, pragmatic and unstable. The family and the couple are often the site of emotional violence, the sado-masochistic oscillation of power relations, and the economic negotiation of self-interest with the demands of social responsibility, and selfless love. As a result, narrative resolution is rarely achieved through romantic coupling or through the reconciliation of a family. This is demonstrated with uncompromising clarity in the final hallucinatory scene of *The Killer Inside Me* in which the protagonist, reunited with his lover Joyce, stabs her and sets fire to his house killing himself and the other occupants.

'Should I stay or should I go?'[3] – ambivalent intimacy

The made-for-television film, *Go Now* (1995), is a good example of the melodramatic treatment of the complexities of intimate relationships explored in Winterbottom's work. The title itself – a song title like several other films by the director – encapsulates the uncertainty of the central relationship. Lensed by Daf Hobson (who shot *Welcome* to *Sarajevo*, as well as the Winterbottom-directed TV dramas, *Family* and *Under the Sun*), and edited by Trevor Waite (a frequent Winterbottom collaborator who won a BAFTA[4] award for this film), *Go Now* is also a good example of Winterbottom's tendency to collaborate repeatedly with certain creative figures. There is none of the stylistic excesses we might associate with film melodrama, but the film's naturalist style is subtly undermined by punctuation with captions and montage sequences of black-and-white stills depicting comic events in the amateur football matches played by the protagonist. Co-written by Paul Henry Powell and Jimmy McGovern[5] (who also devised, and wrote some episodes of the TV series *Cracker* (1993–2006) for which Winterbottom directed the feature-length pilot episode, 'The Mad Woman in the Attic' (1993)), *Go Now* tells the story of a young couple living in Bristol, Nick (Robert Carlyle) and Karen (Juliet Aubrey), whose lives are devastated when Nick develops multiple sclerosis. Nick, who makes plaster architectural mouldings, is a craftsman, a recurrent figure in Winterbottom's films from Jude the stone-mason and Vincent the glazier (*With or Without You*) to Mark the film director (*A Cock and Bull Story*). Its repetition suggests a self-reflexive celebration of creative work as technically special-ised, labour-intensive, masculine and practical.

The film opens with an argument in the changing room after Nick's amateur football team, The Monts, have lost a match and Nick is being berated by his team-mates for missing a sitter (foreshadowing his physical decline). His friend Tony (James Nesbitt) then tells a joke about having sex with a 'cripple', establishing two of the film's inter-related themes: sexuality and disability. These themes are explored through an intimate focus upon the transformation of Nick's body, and the effects of this upon his relationship with Karen. The narrative traces the development of Nick's relation-ship with Karen, whom he meets in a bar after the opening game and who later moves in with him. As the symptoms of his illness become more evident, and he becomes increasingly incapacitated, their relationship is progressively strained. In the early stages their relationship is depicted in positive terms, their affection communicated through shared physical activities as we see them having sex, walking, jogging and playing the piano together and renovating Nick's flat.

Nick is depicted in terms of conventional working-class masculinity, which is rein-forced by the casting of Robert Carlyle whose dominant screen persona as a tough, working-class figure was established by his role as a builder in Ken Loach's *Riff Raff* (1991). A passionate amateur footballer, Nick is athletic, sociable and affectionate but also argumentative and sometimes belligerent, and works as a manual labourer. His social activities and friendship group are oriented around the football team. His illness is thus staged in the film not simply as a threat to his livelihood and professional identity, but, specifically, as a crisis of masculinity that precludes these expressions or performances of gender. After dropping a lump hammer while moving around on scaf-folding – the first clear sign of illness – he experiences double vision and begins wearing glasses (prompting amusement from his friends: 'God! It's Cliff Richard!'). He begins to find walking difficult becoming reliant on crutches and, later on, has to use a wheel chair intermittently. He also becomes incontinent and in one comic episode during a visit to Glasgow to break the news to his family, he sprays his dad and brother with piss while trying to empty his over-full urine bag in a pub toilet. By stages his illness prevents him from working, playing football and exercising, drinking alcohol copiously, playing the piano, driving, seeing clearly, having sex and, ultimately, walking. However, it is notable that the tone of the film shifts repeatedly from romantic melancholy to unsentimental, broad comedy.

Struggling to play pool in the local pub, for instance, Nick explodes with frustration at his friend, who deliberately misses a crucial shot after Nick missed a sitter, 'Don't fucking patronise me, Tony! Okay?' He goes on to explain, 'I want to be told to get my round in. I want a bit of stick, and I want a pastin' on there [the pool table], 'cause I'm still the fuckin' same.' This results in a particularly uncomfortable scene later on when Nick, now reliant on a wheelchair, visits the changing room after a match and Tony enthusiastically complies with Nick's earlier request, telling him, 'You're ugly, you're skint, you're a four-eyed friggin' spazz. The only thing you had going for you was the occasional stiff one and now you can't even give her that.' Not recognising that his banter is edging into humiliating mockery, he goes on to propose that they draw up a rota so that the team can take turns having sex with his partner, Karen. Nick, who is placed ironically in front of a row of naked men in the shower, wheels his chair away without responding, while the rest of the team turn their back on the bemused Tony. Nevertheless, his diatribe staged in the macho environment of the changing room in which the characters are introduced in the opening scene, identifies precisely the way in which Nick's illness is experienced (and disavowed) as compromised virility – physical incapacity and sexual impotence. The insensitivity of Nick's best friend also demonstrates the restricted capacity for intimacy of a particular mode of normative masculinity wherein homosocial affection is expressed paradoxically through jeering and abuse.

As the illness progresses, Nick becomes increasingly angry through a mixture of self-pity, resentment and shame and goads Karen to leave him, perhaps suspecting what the audience has been shown: that she has had an affair with a work colleague. He tells her that on a trip he took to Africa with his friends before she moved in with him he did 'lots of shagging' and taunts her, 'I'm in this chair but it's you that cannae move. If there was nothing the matter with me you'd have spat in my face and walked, so do it.' He then slaps her in the face to provoke her and they fight before becoming reconciled. This ambivalence is crystallised in the lyric of the 1964 Moody Blues song, 'Go Now', which Tony and Nick play on Karen's piano early in the film, and which is also played by the band at Nick and Karen's wedding reception in the final scene. In the song, which captures a crisis point in a relationship, the singer importunes his lover to leave while insisting that he does not want her/him to go. The final line, 'I don't want to see you go but, Darling, you'd better go now' articulates the pain of being in love with someone who does not or cannot reciprocate, and describes equally well the turbulent, contradictory feelings of both Nick and Karen at different points in the film both of whom are uncertain about whether they want to stay with the other.

The wedding comprises a happy (and unexpected) ending of sorts, and the final shots are of Nick and Karen dancing and laughing, but it has been established that multiple sclerosis is an incurable disease and so this is a brief interlude. Although there are sequences in which the disease goes into remission – we see Nick playing pool and jogging again with Karen – we understand that he will become more and more incapacitated. The song, 'Go Now', plays over the closing credits but by this point in the film, it can also be taken to refer to Nick's decline (as well as announcing to the viewer the end of the film). *Go Now* belongs to the tradition of the 'male melodrama', films such as *Rebel Without a Cause* (Nicholas Ray, 1955) that concentrate upon 'feminised' male characters or, rather, upon characters whose masculinity is rendered as unconventional and complex or sexually ambivalent through their deep emotional expressiveness or their forced passivity. In this respect, melodrama is a framework through which the film interrogates gender relations.

In *Go Now*, the relationship between Nick and Karen is jeopardised by Nick's illness, but, given that he is represented so clearly in terms of conventional masculinity, what threatens the relationship is not simply the difficulties of living with disability and incurable illness (and the bodily estrangement or abjection that accompanies that), but the reversal of traditional gender roles it entails. Among its various effects, multiple sclerosis places Nick in a position of dependency upon his partner and his friends. Thus, the film explores the effects of a particular illness through the shifting dynamics of an intimate relationship which is shot through with a painful and complex combination of betrayals, rejections and reconciliations, silence and communication, strength, weakness and self-exposure.

Masculine intimacies

Romantic and intimate relationships in Winterbottom's films are haunted by loss, failure, rejection and withdrawal and also by uncertain futures. Indeed, characters are often engaged with the active, self-harming dismantling of relationships, rather than with the constructive investment in secure partnerships. *The Trip*, a six-part UK TV series,[6] also made for the BBC, is concerned with the comically awkward nature of the friendship between two straight male actors, and the way in which, for these men, the expressions of intimacy is obstructed by emotional awkwardness and sexual anxiety, and is mediated and displaced through the adoption of various personae and self-conscious performance.

The premise of the series is that Steve Coogan, playing himself, has been commissioned by a national newspaper to write an article reviewing restaurants in the north of England. Coogan had intended to travel with his American girlfriend, Mischa, taking the opportunity to introduce her to areas of the country that he knows and loves. However, with his girlfriend having left him to return to America, he asks his friend Rob Brydon, also playing himself, to accompany him. Thus, Brydon finds himself awkwardly occupying Mischa's role in what was conceived as a romantic excursion, demonstrating that the series is an exploration of the dynamics of a couple as well as an examination of middle-aged masculinity.

The series, a road film derivative with extended interruptions, is effectively a sequel to *A Cock and Bull Story* since it centres on the interplay of the two actors who were the protagonists of the earlier film in which they also played themselves (in more or less the same characterisation as in this series), although there is no reference to the fact that they have each previously appeared in two of Winterbottom's films. The narrative premise of a road film featuring a same-sex couple is a flexible format in Winterbottom's work and is shared with *In This World* and *Butterfly Kiss*. It isolates two characters in close proximity – the car is a particularly effective device for this, a parody of the confines of a relationship wherein the characters are strapped in to their seats, side by side – and tests their relationship by moving them through a series of encounters and unfamiliar locations. The car, in which the characters sit immobile (but travelling through space) looking not at one another but at the screen in front of them is also a reflection of the spectator's position, inviting us to identify or to recognise a parallel. As Julian Stringer observes, while the protagonists of road films appear to be driven by two alternate solipsistic impulses – escape and self-discovery – these films tend in fact to be centrally concerned with social interaction of individuals encountering one another in unfamiliar contexts. 'Paradoxically, then, in masquerading as one of the most anti-social of all cultural forms, road movies constitute a polar opposite. Presenting characters who travel through expansive landscapes in self-enclosed vehicles, they situate the work of ideology in the creation of new intimacies' (Stringer 1997: 166). That is to say, regardless of their intentions, these characters are unable to escape ideological determination in their interaction with others during the trip. They are returned to themselves. 'Road movie protagonists may look through the window and see the whole world ahead of them, but they usually end up becoming intimate with people just like them-

'Gentlemen, to bed, for we rise at daybreak!' – Coogan and Brydon extemporising a costume drama

selves' (Stringer 1997: 166). Tellingly, when Coogan and Brydon look through the windows of their Range Rover they see a film set in which they are acting. As they drive through Cumbria, Brydon suggests, 'You could have a costume drama here, couldn't you?' Coogan responds excitedly, 'Do you know what? I'd just love to do a costume drama in these hills, just leaping, vaulting over dry stone walls with a scabbard, that dead look in my eyes because I've seen so many horrors I'm immune to them.' They then spend several minutes exchanging heroic dialogue and mocking the conventions of the genre.

Much of the dialogue in *The Trip* appears to be improvised and, as a result, certain scenes have an 'authentic', confessional quality where the actor behind the performance appears briefly to be exposed as in the flashes of anger, jealousy, angst and arrogance with which Coogan responds to Brydon's conversation. The naturalism of the performances by Coogan and Brydon makes it difficult to determine to what degree the film is fictional as opposed to 'authentic', but this is exacerbated by the fact that they are playing professional performers and celebrities, who are inevitably self-conscious about their presentation, and it is redoubled by the fact that this is a performance of awkwardness – of two male friends placed in uncomfortably intimate circumstances. There are inseparable layers of artifice, self-reflexion and a concomitant absence of self-awareness in these performances.

In each half-hour episode they visit a different restaurant and the focus of the programme is on their conversations conducted during the meal, while driving through the winter landscape of Yorkshire, Lancashire and the Lake District and during visits to local tourist attractions such as Wordsworth's cottage and Coleridge's house. This simple structure is repeated in each episode as the two actors discuss the food and drink, reflect upon their experience of ageing, sing pop songs together, exchange acting techniques and observations, competitively perform impersonations for each other, occasionally slipping into improvised routines, and defensively compare the success of their careers. As Coogan asks Brydon in the third episode (in a typically self-reflexive comment upon the series):

Do you think we have the same conversation in every restaurant? … We start out being a bit awkward with each other, have a little bit of wine, exchange a few frivolities … Have a bit more wine, get cantankerous, pick faults with each other, and it descends into a kind of bitter, unhappy end to the meal.

The sado-masochistic dynamic of the couple is that of a male comedy double act like Laurel and Hardy in which a vain, self-important but frustrated character continually abuses and humiliates his gentler, tolerant but resentful counterpart. The pair find themselves repeatedly thrust together not through choice, but through a certain fatal affinity and it is only when Coogan is asked by his son how long he's known Brydon that he comes to acknowledge with surprise both to his son and himself, that 'He's a good friend'. The sexual dynamics of the classic male comedy double act typically remain unacknowledged in any direct way by the characters or the film's narration, but they are nevertheless often a crucial comic component. Despite the fact that Laurel

Two-shot – Brydon and Coogan dine at the Inn at Whitewell

and Hardy are frequently shown sharing a bed, cross-dressing, and in one short (*Our Wife* (James W. Horne, 1931)), are accidentally married by a cross-eyed J.P., they tend to be presented either as infantilised and asexual, or as chastely heterosexual husbands. As Jonathan Sanders has demonstrated, however, in a thorough thematic study of their films, the films of Laurel and Hardy consistently explore and derive comedy from gender instability and nonconformity: 'Childhood and adulthood, masculinity and femininity, heterosexuality and homosexuality: polarities such as these are synthesized into comic ambiguities, which in turn are combined with each other to create a world in perpetual flux' (Sanders 1995: 3). The pair are sometimes figured as a parody of a battling, vindictive married couple, sometimes as an idealised couple united in their difference from the hostile social environment.

Coogan's discomfort with the 'comic ambiguities' of their intimate coupling is a running theme of *The Trip* as he repeatedly expresses his anxiety that they might be misperceived as a gay couple. This is superficially funny since, in a depiction that is consistent with his celebrity persona as it has been constructed by intrusive press reports on his 'private life', the Coogan character is depicted as a Lothario who sleeps with two women in the course of the trip while simultaneously trying to patch up his relationships with his girlfriend and with his son. However, this promiscuity and his disavowal of sexual intimacy with Brydon is, of course, poignantly underscored by a desire for intimacy. He will not allow the newspaper's photographer to take a picture of the two of them together and he makes clear to Brydon in the opening scene of the series that he invited him on the trip only after failing to find another travelling companion, explaining, 'It's a job; I'm not asking you to go on holiday with me, or anything weird'. He is flatly insistent that they cannot share a bed when, in a comic cliché, they are booked into a single room by mistake. The awkward dynamic of forced proximity is a common feature of road films so that, Robert Lang suggests, 'Almost every mainstream road movie in which two men travel together … contains at least one scene that turns on homosexual anxiety and the taboo of same-sex attraction' (Lang 1997: 334). This generic convention is made excessively obvious in a scene where Coogan recoils when Brydon playfully leans in to kiss him, snapping, 'Don't do that.' Recovering his composure and attempting to gloss over this brief exposure of his anxiety, he jokingly explains to the two women they have just met, 'There's been none of that. Heavy petting … but no penetration.' His ironic disavowal exposes precisely the erotics of their relationship. Discussing the emergence of (primarily American) queer independent road movies in the 1990s, Lang suggests that the road movie has emerged in this period as a particularly effective vehicle for exploring the nuances of male friendship: 'Fifty years after *Road to Morocco*, the road movie can explore some of the erotic complexity of male-male friendships, without prohibitive cultural anxieties and Production Code pressure making comedy the only genre in which such questions can be honestly addressed' (Lang 1997: 335). In *The Trip* this flexible cinematic tradition is fused with the conventions of the TV sitcom.

Coogan has appeared in a number of high-profile films,[7] although his character explains to Brydon's (in an ironic comment upon his relationship with Winterbottom), 'I don't work with mainstream Hollywood directors. I work with auteurs.' However, both actors are best known in Britain as comic actors and skilful impressionists on radio and TV. In conversation with one another and with other characters they encounter during the trip they launch continually into comic voices or impressions of famous actors, adopting and exaggerating their voices, facial expressions and physical mannerisms. Over the course of the series the frequency with which they perform this masquerade begins to seem almost pathological. Brydon's irrepressible readiness to launch into an impression at the slightest cue prompts Coogan to suggest that he is an 'autistic impressionist', adding that, 'I think anyone over 40 who amuses themself by doing impressions needs to take a long hard look in the mirror'. Nevertheless, they both constantly fall back on impressions during conversation and seem more comfortable behind the persona of Al Pacino or Woody Allen. While it is underpinned by disavowal, particularly, for Coogan, masquerade for the two of them is also a means of intimate communication rather than an obstacle to it. Brydon, for example, continues to rotate through different voices during his flirtatious, playful and self-mocking phone calls to his partner from his hotel bed at the end of each episode, making it clear that intimacy and performance are not incompatible. On the contrary, the drama demonstrates that intimacy and authentic expression is something that is performed and that is structured by cultural knowledge. The joyful sequences where Coogan and Brydon sing kitsch pop songs in harmony and act out conversations in character are brief intervals of relaxed, pleasurable, intimate communication. In this sense, the question raised by some of Winterbottom's other films about the relationship between documentary and fiction is addressed in a different way since, for these actors, adopting someone else's voice – usually a comically exaggerated version of a famous film actor such as Michael Caine, Anthony Hopkins or Roger Moore – enables them to express themselves in a nuanced way. On a visit to Bolton priory, Coogan berates Brydon for reciting an extract from Wordsworth's poem 'The White Doe of Rylstone' (1807),[8] in the voice of actor Ian McKellen: 'It was a lovely poem. What would have been really nice is if you'd got up this morning ... and said the poem in your own voice and meant the words.' Brydon calmly replies, 'I chose the voice to suit the mood'. For Brydon, imitation and the conscious adoption of personae is a means of sincere and personal expression, a sensitive response to a specific context. Indeed, one of the most oddly moving moments in the series comes when Coogan, looking despondently at himself in a hotel bathroom mirror (echoing his earlier advice to Brydon), says in his childish 'silly cartoon voice', 'I don't care about silly voices. They're stupid.' This performance before the mirror is a moment of self-recognition and self-condemnation (and jealousy of Brydon's popularity), voiced through the most bizarre of all the voices employed by the two actors.

Significantly, Coogan's frustration is triggered by his inability to reproduce Brydon's uncannily accurate impression of the muffled voice of a 'small man trapped in a box'. This has become one of Brydon's most well-known impressions – they are able to get access to Dove cottage at closing time when Brydon performs it for the star-struck attendant, who is utterly uninterested in Coogan. It is, of course, also a vivid metaphor for repression, the psychic defence mechanism whereby thoughts and memories that might be troublesome if voiced or acted upon, are deflected into the unconscious. More precisely, it is a metaphor for the impossibility of masculine intimacy.

In one respect Coogan's unhappiness is due to dissatisfaction with his lack of success in America. Anxious about being trapped in 'the box' (British slang for 'television'), he explains to his agent at one point, when offered a role in the science fiction series *Doctor Who*, 'I don't want to do British TV', adding, 'I want to do films. Good films!' The fact that the two of them repeatedly imitate the voices of much more famous actors underscores their comparative lack of success. We are given an intimate insight into the character's egotism and anxiety through a dream sequence in which Coogan is addressed by Hollywood star, Ben Stiller.[9] The actor tells Coogan that everyone wants to work with him, listing Tony and Ridley Scott, the Coen brothers, the Wachowskis, Todd Haynes. 'They're all geniuses,' Stiller assures him, 'and they wanna work with the genius.' 'I can't believe it's happening', gasps Coogan, to which Stiller replies ambiguously, 'You're living the dream, Steve. It's all a dream.' However a later dream reframes Coogan's anxieties about success and 'performance' more precisely in terms of masculinity. In the second dream he is dismayed to meet a man coming out of a village newsagent holding a tabloid newspaper bearing the headline, 'COOGAN IS A CUNT SAYS DAD'. This is an equally vivid figure for Oedipal hostility and emphasises that what motivates Coogan, much more so than Brydon, is repression. He is the small man trapped inside a box, which is precisely why he cannot reproduce Brydon's impression, why he cannot find a voice for this diminutive version of himself and why easy intimacy remains an impossibility for him. This is true of his relationship with Brydon and also with others, since Coogan is separated from his partner and children, and is 'chasing women', as Brydon puts it, sleeping with two women during the trip while also trying to resurrect his relationship with the absent Mischa.

There is some sense that the two characters have got to know one another more fully during the journey, but the terms of the relationship are not altered substantially so that at the end of the series the characters return to where they began literally and symbolically. The trip has traced a circle rather than a progressive line. Coogan drops Brydon back at his house, driving off impatiently as Brydon suggests that they phone one another to arrange to get together. He then returns to the empty, pristinely minimal tower-block apartment where we saw him at the beginning of the first episode. Whereas Brydon is welcomed home by his partner, Sally (and continues to do impressions during dinner with her), Coogan sits alone watching a video of him and his estranged girlfriend,

Small man trapped in a box – Coogan at home after the trip

Mischa, on his phone. He then calls his agent to tell him that he's turning down the offer of a starring role in the pilot for a US TV series because, 'I've got kids.' However, it's unclear whether this is genuinely based on a renewed determination to invest in his own family, whether it is a pretext for not taking up a job that may have led to a seven-year commitment, or whether it is an indication that he has reconciled himself to a less spectacular career. The series ends with a series of shots of the London skyline at night, reprising the daytime shots the series opened with.

Sex and intimacy

A consistent feature of Winterbottom's films is the reiteration of sex as a component of intimate, adult relationships. In some films, such as the romantic comedy, *With or Without You*, in which procreation and fertility treatments are a theme, the matter-of-fact depiction of sex within (and outside) a long-term relationship is unsurprising, but in other films such as the costume film, *Jude*, a sequence showing the two protagonists having sex is rather more unconventional – and is a creative elaboration upon the source novel. In this sense, from *Butterfly Kiss* onwards, Winterbottom's films have been quietly pushing back a boundary, testing a censorious convention that requires representations of sex in mainstream film and television to remain implicit. Appropriately, given an insistence upon its ordinariness, the films are not radically formally unconventional in their depiction of sex, although they are sometimes more explicit than the genre context might suggest. As Jackie Stacey observes of the staging and filming of sex in *Code 46*, for example:

Maria's appearance in her black cap and coat, with cropped hair and urban self-confidence, also places her within an aesthetic of metrosexuality, with a distinctly queer urban feel […] These homoerotic connotations are extended into the filming of the lovers' first sex scene, which cuts between the two evenly, emphasizing not sight but touch in the close-up shots of their hands and mouths. Such mutuality and visual symmetry is rare within the scopic economies of penetrative heterosexual sex on the cinema screen, and the scene emphasizes similarity and reciprocity. (Stacey 2010: 167–8)

The next section of the chapter will explore the issue of the representation of sex in cinema through a discussion of the two films of Winterbottom in which sex is most central, *Code 46* and *9 Songs*. Both films are characterised by self-reflexivity and can therefore be understood as commentaries upon cinematic sex in quite different ways. This chapter will also explore the complex play of distance and proximity in relation to sexual intimacy as it is depicted in these two films.

Code 46, a science fiction film set at an unspecified point in the future where, perhaps due to advanced climate change, the inhabitants of Shanghai sleep during the day to avoid the dangerous sun, while all of the land we see outside the city is desert and ruined buildings occupied by an underclass which is denied passage across the border into the city. In this inverted society advances in genetic engineering and reproductive technology have led, through cloning, artificial insemination and *in vitro* fertilisation, to a situation where it is possible that apparently unrelated individuals might be genetically identical. As the opening expository caption explains, 'the relations of one are the relations of all'. 'Code 46' is the consequent law that has been introduced to prohibit 'accidental or deliberate genetically incestuous reproduction' through the requirement that all prospective parents are genetically screened before conception. Foetuses resulting from unplanned pregnancies must also be screened and terminated if the parents are 25%, 50% or 100% genetically related and it is a crime for parents who know they are genetically related to conceive. Thus, the film belongs to a tradition of dystopian science fiction films such as *THX 1138* (George Lucas, 1971), *Z.P.G.* (Michael Campus, 1972), *A Boy and His Dog* (L. Q. Jones, 1975), *Nineteen Eighty-Four* (Michael Radford, 1984), *The Handmaid's Tale* (Volker Schlöndorff, 1990), *Children of Men* (Alfonso Cuarón, 2006) that are concerned with the intrusive biopolitical regulation of sexuality and procreation by surveillance societies or totalitarian states, or with apocalyptic futures marked by infertility and a declining birthrate. *Code 46* is framed by these captions as a film that is thematically concerned with the social and legal regulation of sex through the legislative incorporation of the incest taboo. Thus, the most intimate, private of exchanges is figured here as a matter of public interest and sexual partners effectively require the consent of the state. Sex is separated from intimacy or, rather, the intimate relation is a relation with the state and the medical-judicial infrastructure, rather than with an individual sexual partner.

The film thus also follows in a tradition of science fiction and fantasy films concerned with genetic engineering and reproduction, medical science, and the technological transformation and supersession of the flawed, fragile, differentiated body. As Steven Shaviro observes, most science fiction

> is not about literally predicting the future. Rather, it is about capturing the latent futurity that already haunts us in the present [...] Especially in times of great social and technological change, we *feel* the imminence of the future in the form of gaps and leaps in temporal progression and shifts in the horizon of what is thinkable. Of course it is impossible to know what changes the future will bring; but the signs of this impossibility – the intimations of instability, the shifts of perspective, and the incipient breaks in continuity – are themselves altogether real. (Shaviro 2010: 66–7)

Indeed, *Code 46* is economical in its elaboration of the future. There are a number of elements that code the film generically as a future fantasy, such as minimalist interiors, VR headsets and windows that function as touch-screen video monitors, as well as synthetic viruses. However, the film's depiction of the infrastructures and topography of this future society is sketchy, which confirms that the film is not interested in the future except in so far as it offers a shifted perspective on the present. As Jackie Stacey suggests, in a detailed discussion of the film in relation to cinema's engagement with 'the genetic imaginary', the spaces of the film are a symbolic articulation of a problematic intimacy, so that, 'we might approach the cityscapes in *Code 46* not as settings, but as projections of the modern subject's anxieties about the changing significance of the body's interior' (Stacey 2010: 138). The city, which recurs repeatedly in Winterbottom's films as a symbolic stage or backdrop, is here figured as a visual figure for a technologised, deindividuated, post-human subjectivity. As Stacey observes, questions about the permeability or transparency of the body's boundary reverberate through questions about the mobility of bodies across borders between the interior and exterior – significantly, characters refer to the blasted landscape beyond Shanghai's boundary simply as 'outside'.

As with several other films by the director, *Code 46* is a composite or, appropriately given its thematic orientation, a hybrid of several genres. Both visually, with its tenebrous lighting scheme, and in terms of its plot, it is a *film noir* (a genre also explored by Winterbottom in *I Want You* and *The Killer Inside Me*) whose story concerns a detective falling for the sexually independent woman who is the object of his investigation. In doing so, his professionalism and the integrity of his family are compromised.

Shanghai – futuristic metropolis

William Geld (Tim Robbins) is a corporate investigator hired by Shanghai company, The Sphinx, which makes 'papels', or 'cover': visas that permit people to travel in and out of the city. Geld uses an 'empathy virus', which enables him to read other characters' unspoken or unconscious thoughts as they speak to him, to identify the employee, Maria Gonzales (Samantha Morton), who is smuggling counterfeit visas out of the factory to distribute them to people unable to obtain 'cover' for various reasons. Perhaps due to the virus he is infected with, Geld becomes infatuated with Gonzales and deliberately identifies another employee as the forger. He then pursues Gonzales and they sleep together before Geld returns home to Seattle and his wife and son. Despatched back to Shanghai to resolve the case after it becomes clear that the distribution of forged papels is continuing, Geld seeks out Gonzales and discovers that she is in a medical facility having had a pregnancy terminated and her recent memory wiped and replaced with a synthetic (screen) memory. He arranges her release and then proves to her that they have already met by showing her video footage of the two of them together, telling her that he fell in love with her during the fraud investigation. While she sleeps he takes a sample of her hair to a pharmacy for screening and learns that she is his mother's genetic twin. On learning this, Geld tries to leave Shanghai but finds his visa has expired and so he asks Maria for a forgery and, when she meets him at the airport, the two of them fly to Jebel Ali and take a room in a hotel. When Geld touches her and she recoils, he explains that she has been infected with a virus by the Sphinx. She wants to have sex nevertheless and so, in a particularly disturbing scene, she allows herself to be tied to the bedhead and undressed. She then writhes, whimpers and cries while Geld has sex with her in an act of what Stacey describes as 'consensual rape', as she instructs him, 'Make me make love to you' (Stacey 2010: 169). This sequence is made more uncomfortable as much of the scene shows her suffering face in close-up from Geld's point-of-view, aligning the spectator (spatially, at least) with him. The following morning she awakes and, without realising, makes a telephone call to report a 'Code 46 violation' before returning to bed. Geld then wakes her, aware of what has taken place, buys a car, and they flee into the desert where they crash trying to avoid a camel train. In the film's conclusion Geld has been returned to Seattle, having had his memory wiped and he is reunited with his family. Gonzales meanwhile has been cast into exile 'outside' (*al fuera*) and left with her memories intact – in an inversion of *film noir* conventions, the voice-over narration throughout the film is provided by her rather than the investigator, rendering Geld a distant, unsympathetic figure whose motivation is difficult to infer. She is seen in the film's last shots living in a desert

The bare life of exile –
Maria al fuera at the
film's conclusion

shanty town that resembles the Shamshattoo refugee camp in Pakistan, depicted in the opening scene of *In This World*.

There are other frameworks the film might be read through. It is a border film depicting a future in which social inequality is compounded by a hierarchy of mobility wherein some characters can cross regional and national boundaries while others are stranded at checkpoints. The fact that the shots of present-day Dubai, London, Hong Kong and, in particular, hyper-modern Shanghai stand for future cities indicates that this is by no means a remote, exotic future. It also depicts a thoroughly multi-cultural, Orientalised future, which is marked by the hybrid language spoken by the characters, in which English is peppered with words from other languages, recalling the 'city-speak' of the inhabitants of Los Angeles in *Blade Runner*. *Blade Runner* is an important reference point both for this film's visual imagining of the spectacular spaces and cultures of future cities, extrapolated from the present,[10] and for a scenario in which ubiquitous genetic engineering challenges the category of the human and the natural.[11] The world of *Code 46* is a highly but unequally bio-technologised future in which characters can use synthetic viruses to enable them to sing, learn languages, enhance their intuitive abilities, and in which they can download their memories directly into 'photograph' albums.

The inter-generic status of Winterbottom's films means that one of the challenges of writing about them and framing them critically lies in identifying and naming affinities and continuities. The films lend themselves to a variety of provisional groupings. For example, Yosefa Loshitzky groups *Code 46* alongside *In This World* and *The Road to Guantánamo* calling them 'The Camp trilogy', since the three films can be read as an elaboration of Giorgio Agamben's contention that, in their exercise of sovereign power, contemporary liberal democratic states tend to reduce certain groups of people to the exceptional condition of 'bare life' experienced by inmates of Nazi concentration camps and extermination camps. In a study of power and political modernity, Agamben proposes that we might 'regard the camp not as a historical fact and as an anomaly belonging to the past (even if still verifiable) but in some way as the hidden matrix and *nomos* of the political space in which we are still living' (Agamben 1998: 95). Moreover, Agamben suggests, 'the birth of the camp in our time appears as an event that decisively signals the political space of modernity itself', and thus we can find spatial echoes of the camp in a wide range of places including immigrant detention centres, black prisons, refugee camps and travellers' sites (Agamben 1998: 99). Within the camp, normal legal safeguards are suspended so that incarcerated individuals are effectively reduced to the state of *homo sacer*, a legal category of Roman law wherein a criminal was relegated to the accursed status of a person who could be killed with impunity. The condition of *homo sacer* constitutes 'bare life', in which individuals are stripped of rights, citizenship and political agency. Agamben argues that the state of exception that permits the suspension of normal laws – legitimising the concentration camp that reduces individuals to bare life – has become a permanent, constitutive feature of the exercise of power by the modern nation-state. The camp has a paradoxical status wherein it becomes a normal part of the 'juridico-political paradigm' – an internalised exceptional space: 'The state of exception, which was essentially a temporary suspension of the juridico-political order, now becomes a new and stable spatial arrangement inhabited by the bare life that more and more can no longer be inscribed in that order' (ibid.). The camp, Agamben proposes, 'is now securely lodged within the city's interior, is the new biopolitical *nomos* of the planet' (ibid.). With reference to Agamben's argument, Loshitsky proposes that, 'In his trilogy Winterbottom, represents the camp as a space of exclusion, punishment, and torture to which people are exiled, not in Western-style entertainment shows promoting and celebrating free-market competitiveness and neo-capitalism's survival of the fittest (i.e., the most aggressive), but camps they are forced to inhabit' (Loshitzky 2010: 119).[12]

However, the film's narrative spine is Geld's infatuation with Maria. This is a romance narrative of sorts, but it is one that deviates from convention in a way that invites us to reflect upon the underlying logic or morality. For one thing, it appears to be prompted by the empathy virus that is a tool of Geld's trade, which suggests that this is a romance structured by synthetic emotion. Although it is Geld who actively pursues Maria and both overlooks and instigates her forgery, he is unpunished at the film's conclusion, retaining his job and being returned to his family (establishing that the nuclear family remains a socially and ideologically central institution even in this speculative future). Maria, however, is cast into exile, consigned to a future that, as the taxi driver who chauffeurs Geld from the airport at the beginning of the film explains, is 'not living, just existing' – bare life. The future depicted in this film remains as misogynistic, patriarchal and class-bound as the period depicted by classic *films noirs*.

The screenwriter, Frank Cottrell Boyce, a regular collaborator with Winterbottom, has explained that with this film, 'Michael's starting point was the Oedipus myth about the inescapability of fate.'[13] Indeed, the film is a loose retelling of Sophocles' *Oedipus Rex*, a narrative Raymond Durgnat describes as 'the first detective thriller' in his genealogical history of the *Film Noir* (Durgnat 1996: 37) (which suggests an additional logic underlying the *noir* stylings of the film). In Winterbottom's reworking Geld occupies the role of Oedipus, the king of Thebes who is called upon by the Thebans to rid the city of a plague that is supposedly due to the murder of the former king, Laius. It transpires that Oedipus, who is now married to Queen Jocasta, had himself already unknowingly killed Laius in a dispute on the road. Oedipus asks a prophet, Tiresias, to help him find the murderer and Tiresias reluctantly informs him that Oedipus *is* the murderer and that he is both brother and father of his own children and husband and son of his mother. As the play continues Oedipus learns that he is in fact the son of Jocasta and Laius and had been abandoned at birth because of a prophecy that he would kill his father and have children with his mother. On learning that the prophecy has been fulfilled his wife/mother hangs herself and Oedipus blinds himself. The ominously powerful Sphinx corporation in *Code 46* also takes its name from the play since, in the period before the narrative begins, Oedipus solved the sphinx's riddle which led the repressive creature to kill itself. This released the Thebans from the grip of pestilence and Oedipus was made king in gratitude.

Reading *Code 46* in relation to *Oedipus Rex* directs us towards a consideration of the relationship between genetics and self-determination, as well as to the implications of genetic engineering for our concept of unique human identity and capacity for self-knowledge in a society in which anyone is liable to discover, as does Oedipus, that her/his sexual partner is the genetic twin of a sibling or parent. This is addressed by the pharmacist who performs the DNA test on Maria's hair and who tells Geld that, 'We aren't prisoners of our genes'. However, while it may be the case that identity remains largely a matter of environment, the cautionary message of the film is that the institutions responsible for the medical technology that permits cloning and gene splicing are also involved in the reprogramming of the protagonists – the rewriting of their memories and, in so far as memory is a fundamental constituent of them, their identities.

What is more clear in *Code 46* than in any of Winterbottom's other films is the relationship between intimacy and identity. In its thematic focus upon genetic relations, the film is concerned with the intimate composition of identity and the possibility that identity is reducible to, and therefore commodifiable as, a particular gene sequence. In this future, in which 'the relations of one are the relations of all', technoscience has rendered individuality obsolete as one 'individual''s (genetic) identity overlaps with, or is doubled by, another's. *Code 46* imagines a society in which commercial biotechnology is a state apparatus responsible for constructing a docile, self-policing citizenry – the military-industrial complex superseded by the biopolitical-biotechnological complex, and the government superseded by the corporation. In this respect, the vast industrialised city of *Metropolis* (Fritz Lang, 1927) is a key visual, spatial and thematic source for *Code 46*, with Maria Gonzales an echo of the worker Maria and her robotic double while Geld is the double of Joh Fredersen, the aristocratic outsider drawn to the lower levels of the city by his fascination with Maria: 'While William is the privileged outsider who views the city from above, Maria embodies the city in the sense that she inhabits its underground capillaries and whispered secrets' (Stacey 2010: 145). As with much science fiction, however, the projection of certain features of contemporary society into a near-future diegesis in which these features are advanced, exaggerated and foregrounded, is a means of making visible processes that are already under way. In this respect, *Code 46* offers an account of the present, of a contemporary intimate surveillance society.

Shots of CCTV monitors are a visual motif of the film emphasising the organisation of the social space around panoptic principles. As Peter Marks observes, in a discussion of the film's depiction of a surveillance society, the film explores the ambiguity of screening as a process of exposure (genetic screening) and enforced visibility, and also as a process of repression and concealment (Marks 2008). However, this is

CCTV shot of the Sphinx corporation's papel workshop – the corporation as microcosm of control society

not a society modelled on the paranoid principles of the prison in which the rebellious, resistant tendencies of inmates must perpetually be contained and dissipated, so much as a control society in which individuals are self-policing, programmable software susceptible to modification by unstable viruses. The film's title thus evokes the source code of a computer programming language, the genetic code by which information is stored in proteins within cells (since there are 46 chromosomes in each human cell), and the legal article quoted in the introductory captions.

The society adumbrated in this film corresponds closely to the society of control described by Gilles Deleuze in the early 1990s. Following Michel Foucault's argument that the 'disciplinary societies' of the eighteenth and nineteenth century were in crisis, Deleuze suggested that we were witnessing the emergence of a new capitalist regime in which the 'environments of enclosure' of the disciplinary society through which power relations were established and stabilised – the school, the factory, the prison, the hospital – are replaced by 'efficient', 'responsive', dispersed structures in which power relations become mobile or invisible. 'For example, in the crisis of the hospital as environment of enclosure, neighbourhood clinics, hospices, and day care could at first express new freedom, but they could participate as well in mechanisms of control that are equal to the harshest of confinements' (Deleuze 1992: 4). One of the clearest signs of this transition from one regime to the next, from industrial capitalism to a capitalist society in which production is outsourced – which, Deleuze suggested was well under way – was the displacement of the factory by the corporation, which is, 'a spirit, a gas' (ibid.). The Sphinx corporation exemplifies this new regime in which the corporation takes on superhuman characteristics. 'We are taught that corporations have a soul, which is the most terrifying news in the world', Deleuze writes, and this is voiced by several characters in the film who observe that 'The Sphinx knows best' (Deleuze 1992: 6). George Orwell's disciplinarian Big Brother has been replaced in *Code 46*'s dystopia by a vastly powerful corporation. In characterising the society of control, Deleuze suggests that the serpent is the most appropriate metaphor for the undulating, liquid mobility of the contemporary condition: 'The old monetary mole is the animal of the spaces of enclosure, but the serpent is that of the societies of control. We have passed from one animal to the other, from the mole to the serpent, in the system under which we live, but also in our manner of living and in our relations with others' (Deleuze 1992: 5). However, the vicious mythical sphinx is a far more apt figure – a hybrid of human, lion, eagle and serpent, predators all, it is a symbol for a post-human concept of individual identity as a bricolage of structural elements at the molecular level, as well as a symbol for the Borg-like[14] cultural hybridity of advanced corporate capitalism, which attempts to assimilate everything indiscriminately. It is also an appropriate symbol for power since it is impossible and evanescent, an image existing in the imagination rather than a real entity, concrete, physical and locatable.

Whereas, disciplinary societies drew a distinction between the individual and 'the mass', the new regime does not recognise this distinction since the individual is understood in abstracted terms as a particular (more or less valuable) configuration of information. It follows then, that the crime under investigation in *Code 46* is not financial, but the forgery of papels, 'letters of transit' permitting cross-border travel. In societies of control:

> what is important is no longer either a signature or a number, but a code: the code is a password [...] The numerical language of control is made of codes that mark access to information, or reject it. We no longer find ourselves dealing with the mass/individual pair. Individuals have become 'dividuals', and masses, samples, data, markets, or 'banks'. (Ibid.)

Consequently, the issue of repression or control is no longer a matter of physical enclosure or internment *within* the boundaries of the state or the region. When the Shanghai resident, Maria, violates code 46 a first time, her pregnancy is terminated and her memory is over-written. The second time it happens she is simply cast outside the borders of the city, set free. As Deleuze suggests, control society is interested in individuals only in so far as they are financially productive, which is to say, in a post-industrial economic system that thrives on credit, debtors:

> Man is no longer man enclosed, but man in debt. It is true that capitalism has retained as a constant the extreme poverty of three quarters of humanity, too poor for debt, too numerous for confinement: control will not only have to deal with erosions of frontiers but with the explosions within shanty towns or ghettos. (Deleuze 1992: 6–7)

The concluding shots of the film that contrast Geld's return home to the US (now, like Oedipus, 'blinded' due to his amnesia) with Maria's exile to the desert dramatise this radically unequal situation. Thus, we can read *Code 46* as a cautionary account, set a short distance in the future, of the reorganisation of the globe by neo-liberal capitalism that is happening right here, right now.

The film's invocation of the Oedipus myth suggests another thematic reading of the film, however. Sophocles's drama provided Sigmund Freud with a schematic narrative to explain the organisation of human sexual desire (see Freud 1976: 363–5). Freud proposed that the 'Oedipus complex' marks a stage in psycho-sexual development in which a young child's sexual desire is directed towards the parent of the opposite sex and a consequent hatred for the parent of the same sex emerges. For male children, this hatred of the father, perceived as a rival for the mother's affections, can manifest itself unconsciously in castration anxiety, the fear of punishment by the father for desiring the mother who, the child imagines in an attempt to make sense of physical sexual difference, must already have been castrated. It follows, then, that Geld is named after the act of castration, and also that when Maria's pregnancy is terminated, she is given a false memory of having been hospitalised in order to have a severed finger replaced, a restoration of a castrated body part.

Code 46 is, thus, a film about culturally embedded conceptions of male sexuality, understanding Geld's behaviour through the psycho-sexual narrative frame of the Oedipus complex. For Freud, the development of sexuality is indeed a narrative process that follows several possible trajectories depending on the extent to which the child's desire for the parent of the opposite sex is diverted towards a substitute 'object-choice', a figure who takes the place of the desired parent. To varying extents, however, the Oedipus complex continues to structure an individual's sexual desire beyond infancy and through puberty into adulthood. This is played out by Geld in his infatuation with Maria, his mother's double. As Maria explains on the voice-over his attraction was due to a 'distortion of judgement' caused by the empathy virus with which he was infected – sexual desire as pathological symptom, but it is also possible that it is prompted by narcissism: 'The sense that William and Maria's mutual fascination lies in some kind of recognition of their uncanny similarities is established in their first evening together, with their common tone-deafness and their strikingly "doughy resemblance" (as one reviewer put it)' (Stacey 2010: 167). In its oblique references to Freud, the film perhaps demonstrates the limitations of Freud's thought when confronted with female sexuality, since Maria remains a disposable, negligible character whose desire is unexplained and uncontainable. Their relation is treated by the transnational authorities as a symptom of Geld's infection and while Geld is rehabilitated and returned to his family after their breach of code 46, she is punished with expulsion.

Whatever the clinical accuracy of Freud's account of sexual development, it has been profoundly important in shaping popular and scientific understanding of human sexuality in a variety of fields. As Frank Cottrell Boyce proposes, however, the impact of Freud's work was felt across a much broader spectrum, the technical vocabulary of psychoanalysis entering into everyday discourse: 'The 20th century was the Freud century and the 21st century is going to be the genetics century'.[15] Freudian psychoanalysis was very influential upon surrealist art and literature in the 1920s, for example, and by the 1940s was influencing the themes, characterisations and imagery within Hollywood thrillers such as *Spellbound* (Alfred Hitchcock, 1945), musical fantasies such as *The Red Shoes* (Michael Powell & Emeric Pressburger, 1948), and family melodramas such as *Now, Voyager* (Irving Rapper, 1942). In its framing as a narrative about sexual development, this science fiction film can also be understood as a film about cinematic sexuality.

Psychoanalytic film theorists have argued that conventional mainstream film narratives track an 'Oedipal trajectory' in which the male protagonist is required to negotiate of a series of obstacles and characters in order to reach a successful resolution. Given the heteronormative values underlying mainstream culture and the frequency of romance narratives in popular cinema, this resolution will often involve marriage or coupling with a woman, or the restitution of stable family relations. Thus, arguably, mainstream films repeatedly retell and reproduce the same normative story about (male) sexuality and masculinity.

Code 46 largely follows this narrative schema, but the film employs several alienating devices that ensure that the spectator is held at a distance from the action, emotionally disengaged from Geld, despite several close-ups where Maria directly addresses Geld/us. The voice-over delivered by Maria situates her as the more significant, more knowledgeable character, the one who fully understands what is taking place; at the film's conclusion, Maria's memory is left intact, perhaps in order to make the experience of punitive exile more painful. The fact that Geld's actions are motivated (to some extent, at least) by a virus, also makes identification with his behaviour less straightforward. For example, we are given no explanation for his instantaneous fixation upon Maria except for the effects of the virus. The film intermittently employs slow-motion, unfocused shots, jump cuts and chronologically discontinuous transitions, unexplained images (such as a brief shot of Geld reflected in Maria's iris that disappears when she blinks), and frequent cutaways to the dream of travelling on a subway train that Maria has every year on the eve of her birthday. The effect of this is that the whole film is suffused with a non-naturalistic, dream-like quality. As a result, rather than functioning to suture us into the futuristic diegesis, the romance in *Code 46* is rendered strange and implausible. Maria's infatuation with Geld is perhaps less strange since he is a confident exotic foreigner, who, through viral hyperacuity appears to be able to read her thoughts, but as she points out, drawing attention to the salacious, exploitative nature of his relationship with her, the virus is like wearing X-ray specs to look at girls' underwear. While *Code 46* tells the story of desire through familiar cultural and cinematic narratives, it also proposes a radically different and anti-romantic genomic model of desire in which overwhelming sexual desire is intelligible not in relation to childhood experience but as symptom of infection and (dysfunctional) genetic selection.

9 Songs – sex and intimacy

9 Songs, which was shot over a period of five months and premiered at the Venice Film Festival just nine months after the release of *Code 46*, is a further exploration of possible configurations of the cinematic romance narrative. Like *Code 46* (and also *The Claim, A Mighty Heart, Genova* and, to a marginal extent, *I Want You, The Road to Guantánamo, The Trip* and *Trishna*), this is a transnational romance in which lovers from different countries and cultures find themselves briefly united. In this respect, despite the apparent thematic distance between them they can be considered companion pieces, although its comparatively short running time of 73 minutes, its minimalist, fragmented structure, the absence of stars, the reliance upon improvisation in the absence of a script, and, most obviously, the film's explicit depiction of sex, mean that it is situated at a greater distance from the mainstream than *Code 46*. By contrast with the thematic complexity of *Code 46*, *9 Songs* is much more narrowly concerned with the play of intimacy and distance within a sexual relationship.

Sharing with *The Trip* a narrative focus upon the tense interaction of a couple, the film tells the story of a relationship between a British glaciologist, Matt (Kieran O'Brien), and an American student, Lisa (Margo Stilley). This story is told through flashbacks, with expository voice-over narration delivered by Matt, and the film is bookended and punctuated with visually arresting, symbolically suggestive sequences, presumably set in the present, that show Matt camping and hiking in the Antarctic, and flying over the frozen sea. Within this framework, the presentation of the relationship seems to be chronologically linear and depicts its progressive disintegration as the couple, who are initially playful, passionate and enthusiastic, become distant and irritable until, finally, Lisa returns to America for an indefinite period.

As with Abbas Kiarostami's films, *Ten* (2002) and *Five* (2003), Lars von Trier's *The Five Obstructions* (2003) or François Girard's *Thirty-Two Short Films about Glenn Gould* (1993), the title initially draws our attention to the film's structure rather than the thematic content, since the relationship is measured by Matt's attendance at nine concerts, from the first at which he meets Lisa, through to the concert at the film's conclusion, that he attends by himself after they have separated. The title indicates that *9 Songs* may be read as an exercise in the construction of a film around a set of self-imposed formal restrictions as well as a story. One of the most unconventional formal features of the film is the presentation of complete songs, as if the compartmentalised structure schematically – or perhaps parodically – reproduces that of a classic Hollywood musical, emphasising the disjointed form of such films. Apart from being simply the sorts of bands a hip young couple living in London might have been to see, it is possible to read the musical numbers as an expressive, meta-narrative commentary upon the relationship – in the early stages of the relationship we see a performance of the euphoric song, 'Movin' on Up' by Primal Scream, while towards the end of the film they attend a concert by Michael Nyman, whose solemn piano instrumental, 'Nadia' (which, in a characteristic gesture of authorial self-reference, is from the score for Winterbottom's *Wonderland*), prefigures Lisa's announcement that she is returning home. The refrain of the final song by Black Rebel Motorcycle Club, is 'Now she's gone, love burns inside of me', however, it is the increasingly melancholy tone of the songs, rather than their sometimes oblique lyrical content, that functions most directly to frame the romance.

The decision to show complete songs exemplifies the inverted narrative strategy underlying the film. Where we might expect a film to show a courting couple going to the cinema or going to concerts, cafés and restaurants – indeed it is something of a cinephiliac cliché to show couples in love entering and leaving cinemas, and *The Killer Inside Me* features just such a montage sequence – we would not expect to see much or any of the actual concerts. In the concert sequences of *9 Songs*, however, although Matt and Lisa are occasionally glimpsed in the audiences, their dialogue is indiscernible and the focus of these sequences is the performance. Shot and edited as if they belong to a concert film, the sequences are assembled from footage taken with hand-held cameras from various points around the auditorium and within the crowd in front of the stage – consequently, the framing is shaky in many sequences as the camera is

One song –
documented performance

jostled by dancing, bouncing spectators and many shots are out of focus, obstructed and indistinct in the low light, or 'blown out' by the stage lights. Whereas a promotional concert film typically offers an unimpeded view of the performers, sometimes placing the spectator/camera in a 'privileged' position onstage with the performers, the concert sequences in *9 Songs* place us in the throng. Comprising more than a third of the film's running time they function as lacunae or interruptions rather than as extensions of the relationship. These sequences also exemplify the documentary principle informing the film, since, rather than depicting specially-staged performances, the nine songs we see were selected from over one hundred that were recorded at various concerts that took place during the production period.

The depiction of Matt and Lisa's interaction follows a similar principle of inversion. For a complex variety of reasons including performers' reservations, obscenity legislation and commercial prudence, the situation of the film theatre within the public sphere, censorious representational conventions and the principles of classical continuity, sexual activity in mainstream films tends either to be implied or depicted discreetly through montage sequences assembled from low-key close-ups of faces and body parts that leave genitalia off-screen. By contrast, *9 Songs* omits many of the sequences through which a cinematic romance is conventionally emplotted – meals in restaurants, shopping, walks in the park, parties, confessional conversation – and instead orients the depiction of the couples' relationship around their sexual interaction. The couple are shown having penetrative sex, playing bondage games with blindfolds and stiletto heels, sharing a bath, engaging in oral sex and, in a sequence that functions as a defiant guarantee of the documentary authenticity of these scenes, Lisa masturbates Matt to ejaculation. Although the couple take a trip to the beach[16] (where Matt strips off and runs into the cold sea to show Lisa that he loves her), and we see them in a holiday apartment and a hotel room, most of the interaction takes place in Matt's flat. The effect of this focus is to emphasise and evoke the claustrophobic insularity of the relationship. Apart from a brief scene in a lap-dancing club, we barely see them interact with anyone else. Friends, family and colleagues remain off-screen and except for a glimpse of Matt at work in a laboratory analysing an ice sample, there is very little sense of what they are occupied with the rest of the time; we do not learn where Matt works and lives, nor where Lisa studies or what she is studying, or even their full names. It is as if the film is comprised of the ellipses from a mainstream romantic drama. Winterbottom has explained that the film was conceived as 'an experiment to see whether you could convey what it's like to be in love by watching people together as opposed to creating a narrative', and many of the moments in which Matt and Lisa are seen together are inconceivable in a conventional narrative film.[17]

However, the film strikes a fine balance between narrative disintegration and coherence, rigorous formal experimentation and conventional structure. Underlying the film is not an *avant-garde* contrarian's desire to pulverise conventional narrative comprehensively, but rather a modernist project of reducing a work to its essential formal elements. Thus, for example, some of the songs are interrupted by cutaways to shots of the couple, emphasising the continuity between these distinct narrative components, rather than setting them carefully apart. Also, despite its formal experimentation, *9 Songs* does not dispense with linearity; there are few points at which the chronological relationship of shots and scenes is confusingly incoherent. And, of course, in a refusal of formalist purity, of the nine concerts featured, only eight of them consist of songs.

The film belongs to a tradition of international art cinema that has tested and challenged conventions around the representation of sex through increasingly explicit depictions of bodies and sexual activity both in the interests of realism, as a means of establishing a distance from commercial entertainment culture, but also to redirect that culture, and in order to provoke spectators. Winterbottom is one of a number of contemporary directors, including Andrea Arnold, Bertrand Bonello, Catherine Breillat, Virginie Despentes, Patrice Chéreau, Vincent Gallo, Gaspar Noé and Lars von Trier, to incorporate explicit depictions of sex into narrative film often in the context of unconventional narrative structures. While a staple image in 'hard core' pornographic film and photography, the depiction of a performer's erect, ejaculating penis within Winterbottom's film remains a particularly striking and narratively disruptive image. As Linda Williams observes, the 'money shot' is the 'hard core fetish par excellence', functioning as visible proof of the performer's pleasure, although, as Williams observes this image also comprises a 'crisis of representation', since 'this particular "erotic organization of visibility" cannot satisfy the genre's increasing curiosity to see and know the woman's pleasure' (Williams 1989: 271).

The world-wide web has allowed hardcore pornography to become an immanent, hyper-visible background to contemporary western consumer culture – and it is against this background too that Winterbottom's film was awarded an '18' certificate for commercial release by the British Board of Film Censors, permitting the film to be shown in all cinemas rather than being restricted to licensed adult cinemas and sex shops. Nevertheless, a realistic depiction of sex potentially remains a compositional problem in narrative cinema. As Slavoj Žižek argues, 'The fantasy ideal of a perfect work of pornography would be precisely to preserve this impossible harmony, the balance between narration and explicit depiction of the sexual act' (Žižek 1991: 111). However, he suggests that 'harmony, congruence between the filmic narrative (the unfolding of the story) and the immediate display of the sexual act, is structurally impossible … because as soon as we "show it all," the story is no longer "taken seriously" and starts to function only as a pretext for introducing acts of copulation' (Žižek 1991: 110–11). The schematic characterisation of the protagonists and the disjointed structure of *9 Songs* is perhaps an acknowledgement of this structural impossibility wherein 'the sexual act would function as an intrusion of the real undermining the consistency of this diegetic reality' (Žižek 1991: 111). Although in one sense, the public performance of sex is no more authentic or any less staged than any other performance of intimacy by an actor – seeing a screen performer laugh or cry or orgasm raises the same questions about the possibility of distinguishing simulated affect from spontaneous embodied response, or a consciously controlled performance from contingent, uncontrolled reaction – it nevertheless connotes documentary reality. In this sense, the depiction of sex has a similar ontological status within the diegesis to the footage of the concerts and is consistent with the dominant aesthetic of Winterbottom's cinema in which the boundary between actuality and fiction is repeatedly blurred, shifted and transgressed.

In some respects, the compositional problem described by Žižek above – the containment and integration of spectacular disruption within a smooth narrative flow – is the structural impossibility encountered by all narrative cinema. With *9 Songs*, however, the problem of narration is as much a matter of a certain impossibility of depicting intimacy or love. In this respect, the impossibility of cinematic intimacy describes both thematic and representational dynamics within the film. As Melanie Williams notes, Winterbottom has said that, 'In a way, being in love doesn't have much narrative; if you think about love poems and love songs, they're much more successful at capturing what it feels like to be in love because they're not so concerned with narrative' (Williams 2006: 61). In other words, for Winterbottom, mainstream cinema's preoccupation with narrative continuity and coherence precludes a convincing representation of that experience. Williams goes on to suggest that, as a result:

> His approach is to jettison all that and get to the heart of what we really remember about a past love affair: the rush of physical intimacy and the music that we were listening to at the time – the melodies that "haunt our reverie" and transport us back to the past. The film is thus dominated by the presence of these two ordinary forms of transcendence from the everyday – sex and music – as a means of getting to the quintessence of love. (Ibid.)

2 scenes

9 Songs is purportedly the most explicit film to have received a certificate for general release in the UK without cuts being demanded by the BBFC. In this sense it could be considered a radical or progressive film, demonstrating that a 'mainstream' film can incorporate explicit sex in its account of a romantic relationship, albeit within the non-classical framework of a compartmentalised narrative structure. One scene, mid-way through the film, opens with the couple lounging half-undressed on Matt's bed during the day, as Lisa begins to read aloud a sexually explicit passage from *Platform*, Michel Houellebecq's novel about sex tourism in Thailand. This prompts the two of them to begin having sex, Matt tying Lisa to the bedstead and blindfolding her with a stocking before licking her vulva while she continues to recount a tale of sex on a Thai beach, and then putting on a condom and penetrating her.

Visually and structurally, the depiction of sex in this scene is organised in the same unspectacular manner as other sequences in the film. Lit with grey light from the windows, the scene is elliptically edited, showing us a condensed sequence of moments from the encounter. The scene is shot from a variety of angles and distances, alternating long shots of the couple on the bed with intimate close-ups of faces, hands and genitalia.

Initially there is no incidental music as Lisa reads to Matt and then, at his instruction, begins to describe a fantasy scenario of sex on a beach in Thailand while he licks her. The absence of intrusive, non-diegetic sound stresses the intense intimacy of the encounter. After a while, Lisa instructs Matt to fuck her and a reflective piano solo by Melissa Parmenter is introduced on the soundtrack playing over the final two-minute

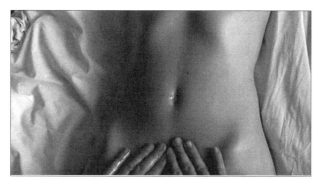

Cool realism and fantasy

shot, a high-angled over-the-shoulder shot looking down on the couple as they have sex. The shot ends with a fade to black before the next concert scene fades in.

In its staging, cinematography and cutting this scene recalls the disturbing 'consensual rape' scene in *Code 46* in which Geld ties Maria to a bed in order to have sex with her, and placing the two scenes alongside one another is instructive with regard to the question of how the depiction of sex might be incorporated into a narrative film. As with *9 Songs*, penetrative sex is directed by the woman who instructs Geld to, 'make me make love to you' and both films – shot by Marcel Zyskind – use similar framing and long takes. The scene from *Code 46* is the more uncomfortable to watch as it is oriented around lengthy subjective point-of-view shots that show us Maria's face in close-up from Geld's position above her as she moans and struggles in a mixture of distress, discomfort and (perhaps) pleasure, returning his/our gaze.

Thus, as viewers, we are intermittently positioned as the perpetrator of this technically incestuous sexual violence, and this discomfort is exaggerated by our knowledge of

Maria's agony/ecstasy

Geld's 'lack of disclosure (of their relatedness)' (Stacey 2010: 170); he knows that they are genetically similar but has withheld this knowledge from Maria. In different ways both scenes explore, within the context of a film narrative, the unequal or unstable power relations and potential violence that underlie sexual relations as well as the unconventional formal possibilities of the representation of the sex act. Despite the formal similarities, the effect of the two scenes is quite different.

The sexual encounter in *Code 46* is organised around conventional sexual power relations in which the woman is figured as masochist, and this is doubled at the level of the image which leaves Robbins largely off-screen and presents Morton as the emphatic object of the cinematic gaze, pinned down by the lengthy close-ups of her face. In this affectively ambivalent scene at least, she is not the point of identification. Rather, as Laura Mulvey suggests of Hollywood cinema, 'As the spectator identifies with the main male protagonist, he projects his look on to that of his like, his screen surrogate, so that the power of the male protagonist as he controls events coincides with the active power of the erotic look, both giving a satisfying sense of omnipotence' (Mulvey 1992: 751). This identification is reinforced by the 'invisible style' of classical cinema in which the viewer attends not to the construction of the image – the way in which a shot or a sequence has been staged and structured – but to the ostensible content of the image, so that we are able to see what the protagonist sees. What is unconventional about the scene, however, is the way that Morton stares at the camera, foreclosing the pleasurable illusion for the spectator of voyeuristic invisibility (although it might be noted that direct address is a regular motif in Winterbottom's films). In its refusal of erotic pleasure, the scene functions as a critique of mainstream cinema's representational regime. While, in mainstream cinema, 'The male protagonist is free to command the stage, a stage of spatial illusion in which he articulates the look and creates the action', in looking back, Morton breaks the illusion of invisibility and also of non-complicity (ibid.). Like the final shot of *Welcome to Sarajevo*, it is an ambiguous image that carries an implicit accusation.

By contrast with this scene, the sexual encounter in *9 Songs*, initiated by a fictional novel which sits on the bed during the scene as a sign, is conducted as a playful enactment of a fantasy scenario. The interaction of the protagonists remains awkward, tentative and slightly embarrassed, tender rather than aggressive. The depiction of the male performers' bodies is a crucial marker of the difference between the two scenes. Although *9 Songs* is far more graphic, the bodies of Samantha Morton (or occasionally her body double) and Margo Stilley are on display in each film, with explicit close-up shots of their genitals inserted into the sequences. However, whereas Tim Robbins's body remains largely off-screen save for a close-up of his face and a medium shot of his shirtless torso, Kieran O'Brien's naked body, sporting an erection, is fully visible during this scene. The film thus rejects mainstream cinema's conventional reproduction of sexual difference and social inequality wherein 'In their traditional exhibitionist role women are simultaneously looked at and displayed, with their appearance coded for strong visual and erotic impact so that they can be said to connote *to-be-looked-at-ness*' (Mulvey 1992: 750). Presenting O'Brien's body to be looked at in this way is by far the most radical element of these two scenes, but it is the earlier film that is the

most uncomfortable. This suggests, with regard to Žižek's comments on the narratively disruptive effect of graphic sex, that it is not the smooth incorporation of a representation of 'unsimulated' penetrative sex into a film that is unthinkable, but the exposure of a male star's sexually aroused body. In this sense, the two scenes test and redraw a representational and ideological limit of narrative film.

Winterbottom has suggested that *9 Songs* emerged from a failed attempt to develop an adaptation of that novel: 'One thing that happened before we made *9 Songs* is that we'd asked Michel Houellebecq about the possibility of making a film of *Platform*. He said that he wanted to direct it, so it wasn't possible'.[18] Among other things, this genealogy suggests that the film is the result of attempt to transpose the sexually explicit passages that are integral to the subjectivity and inter-relation of the characters in Houellebecq's novel into a different medium.

Winterbottom has described the film as a 'love story' but because of the minimal characterisation the characters remain distant and difficult to identify with, which perhaps also ensures that the sex scenes are less arousing than might be the case with conventional pornography. Approached from one angle, hardcore pornography is a limit case of cinematic intimacy both in its visual and narrative preoccupation with bodily intimacy (with intimate contact between bodies and with exposing intimate areas of the body), and in its aspiration to make intimate contact with the spectator, to elicit a physical response. For this reason, Linda Williams classes pornography alongside melodrama and horror as an excessive, sensational 'film body genre', since these types of film are marked by 'an apparent lack of proper aesthetic distance, a sense of overinvolvement in sensation and emotion' (Williams 2003: 145). While the frank depiction of heterosexual sex clearly invokes pornographic film, *9 Songs* is distinct from pornography in several ways. While, in its single-minded focus upon sex, 'Porn today deploys sex as something to be treated outside of other human and social relations', *9 Songs*, like other films by the director, depicts sex as expressively integral to human relations (Power 2009: 47). Secondly, in insisting upon the centrality of sex to the relationship between Matt and Lisa, the film refuses pornography's conception of sex as alienated labour (and competitive performance) wherein 'The sheer *hard work* of contemporary porn informs you that, without delusion, sex is just like everything else – grinding, relentless, boring, albeit *multiply* boring. The pneumatic Calvinism of rubberized piston-porn duty, the grim orgasm of unsmiling physical moil' (Power 2009: 51). The sex scenes in Winterbottom's film are sometimes tender, sometimes playful and sometimes, as with the bondage games, a little awkward and self-conscious.

Apart from one scene early in the film in which they have sex in front of a window, the sun providing a romantic golden back-light, the sex scenes are also not lit, shot or edited differently from the rest of the film. These sequences are filmed with a hand-held camera, which moves around the couple and is often positioned very close to the performers. It appears that the scenes, which are sometimes very dark, are shot with available light. As with other passages in the film, the scenes are assembled in a compressed montage as close-ups and medium shots of faces, genitalia and other details of the performers' bodies are intercut with long shots. There is little speech and in some of the sequences non-diegetic reflective solo piano music is introduced part way through, sometimes in the absence of diegetic sound – one scene re-uses a musical cue from Michael Nyman's score for *Wonderland*, while two other sequences use Nyman-like pieces by Melissa Parmenter (who went on to score *Genova* and *The Killer Inside Me*). The effect is that most of the sex scenes have a quiet, intimate feel and thus the film's depiction of sex is formally unspectacular and non-confrontational. The film does not present us with images of 'transgressive', violent or otherwise 'extreme' sex, and nor is the style in which these sequences are presented coded as 'transgressive' or shocking (whether in relation to the rest of the film, Winterbottom's body of work, or narrative cinema more generally). If these scenes do have a shocking or sensational register it rests instead in the matter-of-fact way in which they are incorporated into a narrative. The film's title similarly directs our attention away from the sex scenes, implying that they are a minor and unremarkable element of the film. In its refusal of a taboo relating to the literal depiction of sex in mainstream cinema, Winterbottom's film suggests not that 'sex is just like everything else' but rather that sex is just one of the ways in which couples interact. Nicolas Roeg explained that his intention behind the sex scene in *Don't Look Now* (1973) was that 'I wanted to make it as normal as possible' and the effect of the representation of sex in Winterbottom's films is a similar normalisation.[19]

At the same time, there is also little sense that the physical intimacy between the two of them opens onto emotional and intellectual intimacy. As with the other films discussed here, the unfolding relationship that is the core of this film is one in which intimacy remains elusive and fleeting. Matt's description of Lisa on the voice-over – 'She was twenty-one, beautiful, egotistical, careless, and crazy' – is not so much an individualised description as a reductive caricature and the film tracks a growing distance between them wherein sex becomes an expression of this distance. Scenes of Lisa crying in bed, masturbating alone with a vibrator, or ignoring Matt to focus intently upon a seductive lap dancer, appear to signify their growing estrangement, while the playfully rough sex games also seem to develop into, or scarcely disguise, a resentful aggression. As Lisa tells Matt at one point, 'Sometimes when you kiss me I want to bite you. Not in a nice way. I want to hurt you. I wanna bite your lip really fucking hard.'

Images of the Antarctic thus serve as a fatal metaphor for the relationship, bracketing the moments of passion with images of symbolic and literal emptiness. An aerial shot of the Antarctic (actually shot in Norway) in the opening scene, for example, is accompanied by the following voice-over: 'The Antarctic. 13,800,000 square kilometres of ice; a continent of ice. A place where no man had ever been until the twentieth century.' The shot fades out and then a shot of Matt and Lisa kissing fades in, the juxtaposition implying the destiny of this encounter, as well as reproducing a familiar metaphorical characterisation of femininity as mysterious, frigid, unexplored and uncolonised territory, equating the female body with unmapped natural terrain.

Aesthetic reductionism and symbolic landscape – aerial shot of the Antarctic

For example, the combination of these shots with Matt's commentary echoes Freud's proposition that 'the sexual life of adult women is a "dark continent" for psychology' (Freud 1986: 32). The metaphor is reprised later in the film as a sequence showing Matt pitching camp in a white landscape and then hiking up a hill with ski poles and snowshoes is accompanied by the observation that 'Exploring the Antarctic is almost like exploring space. You enter a void. Thousands of miles with no people, no animals, no plants. You're isolated in a vast empty continent. Claustrophobia and agoraphobia in the same place. Like two people in a bed.' The association of woman with void or lack may be intended as an ironic reiteration of a misogynistic cliché, but as a result of the broad alignment of the narrative perspective with Matt's point of view, it registers as a reactionary counterpoint to any claims that might be made for the film's progressive or innovative qualities.

Shots of Matt tramping across the ice recall shots of characters making their way through the snow-covered mountains of *The Claim*, in addition to the numerous landscape shots that are a signature motif of Winterbottom's work. For instance, the aerial shots of the ice and frozen sea with which the film open, aligning the narrator authoritatively perhaps with this god-like perspective, also invoke the aerial shots of the desert with which *Code 46* opens, which demonstrate the 'privilege of calm and uninterrupted travel and solitary individuality. Unbridled by the competing needs of others, or the dull demands of domesticity or locatedness, the privileged white male moves freely across the globe' (Stacey 2010: 142). However, the Antarctic serves an additional hermeneutic function as a metaphor for cinematic form. Lisa gives Matt a book about the Antarctic for his birthday and, while they are lying on a hotel bed, she reads to him this description: 'The ice is everywhere and everything. It spreads to all sides, an unbounded void of alien whiteness and geometric rigour. Antarctica is the highest, windiest, driest continent, its topography and dynamics the simplest on earth, an exercise in reductionism.'[20] We are invited to understand this as a formal ideal for the film with its simple, foregrounded structure. *9 Songs*, by extension is also an 'exercise in reductionism', oriented around principles of geometric rigour and topographic and dynamic simplicity.

Violence, murder and apocalyptic intimacy

The next section will explore the close relation between violence and intimacy in two very different films that focus on the ubiquitous, emphatically modern figure of the serial killer,[21] *Butterfly Kiss* and *The Killer Inside Me*. Violence can be a form of bodily intimacy – the collision of bodies, skin meeting skin – and it can also constitute a form of intimate affective expression – the exposure and communication of an individual's compulsions, desires, rage and anxiety. The murderous violence depicted in these films comprises another correlative form of bodily intimacy – the breaching of boundaries, a compulsive fascination with the physical interior of the body, an addiction to puncturing, damaging, wounding, and letting blood. As Mark Seltzer argues in his study of the figure of the serial killer in American culture, the fascination with serial killing is symptomatic of a historically specific cultural fascination with violence that constitutes 'a *wound culture*: the public fascination with torn and open bodies and torn and opened persons, a collective gathering around shock, trauma and the wound' (Seltzer 1998: 1). In this context, 'Serial murder and its representations ... have by now largely replaced the western as the most popular genre-fiction of the body and of bodily violence in our culture' (ibid.).

As is suggested by the title, *The Killer Inside Me*, narrative accounts of serial killing are often preoccupied with the interiority of the murderer in order to identify the killer's motivation, typically explaining his/her behaviour in terms of the clichés of pop-psychology – what Orson Welles termed 'dollar-book Freud' in a disparaging comment upon the psychological insights into Kane's drives and desires in *Citizen Kane* (Orson Welles, 1942). What makes the serial killer an endlessly fascinating figure, particularly within classical cinema whose coherence depends upon the comprehensible motivation of the protagonists, is the indifference, hollowness or hyper-normality of the killer. The 'typical' serial killer 'appears as the depsychologized subject – that is, as the over-socialized individual' whose identity is indistinct from the surrounding mass of people (Seltzer 1998: 160). The serial killer's most intimate self is an assemblage of appropriated personality traits and character types. He is thus a paradoxical figure who personifies the collapse of distinctions between public and private, intimacy and distance: 'His thorough identification with others ("just like everyone else") – precisely to the extent that it surfaces within the experience of the subject himself – becomes, paradoxically, the measure of his difference, a difference that lies in the traumatic recognition of a fundamental sameness or likeness' (Seltzer 1998: 161). As a result the serial killer personifies a crisis of intimacy, or the impossibility of intimacy: 'In short, the killer appears as the depsychologized individual for whom intimacy appears as an unremitting spectacle of empty social forms' (Seltzer 1998:162–3). For the emptied-out, undifferentiated killer incapable of an intimate encounter with another, the hyperbolic violence of repetitive murder is both a substitute for this intimacy and also a means of achieving a certain form of intimacy. Through a focus upon addictive violence, these two films are thus concerned with characters in search of elusive intimate relations with another.

Butterfly Kiss – the killer inside Mi

Winterbottom's debut feature film, *Butterfly Kiss*, is an account of the brief, violently intense relationship between two women Miriam (Saskia Reeves) and Eunice (Amanda Plummer) – or, as they call one another, 'Mi' and 'Eu' – as they travel around the North-West of England on a killing spree. The film is a European counter-part to the 'new queer road movie' that emerged in American independent cinema in the 1990s:

> The queer difference between a studio-era road movie like *The Wizard of Oz* and an independent one like *My Own Private Idaho*, obviously, is that the narratives of Hollywood, as they do to this day, can achieve closure only if they end on a hetero-patriarchal principle (family and home or heterosexual coming together as *telos* of Hollywood narrative epistemology). (Lang 1997: 342)

With its narrative focus upon what Clare Whatling describes ironically as 'lesbian psycho-killers' and its conclusion with a compassionate murder that Bea Campbell describes as 'an intimate apocalypse', acknowledging the protagonist's biblical fantasies, the film is a love story that is situated at some distance from mainstream film and television (Whatling 1997: 101).

Butterfly Kiss is also a response to the emergence in mainstream cinema of what Shari Roberts terms, 'feminine' road films, such as *Thelma and Louise* (Ridley Scott, 1991), narratives distinguished by their defiantly non-traditional focus upon journeys taken by women: 'Not only do these films upset audience expectations concerning content and protagonist, they also disrupt formal genre norms' (Roberts 1997: 63). This reconfiguration of generic norms can be understood as a refusal of the romanticisation of masculine mobility and solitude embedded in the road film, but, Roberts argues, this refusal is inevitably limited since the narrowly gendered format forecloses this appropriation of the genre: 'although the feminine road films critique dominant ideology, because of their attempted escape specifically into a masculinist genre, these films tend metaphorically to raise their hand in "feminine" despair' (Roberts 1997: 66). However, whereas the eponymous fugitives of *Thelma and Louise* follow a pessimistic trajectory in which they ultimately run out of road, surrounded by police and family members, and with no option but suicide, the couple in *Butterfly Kiss*, are radically free, roaming across an unpoliced landscape. Convinced that she has been 'forgotten' by God, in her damnation Eunice has embraced an existential freedom, unconstrained by morality, which allows her to commit murder readily. Her lover and devotee, Miriam, although reproachful of Eunice's impulsive violence, is also entranced by her courage and authenticity, suggesting that Eunice acted on desires that are normally repressed:

> the things she did, everyone wants to do them really. The emergency thing on the train; everyone wants to pull that one. Everyone wants to break the fire alarm glass. Everyone wants to drive away from the garage without paying. The difference is that she did it, like, you know? She wasn't scared.

Eunice's rebellious difference is crystallised in her embodiment of the comparatively rare figure of the female serial killer in relation to 'the popular model of the serial killer as white-male-sadist-performance artist' (Seltzer 1998: 8). There is a handful of female serial killers within cinema, just as there have been genuine cases of stranger-killing by women – Aileen Wuornos, whose trans-media persona extends across two documentaries by Nick Broomfield and a Hollywood biopic, as well as US made-for-TV-movies and an opera, is the most celebrated example – but the popular characterisation of the serial killer as hyper-normal, sadistic, predatory, rational, voyeuristic, 'invisible' and solitary inevitably corresponds to a stereotype of masculinity. By contrast, Eunice is an ambiguously gendered and polymorphously perverse figure, a composite of masculine and feminine signs. She sports short hair, army boots, black leather overcoat and tattoos, as well as an unfashionable flowery blouse, pink jersey and dirty powder-blue trousers, and is sexually confident and aggressive, stealing vehicles (including a car

with the ominous registration number, B666 XCK), killing and/or fucking strangers with relative indifference.

Situating female characters within the generic framework of a serial killer film and a road film inevitably directs our attention to gender, due to the incompatibility of the female protagonist. However, the protagonists Eunice and Miriam are not the 'authentically real' individuals that we might expect to find in a social realist drama in response to the gender stereotypes of popular genre films. The film is characterised by a disjunctive synthesis of symbolism and naturalism in which a realist register is interrupted by surreal encounters and scenarios, emphasising the intimate complementarity of the absurd and the everyday. We only know them by their first names, and as the diminutives 'Mi' and 'Eu' indicate, they are not fully rounded, psychologically plausible characterisations but narratively expedient ciphers, place-holders that the spectator can flesh out through conjecture. The figure of the sermonising, sado-masochistic, psychotic killer is by now a familiar character from thrillers and horror films and so, although the cinematic female serial killer is very rare, Eunice is a composite of cinematic precedents. Both the American, Amanda Plummer, and Londoner Saskia Reeves struggle unsuccessfully to maintain a Lancashire accent, but the effect of this is to emphasise the symbolic rather than realistic register occupied by the characters, and their disconnection from their environment. Jean Cocteau observed of Orson Welles's imprecise approximation of a Scottish accent in *Macbeth* (Orson Welles, 1948), 'I confess that it did not disturb me … since we have no reason not to expect that strange monsters express themselves in a monstrous language' (Cocteau 1991: 29). It is similarly appropriate that Miriam and Eunice express themselves in an alien dialect as they journey away from the habitus that most people occupy. They are not, however, depicted as monstrous amoral hedonists deriving pleasure from killing like the thrill-seeking media-saturated couple at the centre of the serial-killer road film, *Natural-Born Killers* (Oliver Stone, 1994). The film's rendering of violence is also unsensational – two of the killings are elided so that we see only the resulting corpses, and another two are brief, brutal, but unspectacular. The three male victims are killed after sex, but we are not invited to sympathise with the killers as victims, since Eunice instigates sex – and in the absence of an explanatory back-story, there is no indication that this violence is a response to a history of sexual abuse or rape. For example, we are not offered the pseudo-moral justification of a 'rape-revenge' exploitation film like *I Spit on Your Grave* (Meir Zarchi,

1978) that Eunice and Miriam are conducting a retaliatory campaign against male sexual violence. Indeed the men who appear in the film are broadly benign and include a bemused glazier, a rather shy and philosophical truck driver who thinks 'most people talk too much and it's because they're afraid of silence', and a father travelling with his daughter. Miriam describes the man she kills, travelling salesman Mr McDermott, as a pervert who 'deserved to die', but her murderous act is motivated as much by revulsion and jealousy when she walks in upon the traumatic primal scene of Eunice and McDermott having sex in the bathroom, as it is by McDermott's sexual masochism.

Scripted by Frank Cottrell Boyce, and developed from an idea by Cottrell Boyce and Winterbottom, *Butterfly Kiss* recounts the strange relationship between Eunice and Miriam after a chance encounter when Eunice arrives at the petrol station where Miriam works and pours petrol over herself at one of the pumps. Miriam is a naive, credulous innocent who shares a flat with her pious grandmother, and she is fascinated and overwhelmed by the volatile, extrovert Eunice who describes herself as (literally and metaphorically) 'a human bomb'. Eunice is tormented and desperate and this interior turbulence is externalised as the surface of her pale body is marked with tattoos and piercings, She wears heavy chains beneath her clothes that are wrapped around her torso and run between her legs leaving her skin bruised and rubbed raw. Where the cinematic serial killer is typically characterised by his indistinct visual appearance, Eunice's body is marked as different. Although she is sexually outgoing, this is not sexual fetish-wear but rather a means of self-punishment in atonement for her sinful character. As she explains to Miriam mid-way through the film she is convinced that, 'God has forgotten me, he's forgotten me. I kill people and nothing happens. You'd think he'd smite me and take me into bondage but no. Nowt. I can do what I like. He doesn't see me.' In spite of the distressing conviction that she has been abandoned (both by God and Judith, the objective of her quest), Eunice's worldview nevertheless remains deeply moral. She is a penitent whose chains and padlocks are a form of self-imposed bondage. What she wants, finally, is to be killed, to be, as she explains to Miriam, a 'sacrificial victim'.

The film opens with her walking along the verge of a busy road rehearsing the opening lines of a meeting, 'Look who it is. It's me.' She enters a petrol station and nervously repeats the line before asking the cashier if she has a particular record in stock, a love song whose title she can't recall. After a brief exchange about the song she gives up and then asks the cashier, 'You're Judith aren't you?' She protests that she is in

'A human bomb' – Eunice displays her tattoos and bonds to Miriam and her mother

fact called Wendy, pointing to the name badge on her uniform, and a subsequent shot a few seconds later shows the cashier lying on the floor behind the counter inert and bleeding. This encounter in the petrol station is repeated several times during the film and, for all we know, could have taken place dozens of times already with Eunice locked into a compulsive repetitive loop of misrecognition. As she later explains to Miriam, after they have buried a body among the trees, 'I always get lost and I always end up in the woods. Always in the woods. Over and over again. Like *déjà vu*.' The comment invokes the repetitive narrative framework of fairy tales and horror films as well as the film's repetitive structure and Eunice's traumatised subjectivity. When she does finally encounter a cashier called Judith, breaking the circuit, Eunice responds with anger and disbelief that the alarmed woman fails to recognise her, and has to be escorted from the shop by Miriam who holds and comforts her.

The film provides almost no personal history about Eunice and there is some doubt as to whether the Judith she seeks and whose letters she carries is a real person or a fantasy object derived from her apocalyptic worldview, since she refers at various points to Judith of Holofernes, the divinely inspired biblical figure who decapitates the general of an army besieging her town. As Miriam explains of Eunice's behaviour in retrospect, 'I see it now, it's not like there was someone missing, it's like there was something missing in herself.' Nevertheless, the quest indicates that a central theme of the film is Eunice's frustrated search for love or intimacy and she rationalises her addiction to killing as the result of a lack of reciprocation: 'People who nobody loves, they always end up killing someone.' It is a love story insofar as it is a story about killing.

Although the film is about the erotic and emotional interaction of a couple – and the characters' diminutive names, Mi and Eu, suggest an archetypally romantic intimacy – this is a dynamically unstable, unequally reciprocal relationship formed against the background of extreme violence. Eunice is distant and distracted, affectively unpredictable, and sometimes aggressive and bullying towards the credulous, sexually innocent Miriam and there is an attendant possibility that Miriam will be the next victim of her violent compulsion. After she has slept with Eunice for the first time, Miriam wakes to find that Eunice has gone, leaving the message 'YOU'RE NOT JUDITH' written on the bathroom mirror, and Eunice later taunts her, 'You think you'll make me good? I'll make you evil before you make me good'. Although there are passages in which she is affectionate towards Miriam, she is also unpleasant and at one

Woman trapped 'in a glass case' – Miriam reflects on her trip with Eunice

point orders a reluctant Miriam to have sex with a lorry driver in the cab of his vehicle, explaining to the driver, 'She'll do what I tell her to.'

The film is bookended and punctuated intermittently with black-and-white video sequences in which Miriam, shot in close-up against a tiled wall, addresses the camera/spectator directly, commenting retrospectively upon the events depicted in the film. The titles, accompanied by Helen Shapiro's jaunty song, 'Walkin' Back to Happiness' (1961), in which the singer reflects upon a past relationship, are a jump-cut montage of Miriam pulling expressions that range from bored and reflective to amused and happy. As the film progresses it appears that these are police video evidence tapes, or perhaps records of an institutional interview in a psychiatric hospital. These insertions have an expository function, providing additional information about events within the story, but they are also the forum for Miriam's reflections upon Eunice. Miriam is devotedly loyal to Eunice throughout the film; although shocked by Eunice's violence she is prepared to overlook it in order to remain close to her. When she first discovers one of Eunice's victims, she says, 'You must have had your reasons', and in the retrospective commentary she observes that although following Eunice was 'the worst thing I ever did, I don't regret it. None of it.' Miriam is a simple character, who is unsophisticated, childish and who wears a hearing aid symbolising (and producing) a disconnection from her surroundings – she describes living with hearing impairment as 'like being in a glass case'. She and Eunice share an affective disjunction so that initially she attempts to disregard Eunice's killing in order to concentrate upon her positive qualities – 'if you want all the good things you've got to put up with all the bad things' – and later goes on to commit a vicious murder herself, bludgeoning to death an acquaintance, Mr McDermott, whom she discovers having sex with Eunice; although she is upset by the deaths she witnesses and participates in, she is also quick to dismiss them as regrettable 'collateral damage'.

Partly because we are reliant upon Miriam's limited insight into Eunice's character, Eunice remains rather opaque, an exotic, fantastic, eccentrically dressed and uprooted figure drifting through the empty spaces of northwestern England. For Miriam she is also an object of desire and over-identification. Eunice's first line in the film is, 'Look who it is. It's me [Mi]' and as Mark Seltzer observes, it is a film on 'female serial violence/compulsive identification … the two female characters – Eunice and Miriam – drawn into relation, and engulfed by identification' (Seltzer 1998:156). Indeed, as the film progresses, Miriam develops from witness and accomplice to murderer and, finally, to Eunice's killer completing an exchange of roles. It is only when Miriam has killed McDermott that she begins to seem calmer and a more equal partner in the relationship – and it is significant that she beats McDermott to death with a shower-head in a motel bathroom restaging with a gender-inversion the murder that is the centrepiece of the prototype serial-killer film, *Psycho* (Alfred Hitchcock, 1960).

Violence is a means of achieving intimacy for these characters. After McDermott's murder, Eunice observes, 'Now we're both in hell', the killing having levelled the power relationship and enabled their identification with one another – enabling Mi to become Eu. The equation of violence with physical, sexual and spiritual intimacy is made clear by Eunice who makes the masochistic McDermott clean her leather

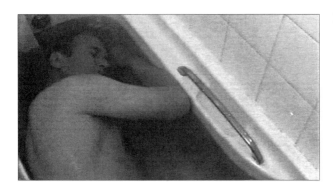

Psycho inverted

boots and then whips him with a chain before kissing and licking a surgical scar on his torso. In a bizarre anecdote he claims the scar is the result of the theft of his kidney while he was attending a Caravan Club rally, emphasising again the violence that is shot through this mundane and apparently unremarkable landscape. 'I love wounds', Eunice tells him, 'We were only singing before, Mi, weren't we? "Deep in thy wounds, Lord, hide and shelter me." I love the bit where St. Thomas puts his hand in Jesus's wound.' Against the bland, anaesthetising background of tower-blocks, motorways and car-parks, violence is a form of intensely affective communication with another.

The intimacy of violence is emphasised most emphatically in the film's conclusion in which Miriam drowns Eunice in the sea in the vast expanse of Morecambe Bay. It is the third time in the film that the couple find themselves at the edge of the land, but the seashore offers only temporary respite from their anxious, haunted journey. The pair arrive at this terminal beach (to borrow the title of a short story by J.G. Ballard) after fleeing from the motel in McDermott's car. There has been no indication during the film that the two of them were travelling purposefully towards a particular desti-nation and their trip seems to comprise a series of chance encounters and diversions. However, as Eunice states, reciting a line from a poem by the apocryphal Judith, 'All roads lead to Rome', and it is certainly the case that narrative convention dictates that all road films must end, however abruptly or arbitrarily (and of course, the compara-tively small size of the country means that the protagonists of British road movies such as *Radio On* (Christopher Petit, 1979), *Soft Top Hard Shoulder* (Stefan Schwartz, 1993), and the condescending comedy, *Heartlands* (Damien O'Donnell, 2002), on which Winterbottom is credited as executive producer, quickly run out of road).

In this particular nihilistic journey, it was apparent from the opening that the journey would terminate with death. Arriving on the shore in the dark, Miriam asks Eunice, 'You do believe I love you, don't you? … You've got to, after all I've done.' 'So you think you've done enough, then?', Eunice retorts sharply, and Miriam replies, 'When you know, that's when it'll be enough.' Staring intently at Miriam, Eunice says 'Kill me. That's what I really want. Someone to kill me.' Miriam agrees, they embrace and then Eunice undresses and instructs Miriam to remove her chains. Miriam frees her, illuminated by the car headlights, and Eunice lies down on the grass declaring herself, 'Defenceless. Helpless. Sinless.' The scene has a ritualistic quality as Eunice proposes, 'I'll be a victim, a sacrificial victim. Sacrificial victims always go to heaven.

Intimate violence and
landscape – the final shot

That's the point of them. They're like presents to God.' Miriam, lying against her,
flutters her eyelids against Eunice's cheek explaining that that is how angels kiss, but
Eunice replies that it's a butterfly kiss, the childish gesture of physical intimacy that
gives the film its title. In the morning they walk out across the salt flats into the shallow
sea as Eunice recounts the Old Testament story of Elijah's sacrifice and then recites
lines from the book of Job as Miriam cheerfully responds, 'I know nothing' and 'I
am useless, but he can do all things'. In the black and white insert, Miriam observes
wistfully, 'it's never easy killing someone is it? Especially if you love 'em'. In the film's
final scene, the two of them play in the water splashing one another and laughing until
Eunice stumbles and falls, and then says to Miriam, 'Now'. Miriam jumps on top of
Eunice and holds her struggling body under the water. The image quality changes here,
becoming grainy and dark like 16mm film, and pulsing black. The diegetic sound
drops out briefly and a mournful song by the Cranberries, 'No Need to Argue', in
which the singer reflects on the loss (or death) of a lover, is heard. The final image of
the film is an extreme long shot of Miriam the low sun behind her, sitting in the water,
sobbing and cradling Eunice's body. This concluding scene depicts a compassionate,
generous killing as Miriam despatches the woman she loves, in an act of sacrifice that
is simultaneously an act of baptism.

The film is shot in a flatly realist style (the frontal symmetrical composition of
shots often emphasising the empty uniformity of the spaces) and makes a feature of the
road film's typical topography of roads and motorways, hard shoulders and car-parks,
petrol stations, service stations, roadside cafés and fast food restaurants, motels and
tower blocks, as well as 'Camelot', an Arthurian theme park, whose commodification
of mythic Englishness epitomises this commercialised, industrialised landscape that
has been made over in order to facilitate travel by car. It is significant that the song
Eunice is attempting to identify, mistaking it for a love song due to the refrain, 'one
on one', is in fact a song about football by New Order, entitled, 'World in Motion'.
Its title describes both Eunice's turbulent affective relationship with the world, and
also the world as seen from within a road film (and from within a car), a world that
appears to be in constant, disorienting motion. While *The Trip* emphasises the rolling,
green, picturesque landscape of North West England, tracing a route through visually
striking and culturally resonant natural and architectural landmarks, the same area of
the country is represented in *Butterfly Kiss* as 'ordinary' and unattractive with little to
identify it as nationally or regionally specific. Depicted in grey, overcast light, it is a

The geographically non-specific matrix of the English road network

landscape of alienating, anonymous 'non-places' (Augé 1995) within which people are perpetually in transit, encountering one another fleetingly. Whereas the landscape of *The Trip* was also charged with personal significance for the traveller Coogan, these are impersonal places that mitigate against intimacy, but they are also places marked by anxiety and intensity. It is a landscape occupied by cashiers, waitresses, lorry drivers, travelling salesmen and hitch-hikers.

The Killer Inside Me – cinematic death trip

The Killer Inside Me, which, to appropriate Julian Stringer's term, might be described as a '*film noir* death trip' (Stringer 1997: 167), is adapted from a 1952 crime novel by Jim Thompson, previously filmed in 1976 in a version that Peter Stanfield suggests (in a discussion of film adaptations of Thompson's novels) 'shifts from being a crime story to a horror movie, the generic conventions helping to make the strange familiar' (Stanfield 2011: 173). Intriguingly, the film was also considered in the 1950s as a vehicle for Marlon Brando, Marilyn Monroe and Elizabeth Taylor (Frankel 2010: 22). Stanley Kubrick, who hired Thompson as screenwriter on *The Killing* (1956) and *Paths of Glory* (1957), had considered making the film in the mid-1950s before concluding that such a grim story would not attract studio funding (Baxter 1998: 73). Indeed, Winter-bottom's treatment of the narrative tests the limits of mainstream acceptability in its breathtaking depiction of brutal violence. In placing such unconventionally explicit passages within the context of a narrative, like *9 Songs*, *The Killer Inside Me* is also an examination of the flexibility of cinematic narrative form, testing how far a genre can be reconfigured or distorted before it shatters, becoming incoherent or unwatchable. Journalist Rachel Cooke recounted that while viewing the horrific sequence in which the protagonist beats his lover to death with his fists, 'I was so queasy, I had to go and stand outside. I thought I might actually faint' (Cooke 2010).

Set in the 1950s, the film tells the story of a series of murders committed by policeman Lou Ford, whose name immediately identifies him as a non-individual: 'Ford, the Model T, mass-reproducible person, the hyper-typical sheriff living in the hyper-typical American place, Central City, epitomizes the subject shot through by the social' (Seltzer 1998: 160). Paradoxically, given Ford's affective blankness, the novel is a retrospective, first-person account of events. As it becomes clear that Ford is insane, this puts into question much of what is being recounted to the reader. With the novel's progression we are forced to reflect on how much of this apparently candid account is distorted, selective, and imagined. As a result Thompson's novel poses a formal challenge for film adaptations in addition to the question of how literal the film can be in screening the novel's violent encounters.

24 Hour Party People, *A Cock and Bull Story* and, to some extent, *Butterfly Kiss*, employ the device of the unreliable narrator in different forms, but first-person narration poses a medium-specific problem for filmmakers in reconciling the narrator's perspective with the image. The detective film, *Lady in the Lake* (Robert Montgomery, 1947), famously addressed the problem through the use of subjective point-of-view shots throughout, situating the spectator in the embodied subject position of the protagonist Philip Marlowe. This technically intricate and narratively restrictive device (since only scenes in which the protagonist is present are possible) is rare within cinema but increasingly familiar in other audio-visual media such as first-person video games and TV comedies such as *Peep Show* (2003–10) (which is composed entirely from subjective point-of-view shots from the perspectives of multiple characters).

Transposing the novel's first-person narration into cinematic terms, *The Killer Inside Me* employs the generically familiar device of a retrospective voice-over commentary

'I didn't see that coming' –
Lou Ford (Casey Affleck)
addresses the camera

delivered intermittently by Ford.[22] The style of the film is more or less naturalistic, implying the objective representation of events. This juxtaposition of objective narration (image) with subjective narration (voice-over) seems unproblematic to begin with since we read the images as illustrative flashbacks motivated by his reminiscence, but not restricted by his perspective.

However the combination becomes radically disorienting towards the end of the film when, having been arrested, Ford (Casey Affleck) is unexpectedly committed to a psychiatric hospital. 'I didn't see that coming', Ford observes comically, and the line is coupled with a shot of Affleck smiling at the camera. It is the first moment in which the narrator directly addresses the camera, image and voice-over coming into direct alignment. Although it was already clear that Ford was a psychopathic compulsive killer, the tone of the voice-over is consistently calm and reflective. It is only when the hospitalised Ford begins to hallucinate, seeing family photographs projected on the walls of his bedroom at night, that it becomes clear the apparently lucid, reflective commentary is being delivered by a delusional psychotic. In this respect *The Killer Inside Me* follows the narrational principles of many classic *noirs*. As Karen Hollinger observes of such films, it appears at first glance that the confessional voice-over serves 'to establish within the text a single over-riding male narrational perspective that appears to dominate all other textual elements. As the films progress, however, this single, dominating point of view does not hold, and the films begin to fracture' (Hollinger 1996: 245). Whereas a classical realist text will typically assemble a narrational hierarchy 'in which one perspective – either that of the narrator, implied author, or implied spectator/reader comes to dominate and enclose all others or the three perspectives merge into a unified whole. In *film noir* a narrational hierarchy fails to establish itself and a proliferation of point of view dominates the texts' (Hollinger 1996: 247). As a result, the subjective account delivered in the voice-over has no reliable status as a master discourse and consequently no truths or revelations about Ford or the characters he interacts with are delivered.

Dark light

Shot by regular collaborator Marcel Zyskind on Super 35mm film in warm, sun-bleached colours, and largely natural light, and edited by Mags Arnold, who also edited *The Trip*, the film is a sumptuous depiction of 1950s Texas, with a score that mixes Melissa Parmenter's cues with Mahler, honky tonk, western swing, rock and roll, and jazz music. More consistently than in any of Winterbottom's other films,

Central City – the warm, earthy colour scheme that dominates *The Killer Inside Me*

the contemporary songs offer a direct commentary upon the action. For example, a montage showing Ford and his lover having sex is coupled with a love song whose clichéd lyrics, 'cling to me, baby. Come on home to mama now', dramatise the intensity of Joyce's love for Ford as well as the Oedipal dimensions of Ford's compulsive violence, as we learn that his mother died when he was young. Elsewhere, Ford and his boss, Bob Maples sing Spade Cooley's hit song, 'Shame On You' (1945) while driving. The song, which is reprised over the final shots of the film, is a rebuke to an unfaithful lover whose sinister quality is highlighted in relation to Ford's treatment of his lovers, but its inclusion carries greater meta-narrative resonance since Cooley later beat his wife to death.

The film employs classical editing principles sparely – there are few establishing shots at the openings of scenes, extensive use of montage editing to compress material into short sequences, and hand-held camera-work – but although it is not pastiche, it is nevertheless a careful invocation of the genre. The anachronistic opening titles, set to Little Willie John's hit song, 'Fever' (a 1956 account of the pleasurably painful, enervating intensity of a relationship), consist of a series of monochrome stills of characters and scenes from the film, overlaid with an abstract, suggestively phallic coloured pattern that recalls 1950s graphic design. The production design of the $13m film generates a plausibly detailed reproduction of mid-twentieth century Texas, in which vehicles, street scenes, costumes and interiors evoke the historical interval without ironic allusion to 1950s cinema or excessive emphasis upon the kitsch absurdities of period popular culture or archaic fashions in clothing. The film's aesthetic blends the highly formalised imagery and chiaroscuro lighting schemes of *film noir*, with an extemporary direct cinema aesthetic marked by mobile camera-work and naturalistic performances. As 1st Assistant Camera operator, Robert Rendon observes, the director 'is insistent on a no-rehearsals, no-marks kind of style, almost like a documentary [...]

Pastiche in the film's title sequence

The Killer Inside Me's noir-ish lighting scheme and set design

He often had us roll film and catch the actors on a break, sitting under a tree. Catching those moments is a lot of his style' (Frankel 2010: 22).

At one point, Lou Ford's boss, Sheriff Bob Maples tells him with drunken sincerity, 'It's always lightest just before the dark.' The enigmatic line signals both the symbolic and the visual prominence of light throughout the carefully lit film. Exterior scenes are staged at night and at dusk – the 'magic hour' – or in baking sunlight, while interior scenes are set in dark rooms with bare bulbs and low-key lighting; the first conversation between Ford and local business magnate Chester Conway (Ned Beatty) takes place in a dark wood-panelled room with sun raking through half-closed venetian blinds. One of the primary visual motifs is the contrast between dark interiors and bright exteriors as actors are repeatedly framed against bright windows which are often over-exposed, flaring and out of focus, so that they register as glaring white areas of the frame (prefiguring, *inter alia*, the white room in the insane asylum where Ford will eventually find himself).

The foregrounding of light invites us to understand the film as a critical commentary upon the visually stylised *noir* film. Rather than a nostalgic celebration of *film noir*'s status as a classic genre (insofar as it constitutes a 'genre', rather than a style, 'movement' or a 'cycle' (Root 1985: 93–4)), *The Killer Inside Me* throws light on and makes hyper-visible what is obscured, disregarded or critically sublimated within *noir* films and neo-*noirs* – the violent misogyny that is at the heart of many key examples. As Janey Place writes of the treatment of the female figure in classic *noir* films in relation to debates around the ambiguously 'progressive' potential of the films, 'Visually, film noir is fluid, sensual, extraordinarily expressive, making the sexually expressive woman, extremely powerful. It is not their inevitable demise we remember but rather their strong, dangerous, and above all exciting sexuality' (Place 1978: 36). By contrast, after viewing Winterbottom's film, it is the destruction of the film's female characters

The visual motif of overexposure – the DA, Howard Hendricks (Simon Baker) questions Ford

Ford begins his assault upon Joyce (Jessica Alba), his gloved hand over her face

that is most firmly imprinted in our memory, rather than a disingenuous insistence upon their power.

In this light, the spectacular emphasis placed upon the killer's brutal assaults upon his two lovers, Joyce Lakeland (Jessica Alba) and Amy Stanton (Kate Hudson) may be understood not as a shocking amplification and aestheticised reiteration of mainstream misogyny (although it is doubtless readable in this way), but as a confrontational critical highlighting of an intrinsic component of the genre. This is evidenced most obviously in the radically different treatment of the deaths of men and women. Of the three men killed, two are shot and die suddenly while the third is hanged off-screen. The murder of the two women, however, is prolonged, vicious, and excessively visible.

The murder of Joyce takes place early in the film. Joyce, a prostitute, believes that she and Ford are participating in a con to embezzle money from Elmer Conway, son of the businessman and one of her clients, and that they will use the money to elope. However, after they have had sex while waiting for Conway to arrive, Ford explains, while slowly pulling on a pair of black leather gloves, that she and Conway will both be found dead and it will be assumed that they had a fight and killed one another. 'Well, that doesn't make any sense,' she responds in bemusement. 'How am I supposed to be dead?' He begins to slap her face back and forth gently before holding her nose closed and then punching her several times in the face. Ford then hits her with such force that she is thrown across the room and crashes against the wall, sliding to the floor. He kneels down and continues to punch her face repeatedly as she sits stunned and passive. She gasps, 'Why?', between impacts, while he mutters, 'I'm sorry, baby' and 'I love you'. The scene is shot from multiple angles, the camera in uncomfortably close proximity to the actors, and includes a series of whip pans following his fist as he swings it at her face. The punches are accompanied by the sickening sound of breaking bones, music playing very quietly underneath, and the right side of her face is increasingly smashed and distorted, her torn mouth agape. The D.A. investigating the case later accurately describes her face as resembling 'stewed meat; hamburger'. After a while Ford pauses to open her unresponsive right eye, peering into it and asking, 'Honey, can you hear me? I'm sorry, I'm real sorry. I love you. Goodbye. You're going to be alright'. He lets her lolling head drop and then continues punching her until her body slumps sideways onto the floor, and he is left sweating and out of breath. Although Joyce lives a little longer, she never regains consciousness and dies in hospital. The fatal beating takes two minutes of screen time but, contrasted with the narrative compression that characterises the rest of the film, it feels much longer.

Amy's murder towards the end of the film is equally vicious and occupies slightly more screen time. She arrives at Ford's house smartly dressed and carrying travel bags having similarly been persuaded by Ford that they will elope. She finds him in the kitchen sitting in his vest whereupon he orders, 'Don't say anything', spits in her face and then punches her twice in the stomach. She collapses face-down on the floor, twitching and croaking, and the absence of incidental music or dialogue adds to the discomfort of the scene. She stretches her finger towards his boot while he stands watching her, but he withdraws it and then roughly turns her over, tearing open her jacket and pulling her skirt up over her face – partly to stage this as a simulated sexual assault, and presumably also to avoid her gaze. He sits down and picks up a newspaper agitatedly and watches her, a smile passing briefly across his face as she continues twitching, while urine pools around her body. When the doorbell rings, he kicks her twice very hard in the stomach, which is again accompanied by the nauseating sound of breaking bones, and there is a lingering close-up shot of her lifeless face.

These scenes are so abrupt and so shockingly ferocious in their emphasis upon the physical damage done to these women's bodies by Ford's feet and fists that, as Rachel Cooke's response indicates, they have the potential to derail the narrative progression of the film. Ford attempts to frame other people for the murders, implicating Elmer Conway for Joyce's murder (in order to avenge the death of his brother who was killed working on an unsafe building site owned by Conway's father), and implicating an itinerant worker for Amy's murder when the man, who knows that Ford killed Joyce and Elmer, tries to blackmail Ford. However, the fury of Ford's assaults makes clear that these are not just calculated, instrumental killings and these rationalisations are not enough to explain the viciousness of Ford's attacks. On the contrary, it is as if the schemes offer Ford a pretext for the murders.

In doing so they foreground spectacularly, the misogynistic fantasy that is at the heart of many *films noirs*. *The Killer Inside Me* follows the generic contours of the classic *film noir* more closely than any of Winterbottom's other genre films cleave to tradition, in terms of its style, tone and sometimes complex plot. James Damico's identification of the defining structure of *films noirs* maps closely onto Winterbottom's film:

> Either because he is fated to do so, or because he has been hired to do a job espe-cially associated with her, a man whose experience of life has left him sanguine and often bitter meets a not-so-innocent woman of similar outlook to whom he is sexually and fatally attracted. Through this attraction, either because the woman induces him to it, or because it is a natural result of their relationship, the man comes to cheat, attempt to murder, or actually murder a second man to whom the woman is unhappily or unwillingly attached (generally he is her husband or lover), an act which often leads to the woman's betrayal of the protagonist, but which in any event brings about the sometimes metaphoric but usual literal destruction of the woman, the man to whom she is attached and, frequently, to the protagonist himself. (Damico 1978: 54)

The Killer Inside Me opens with Ford being despatched by the sheriff to run a prostitute out of town. On realising he is a policeman rather than a client she attacks him, whereupon he strips her and thrashes her with his belt, a form of sexual sadism that is Ford's primary fetish. They then have sex and a sexual relationship develops. Learning that Elmer Conway is a client of hers, Ford realises he can settle some scores. Chester Conway, meanwhile, is concerned about his son's relationship with a prostitute, and instructs Ford to help him pay Joyce $10,000 to leave town. Elmer thinks that he and Joyce will use the money to elope together, while Joyce believes that she and Ford will elope together with the money while Elmer is waiting for her to join him. In the event, Ford beats up Joyce and then kills Elmer when he arrives to deliver the $10,000. When Ford returns home, his girlfriend Amy, realises he has had sex with someone else and in order to mollify her he persuades her he had intended to ask her to marry him. An investigation into the murder is conducted by a sceptical D.A., Howard Hendricks, while Ford and his boss, Bob Maples, travel with Chester Conway and the comatose Joyce to Fort Worth where Conway has arranged for hospital treatment in order that she can stand trial for murdering his son: 'I want to see her burn.' Joyce dies while under anaesthetic and, returning home, Ford then learns that a local teenager, Johnnie Pappas, has been arrested for the murders after trying to spend a marked note from the $10,000. Pappas, who was given the note by Ford on the night of the murder, concealed the source of the note assuming that Ford had taken a bribe and that he was being helpful in covering for him. Ford visits Pappas in the police cell and confesses the murders to Pappas before hanging the boy, a death that is initially assumed to be suicide.

Ford starts to become paranoid and is advised by the local union organiser, Joe Rothman, who appears certain of Ford's guilt, not to 'hang around'. In bed with Amy, Ford suggests that they elope and shortly afterwards is visited by an itinerant pipeline worker who saw Ford near Joyce's house on the night of the murder (which explains the insertion of several puzzling point-of-view shots earlier in the film) and demands $5,000 to keep quiet. Ford agrees to pay in a fortnight. Ford kills Amy when she arrives to leave with him and when the blackmailer arrives he is accused by Ford of killing her. Wielding a knife Ford then chases the man through the streets to the main square where the man is shot by Ford's colleague Deputy Plummer. Plummer and Hendricks subsequently arrest Ford for the murders and put him in the cells. Eight days later he is transferred to the 'insane asylum' where he hallucinates that a slide show is projected on the wall of the room. In the penultimate scene, which is undoubtedly a delu-

Ford's hallucination – a slide of Amy (Kate Hudson) is projected onto his cell wall

Intimate apocalypse
– Joyce and Ford are
engulfed by flames at the
film's conclusion

sion, Ford is released from his cell and driven home by a boisterous, tobacco-chewing lawyer, Billy Boy Walker (Bill Pullman). During the drive, Walker asks Ford to tell him his story since it might be useful to him or help someone else. On arriving home, Ford changes his clothes, douses the interior of the house in petrol and alcohol (in a sequence that recalls the conclusion of *The Claim*) and sits in an armchair toying with a knife. Policemen with rifles surround the house and Plummer, Conway and Hendricks enter with Joyce, scarred and unsteady, wearing a neck brace. She says she wanted to see him but he cuts her off saying he loves her too before stabbing her. The policemen open fire and the room bursts into flames. In the final shot the camera tilts up from the burning exterior of the house to show smoke rising into the air.

The Killer Inside Me closely reproduces the dominant tone of many *films noirs* in its narrative orientation around an unrepentant murderer who, as a policeman, represents the collapse of moral boundaries and the bankruptcy of legitimising social institutions. Janey Place's observations on the register of the genre are literalised in the figure of the psychopathic protagonist:

> The dominant world view expressed in film noir is paranoid, claustrophobic, hopeless, doomed, predetermined by the past, without clear moral or personal identity. […] He has no reference points, no moral base from which to confidently operate. Any previous framework is cut loose and morality becomes relative, both externally (the world) and internally (the character and his relations to his work, his friends, his sexuality). (Place 1978: 41)

Ford's behaviour is not fully explained by the film's outlining of his character, and this ambiguity is a barrier to sympathy and identification, holding us at a distance. There is no indication of what it is that triggers this killing spree – whether there is a specific event that cuts him loose from a moral anchor – or whether Ford has a history of killing. The spectator is provided with a succinct indication of the psychic traumas that may have turned him into a killer, although Ford's limited self-reflexive capacity means that our insight into his motivations remains similarly limited. The spectator is not offered a psychologically substantial explanation of his actions, although it is revealed in passing that Ford's mother died when he was young, that he had an adopted older brother, Mike, who was accused of molesting a five-year old girl, that he lives in his dead father's house and that his father was a doctor. At various moments we see Ford listening to classical music, playing the piano (including a piece by Richard Strauss), reading the Bible, contemplating a chess board and writing complex mathematical equations in a notebook. The character sketched by these details is incoherent and incomplete, although two flashbacks provide partial access to Ford's traumatised psychic history. The first, following a present-day conversation about his brother with the local union boss, is a point-of-view sequence in which the young Ford is discovered by his brother, Mike, holding down a young girl in the back of a car, implying that Mike was falsely accused. The second flashback is prompted by Ford's discovery of some dog-eared pornographic photographs of the house-keeper, her buttocks marked with welts. Ironically, he finds the photographs hidden inside the pages of a Bible (which is shelved alongside two volumes of Freud's writing), defeating his search for spiritual guidance by returning him to his sinful past. Ford's discovery motivates a flashback to a childhood encounter in which the housekeeper removes his shirt, incites him to hit her and is then shown lying on the bed in only her bra, smacking her scarred buttocks and inviting him to do the same: 'Wanna be a big boy? Look what your daddy did. D'you wanna do it too? It's okay. I like it when you hurt me.'

Back in the present, Ford stares intently at the photographs as if recovering a forgotten memory, and then burns them in the sink, still studying them closely. These flashbacks suggest that Ford's violence and sexual sadism is a direct product of abuse, and, indeed, his sexual relationship with both Joyce and Amy is characterised by a disturbing sado-masochistic dynamic echoing this early sexual experience – we see Ford spank them and hold his hand over their faces during sex (as he does to the little girl in the flashback), in one scene he holds a belt tight around Joyce's neck and, as Hendricks later observes, the bodies of both women were covered with older bruises. As the invocation of Freud suggests, we can understand Ford's affect and behaviour as a consequence of a particular series of events during his childhood, but the economy with which this personal history is depicted indicates that this psychologising is a minor theme. When Ford tells Johnnie Pappas that he is paralysed by ambivalence, the claim that he is divided sheds little light on his character: 'I've got a foot on both sides of the fence. They were put there early and they've stayed put. I can't move. I can't jump. All I can do is wait until I split. Right down the middle.'

He lives in his father's shadow, over-identified with him, occupying the same space, reproducing his behaviour and restaging the death of his mother in the murder of Joyce and Amy. Ford is not a character that invites pity or compassion, however, since Affleck's understated performance renders him as anaesthetised and affectless, disconnected from reality. Commenting on his sense of paranoid anxiety after murdering Joyce, he imagines himself an unjust victim with no sense of guilt or mortification: 'It was almost like there was a plot against me. I'd done something wrong when I was a kid, and I'd had my nose rubbed in it day after day until like an over-trained dog I started crapping out of pure fright.' Later on, when he lets slip to his boss that he and Amy are going to get married, he observes, 'I feel pretty lucky. I feel like my life's a picture show.' For Ford, a man without qualities, with no individuality, happiness is experienced at one remove – something that he observes rather than experiences directly. Affleck speaks with a quiet, high voice, that is sometimes petulant, but his delivery is laconic and laid-back and rarely reveals or expresses any emotional dynamics. For much of the film his face remains blank and illegible, and even during the violent assaults the performance remains inexpressive (which is to say that it conveys an affective disjunction). Aside from the montage scenes that show him interacting playfully with Joyce and Amy, he smiles only rarely, often after inflicting violence, but these smiles are brief and tight-lipped. As Raymond Durgnat observes, '*Film noir* psychopaths, who are legion, are divisible into three main groups: the heroes with a tragic flaw, the unassuming monsters, and the obvious monsters' and Ford is clearly an example of the unassuming monster (Durgnat 1996: 49).

A distinguishing feature of this *film noir* is the refusal, in its depiction of violence against women, to reiterate the commonplace that active female sexuality is dangerously seductive, or to reanimate the misogynistic figure of the *femme fatale*. As E. Ann Kaplan argues, *films noirs* typically locate the cause of the protagonist's alienated experience 'in the excesses of female sexuality ("natural" consequences of women's independence), and punishes that excess in order to re-place it within the patriarchal order' (Kaplan 1978: 3). While, as a prostitute, Joyce perhaps connotes independent or excessive sexuality, or simply financial independence, her murder takes place so early in the film, and her relationship with Ford is depicted as so carefree, that there is no sense that he is ensnared or compromised by the relationship. Janey Place writes that 'in film noir, it is clear that men need to control women's sexuality in order not to be destroyed by it. The dark woman of film noir had something her innocent sister lacked: access to her own sexuality (and thus to men's) and the power that this access unlocked' (Place 1978: 36). Both Joyce and Amy are depicted as physically confident and sexually active – Amy twice initiates sex with Ford, for example, and they are visually coded as similar since both have dark brown hair and appear on screen in black underwear. Thus, the presentation of these characters eschews the dark/light moral distinction described by Place despite their superficial correspondence to the opposed archetypes of virgin and whore: whereas Maples opines that 'they don't come any better than little Amy', he instructs Ford to run Joyce out of town. However, there is no insinuation that they are responsible for Ford's treatment of them, and they pose no threat of destruction, corruption or moral disorientation. As Ford observes during a montage sequence showing happy, domestic moments from his relationship with Amy, 'For the first time since I don't remember when, my mind was really free.' Insofar as Ford represents the patriarchal order (as lawman and parodic double of his own father), this order is revealed to be paranoid, psychotic, perverse, destructive and indiscriminately misogynistic.

Impossibility of intimacy

To return to the chapter's linking theme, *The Killer Inside Me* explores the impossibility of cinematic intimacy in several ways. The protagonist Lou Ford remains unknowable throughout the film – his affectless exterior and empty interior mean that neither the other characters nor the spectator can establish an intimate understanding of the man. Ford remains a blank, reflective screen (like the white walls of his cell) onto which other characters and the spectator can project an authentic identity or interiority.

Thus, Ford's boss Maples tells him (after Ford brutally murdered Joyce and Conway), 'I know what you are, Lou ... I know you backwards and forwards. I've known you since you was knee-high to a grasshopper, and you ain't never done anything wrong.' As a result of Ford's emptiness, the narrative has a hollow centre since one of the central principles of classical film narration, the delineation of character psychology as the basis of narrative coherence, is absent from the film. An intimate relationship is also impossible for the protagonist, Ford, and the violence he metes out to his lovers is simultaneously both a means of intimate relationship, since physical violence and abuse is closely linked to sexual intimacy for Ford, and a brutal, punitive expression of a horror at intimacy – the four people he kills, Elmer Conway, Johnnie Pappas, Joyce and Amy all imagine themselves to be close friends or intimates of Lou.

As discussed above, *The Killer Inside Me* makes minor revisions to the style, structure and characterisation of the *film noir*, but in so doing, it foregrounds the archetypal misogyny of the tradition. Like *Butterfly Kiss* it constitutes a feminist critique of a classic American narrative film tradition and exposes the historical contingency of intimate relationality, and in this respect it is a further example of Winterbottom's practice of generic revisions and reconfigurations. It also exemplifies the centrality of intimacy in Winterbottom's cinema, which is understood not as a matter of saccharine, sentimental, predictable romance, but as a complex affective field of potentialities and disappointments, ignorance and transparency, violence, physical proximity, joy, arousal and desire, boredom and isolation, continuity, friendship and loyalty, of borders and their transgression. Cinematic intimacy is a form of manufactured public intimacy, which is staged and performed and unfolds in the relation between spectator and screen. This is acknowledged to different degrees by these texts which, in staging a range of scenarios from couples talking, fighting and fucking to women giving birth and prisoners undergoing torture, expose the limits – the impossibility – of intimacy.

Notes

1   We might also note that Kinetoscopes and Mutoscopes, the precursors of film projection and one of the means by which early films were viewed, allowed individual viewers a very acute sense of intimacy as they peered at the moving images through an eye-piece. Viewed in public spaces, such as amusement arcades and fairgrounds these machines, commonly known as 'peep shows' or, in Britain, 'What the Butler Saw' machines, also promised the viewer individual access to private, 'illicit' or titillating images among the other sorts of films that were viewable. In thinking about film spectatorship it is important to note that the film theatre comprises a variety of culturally and historically specific viewing contexts and practices, rather than a universal, a-historical experience.

2   See, for example, Mulvey 1975 on sadism, and Doane 1992, and Studlar 1985 on masochism.

3   This is the title of a song by the Clash and written by Mick Jones. In a moment of ontological uncertainty that is characteristic of Winterbottom's films, Jones makes

a brief appearance singing this song in a karaoke bar in *Code 46* although, in a typically self-reflexive repetition, Jones also made a brief appearance in archive footage of The Clash in *24 Hour Party People* released the year before.

4   British Academy of Film and Television Arts.

5   The co-writers won the Royal Television Society's 'Best Writer' award for the film (http://www.screenonline.org.uk/tv/id/587051/).

6   The TV series was edited into a feature-length film for screening at film festivals.

7   Including, notably, *Coffee and Cigarettes* (Jim Jarmusch, 2003) in which he again plays himself as an unattractively vain, career-obsessed character.

8   The extract makes reference to the abbey.

9   With whom Coogan acted in the Hollywood satire about Hollywood filmmaking, *Tropic Thunder* (Ben Stiller, 2008).

10   Although, significantly, whereas *Blade Runner* imagines a proximate future in which immigrants remain socially and economically marginal within the context of Los Angeles, *Code 46* places Shanghai at the centre of the futuristic diegesis; for *Blade Runner*, thinking about the future meant looking at the US, for *Code 46*, released in the early twenty-first century, it means looking at China.

11   It is notable that Geld, like *Blade Runner*'s protagonist Deckard, relies upon empathy as the primary method of detection. Where Geld employs a virus, Deckard employs the Voigt-Kampff test.

12   Following Agamben's proposition that 'the camps have, in a certain sense, reappeared in an even more extreme form in the territories of the former Yugoslavia', the camp trilogy might also be expanded to comprise a quartet of films along with *Welcome to Sarajevo* (Agamben 1998: 99).

13   *Obtaining Cover: Inside Code 46* (Greg Carson, 2004) – documentary short from the UK DVD release.

14   The Borg are characters introduced in *Star Trek: Next Generation* (1987–2004) and reprised in subsequent series and spin-off films. They are deindividuated cyborgs who are part of a psychically connected 'collective', and they spread remorselessly through the universe 'assimilating' each new species they encounter.

15   *Obtaining Cover: Inside Code 46* (2004, Greg Carson) – documentary short from the UK DVD release.

16   A key Winterbottom location.

17   EPK, UK DVD.

18   'Michael Winterbottom: 9 Songs – interviewed by Adrian Hennigan', 2005. Available from: http://www.bbc.co.uk/films/2005/03/03/michael_winterbottom_9_songs_interview.shtml. Accessed 18/2/11.

19   2002 UK DVD extra.

20   This passage recalls the book that we see Laura (Julie Christie) reading in the first scene of *Don't Look Now*, *Beyond the Fragile Geometry of Space*, which also serves as a description of that film's discontinuous editing and fragmentary rendering of space.

21   In addition to directing these two films, Winterbottom's company, Revolution films, produced *Resurrection Man* (Marc Evans, 1998), a film about a real-life

Northern Irish gangster, Victor Kelly, one of a group who serially murdered Catholics in Belfast in the late 1970s.

22   The fact that one of the few feature films narrated and shot entirely from a subjective point of view, *Lady in the Lake* is also a crime drama indicates that narrative reliability or the unstable hierarchies of discourse is a specific generic property.

CHAPTER THREE

Nation and Genre

This chapter will explore Winterbottom's work through a focus on the inter-relation of genre and nation. It will discuss the value of framing his work in terms of national culture and also the problems with situating his work in relation to the context of British cinema. It will then go on to argue that his work can productively be understood to be engaged in a critical dialogue with key genres, tropes and traditions from British cinema. I will argue that it is engaged with a reimagining or 'reterritorialisation' of British cinema as a shifting field of contradictions and incompatibilities, rather than a historically stable, clearly bounded cultural zone. While Winterbottom can be aligned with other innovative and inconsistent contemporary British filmmakers such as Andrea Arnold, Nick Broomfield, Gideon Koppel, Andrew Kötting, David Mackenzie, Shane Meadows, Steve McQueen, Pawel Pawlikowski, Sally Potter, Lynne Ramsay and Sam Taylor-Wood due to formal affinities and thematic continuity, his films also beg the question of what British cinema might be comprised of. One of the consistent characteristics of Winterbottom's work is a tendency towards genre transformation. Winterbottom's films frequently invoke familiar genres, such as the road movie (*Butterfly Kiss*, *In This World*), science fiction cinema (*Code 46*), hardcore pornography (*9 Songs*) or the *film noir* (*I Want You*, *The Killer Inside Me*), while incorporating unfamiliar, unexpected or incompatible elements into the generic configuration of the resulting films. While genre formats, such as the western or the musical, have a flexible transnational currency that allows them to be reconfigured continually in different contexts, they are also a key means by which mythic stories about national and cultural formations are told (both to and about a nation). Genre serves as a vehicle for the generation, refinement and recirculation of a repertoire of legitimising images, characters, themes and ideological arrays. For example, as Will Wright reflects, in an examination of US cinema in the 1980s, 'The Western, perhaps the most successful myth in history [was] certainly the bedrock of American popular culture for this entire century' (Wright 1982: 120).The inter-generic character of many of Winterbottom's films and dramas therefore means that these films can be understood as an interference with, or a critique of, the reproduction and transmission of such myths. In splicing together components from unlikely and apparently incompatible genres and traditions, the films make visible to us the story-telling and myth-making mechanisms of the cinematic traditions the films draw on.

The films that are the focus of this chapter are reworkings of heritage films or costume films and although this genre does not have the significance of a foundation myth for British popular culture, it has nevertheless been the object of debates about national identity, the relationship between the present and various imagined pasts, and the position of cinema in relation to a national culture. Through a distinctive treatment of visual style, setting and iconography and narrative organisation the films discussed in this chapter prompt the viewer to reflect upon the stories told by filmmakers about national cultures and identities, and also the ways in which the accretion of such stories and images contributes to the formation of national cultures.

The problems with national cinema

The problems with the employment of national cinema as a framing interpretative category are well established and various. The invocation of a stable nation-state, national identity or national culture in discussions about national cinema can serve to reproduce and reinforce repressive nationalist concepts of the nation as naturalised, singular and undivided. Reference to national cinema can also involve a disregard for the transnational character of the financing, production and circulation of much contemporary film as well as to the reading practices of audiences for whom the origins of a film may be indiscernible, misconstrued, or largely irrelevant. The relationship between a national cinema and a corresponding national culture is complex. In so far as a national cinema is identifiable at a particular moment or in a particular context, its constitutive role within a national culture (representing a nation to itself) and its economic significance may be entirely marginal.

National cinema is, as Susan Hayward suggests, both an object and a problem of knowledge. It is an object of knowledge in so far as the scrutiny of certain films allows us to conceptualise and distinguish groupings of film: 'cinema becomes a domain in which different knowledges about national cinema are produced (from production to reception) and are brought into relation' (Hayward 2000: 93). It is also problematic in so far as a critical examination of particular films within the framework of 'national cinema' inevitably exposes the inadequacy of such a framing:

> viewing cinema in a relational and interdisciplinary context ... does not allow for a 'naturalising' of the concept of national cinema but rather it causes a calling of this into question and in so doing generates problems in three areas, the critical, the political, and policy-wise. (Ibid.)

Reterritorialising 'British cinema'

In this context, Michael Winterbottom's inter-generic films can be framed as a body of texts with a complex relationship to 'British cinema', however it is defined. In the exploration of themes of nation that characterise some of the films, in their reworking of genres associated with British cinema, and in their modes of address, these films invite us to consider Britishness as an estranged, defamiliarised and troubled category of identity, behaviours, images and narrative tropes. While this is a limiting framework in some respects that might temporarily obscure the relationship between Winterbottom's work and that of non-British filmmakers, it is nevertheless a framing that draws attention to subtleties in the films, the particular 'structures of feeling' to use Raymond Williams' term, that might be lost or invisible when they are considered as examples of European or transnational cinema, such as the dialogic relation with British television drama and popular culture (Williams 1975a). Framing Winterbottom's films provisionally in relation to British cinema and the categories of film associated with it also highlights one of the persistent strategies employed in his work – the transformation or reconfiguration of genre frameworks. In turn, the problematic fit of Winterbottom's films with the film genres most closely aligned with a national cinema, may demonstrate the restrictive function of such categories.

At stake in discussions of national cinema is the problematic relation between concepts of the nation and discourses of nationalism and the anxious negotiation of the desire for, or the fantasy of, a singular, bounded nation that corresponds to a definable, homogeneous national cinema. As Susan Hayward observes, one of the ways in which such a concept of nation emerges and is reinforced is through narratives that frame the past as coherent, progressive lines of development that lead directly to the present:

> Nationalisms are forged in part in apprehension (a seizing and remodelling) of the past. Nationalisms make use of the past, go back to 'ancestral' traditions or indeed *invent* them. In this regard … nations are a product of a territorialisation of memory. Memory stands here for collective memory, a shared culture, shared memories of a collective past … But memory also means amnesia and, as [Anthony] Smith goes on to say, 'the importance of national amnesia and getting one's own history *wrong* (is essential) for the maintenance of national solidarity'. (Hayward 2000: 90)

It follows that in popular culture since the beginning of the twentieth century, historical dramas and heritage films can be understood to have played a significant role in the invention and remodelling of the past. US president and historian, Woodrow Wilson's observation that D. W. Griffith's racist historical fantasy, *The Birth of a Nation* (1915), was 'like writing history with lightning' is a particularly clear instance of the way in which cinema's seizure and invention of historical fact can be exceptionally persuasive and dangerously effective (given that film's role in the revival of the Ku Klux Klan, for instance). However, far from using an analysis of Winterbottom's films to map out definitively the territory of a national cinema and a corresponding national

identity and national past, I argue in this chapter that Winterbottom's films are exami-
nations of the ways in which the past is used in the cinema and the ways in which films
get history wrong. In different ways the films discussed here are engaged with remem-
bering and re-writing personal histories that are intertwined with and representative
of broader national and trans-national histories. However, in different ways they are
also concerned with the ongoing processes of correction, reconstruction and recognition. In the course of this narration, the picture of a nation that emerges is potentially
complex and productively incomplete and multiple, rather than repressively singular.
As Hayward proposes, it is possible to discuss national cinema in a manner that makes
national cinema an enabling critical concept. Rather than foreclosing debate,

> this approach also carves out spaces that allow us to *revalue* the concept of
> national cinema. It makes it possible to reterritorialise the nation (to rewrite
> Paul Virilio, echoing Deleuze perhaps) not as bounded, demarcated and
> distinctive but as one within which boundaries constantly criss-cross both
> haphazardly and *unhaphazardly.* (Hayward 2000: 93)

Insofar as Winterbottom's films constitute valuable and provocative examples of British
cinema for this discussion, it is precisely because they cross and re-cross the institutional, stylistic and thematic boundaries associated with British cinema.

Romantic comedy: With or Without You

Thus, framing Winterbottom's films in relation to nation need not involve an uncritical
or chauvinist reassertion of a singular concept of nation, but on the contrary can
involve sensitivity towards the social and cultural incompatibilities and divisions that
transect, order and hierarchise Britain. For example, *With or Without You* follows
the model of a romantic comedy, a genre closely associated with the contemporary
British mainstream, and tells the story of a couple, Rosie and Vincent Boyd (Dervla
Kirwan and Christopher Eccleston) whose unsuccessful attempts to conceive a child
lead almost to the breakdown of their marriage as their frustration prompts both partners to sleep with a former lover. The news at the end of the film that IVF treatment has been successful and Rosie is pregnant, brings the couple back together and
brings narrative resolution. However, as Deborah Allinson observes, although the film
belongs to a familiar genre, it is marked by unfamiliar authorial elements: 'its frequent
stylistic flourishes embody the director's ongoing resistance to presenting a narrative in
a strictly conventional way. These include a multitude of split-screens, frames-within-
frames, irises and wipes' (Allinson 2005).

One of the potentially resistant thematic details of the narrative is that Vincent, who
now works as a glazier for Rosie's father, used to be a policeman before being persuaded
to change career. Since the film is set in Belfast, Northern Ireland, this means that
Vincent was a member of the Royal Ulster Constabulary, a police force whose dual
role was to undertake normal policing duties and also to secure the boundary between
Northern Ireland and Éire/Ireland, containing republican or separatist violence within

The disorienting encounter with medical institutions – Rosie (right) receiving an ultrasound scan

the province. Vincent would have been a policeman during the 'Troubles', a period of violent civil disruption from 1969 through to 1998 and thus the character's personal history is interwoven with the fraught political history of the region. Vincent is a condensed, synechdocal sign of the precarious and sometimes violently repressive process of the formation and maintenance of nations and national boundaries. Martin McLoone has suggested that *With or Without You* is one of a number of films emerging from the 'celtic periphery' that are engaged with the project of reimagining British identities as multiple. He argues that such films indicate 'that a process of internal decolonisation is well underway and that peripherality has moved towards the cutting edge of contemporary cultural debate' (McLoone 2001: 190).

While Vincent's former career is referred to only briefly, the fact that he still owns a hand-gun which he fires at Rosie's lover at the film's climax, indicates that the violent history of the region remains volatile and ever-present. In an earlier argument over an arrangement Vincent has made to play golf with his friends and former colleagues, Rosie tells him he does not even like the game and taunts, 'It's just an excuse to dress up in silly clothes and go out with the boys. Why don't you just join the Orange Order and have done with it?' The Protestant 'Orange Order' is strongly associated with unionist politics in Northern Ireland, and Rosie's angry comment suggests sectarianism is a continuing fact of life and that the police in Northern Ireland were historically aligned with the continuation of a British imperialist project of control and subjugation of the Irish.

The banality of political violence – Vincent scanning the newspaper for jobs

Belfast cityscape

Issues of peripherality remain, as it were, at the peripheries of the film but are nevertheless quietly insistent. Framed in relation to questions of national culture, the film's setting and these marginal details permit a superficially anodyne romantic comedy to be read as a reflection upon the violent and enduring effects of colonisation that remain just below the surface. In this light, the spaces of Belfast represented on screen, such as the gleaming, glass-walled concert hall in which Rosie works unhappily as a receptionist and usher, the golf course, fertility clinic, shops, civic buildings and the smart housing estate on which Rosie and Vincent live, have a dual significance. On the one hand they represent the city as modernised, blandly aspirational and equivalent to any contemporary European city, but on the other hand the visual emphasis of these spaces may be read as a commentary upon the disavowal of the specific history of this city. Indeed, the film could conceivably have been set anywhere as the drama does not depend upon the location, and the dramatic finale takes place at the beach – a non-specific, inter-changeable space that recurs in many of Winterbottom's films, no matter where they're set.

This is certainly not the Northern Ireland mapped out in the earlier TV drama, *Love Lies Bleeding*. That film depicts the province as an altogether grimmer politicised and surveyed territory of prisons, watchtowers and checkpoints, working men's clubs, loyalist estates, farmhouses and republican political campaign centres. By contrast, perhaps, the spaces through which the characters move in *With or Without You* represent the architectural and spatial erasure of this past.

Setting *With or Without You* in Northern Ireland involves a reconfiguration or expansion of the conventions and possibilities of the romantic comedy rather than a subver-

The showdown on the beach –
Rosie chases Vincent

sion or dismantling of them. Formally, one of the means by which the genre is recon-figured is through the film's invocation of social realist traditions. Discussing the film's production, Christopher Eccleston observed that Winterbottom often talked about 'documentary style' during the shoot, and the collision of mundane, dour documen-tary realism with the apparently incompatible tradition of the romantic comedy, which is dismissively regarded as marked by fantasy and idealism, represents the awkward marriage of two traditions that are closely associated with British popular cinema.[1]

One of the effects of this is to establish a certain critical distance from the idealism and reductive optimism associated (however problematically) with romantic comedies. There is a poignant gap between the fantasies of uncomplicated romance, which we might associate with romantic comedies, embodied here by the exotic figure of Benoît, Rosie's boyfriend from the past – a sensitive, bohemian Frenchman who appears unannounced and who cries while listening to a symphony – and the mundane realities and responsibilities of Vincent and Rosie's lives, which are organ-ised around unfulfilling jobs.

For example, much of the film's comedy is derived from the way that their desire for a child consigns them to mechanical and progressively more passionless sex as they follow medical advice on when and how regularly to do it. Having a child becomes another laborious, routinised physical activity, rather than a spontaneous expression of passion, that takes place under medical supervision, a point that is made clear by a cut from the couple having sex to a series of black-and-white microscopic images of semen, and then to a scene in which the couple are being interviewed in a fertility clinic.

While the film can be understood as a 'resistant' critical revision of the romantic comedy, it retains enough of the structure of such films to allow it to be viewed as an unconventional variation on the model, rather than a distortion or disassembly of it. The film retains a familiar narrative trajectory in which the integrity of the marriage is threatened by the disruptive appearance of former lovers, Benoît and Cathy, their vain and increasingly medicalised attempts to conceive, and their alienation from their jobs. The moving conclusion on the beach in which Vincent presents Rosie with a letter from the fertility clinic confirming her pregnancy restores the marriage and leads to the resolution in which, following an ironic iris-in on the delighted couple embracing on the sand recalling the closing shot of a Chaplin film, family and friends attend a cheerful christening party for the baby.

The film's title, which, like several of Winterbottom's other films is a song title, refers to a very well known 1987 love song by Irish rock group U2 and reiterates the status of the film as an unconventional but mainstream romantic comedy, its refrain describing a recognisable romantic scenario, 'I can't live with or without you'. Indeed, the ambiguity of the title relates to the dual mode of address employed by the film. Outside Éire or Northern Ireland, the significance of the narrative setting is likely to register much less strongly. For instance, one review concludes that 'Winterbot-tom's one real achievement is to make a movie set in Belfast in which, for once, the Troubles don't intrude'.[2] The film avoids reproducing simple national stereotypes for international consumption, but the fact that the Troubles remain an insistent presence means that the film has a regionally specific address. There are elements of the film

The family reunited

that are non-narrative, or apparently narratively unmotivated or arbitrary, that convey something of the specific texture of everyday life. These components correspond to the 'image facts' that André Bazin identified as characteristics of the realist aesthetic exemplified by Italian neo-realist cinema. 'Image facts' are distinguished by Bazin from shots insofar as they retain the irreducible, excessive ambiguity and autonomy of material reality, whereas a shot is an intrinsic element of a narrative. In a discussion of *Paisà* (Roberto Rossellini, 1946), Bazin defines the image fact as 'a fragment of concrete reality in itself multiple and full of ambiguity, whose meaning emerges only after the fact, thanks to other imposed facts between which the mind establishes certain relationships' (Bazin 37: 1971).

While the director (along with his various collaborators) has undoubtedly selected these images judiciously, Bazin suggests that neo-realist cinema is characterised by an attempt to retain the 'factual integrity' of these images. The effect of the incorporation of these 'useless facts' into the fabric of the film is that the resulting scene displays a 'concrete density', rather than a transparent significance. While *With or Without You* bears little direct stylistic or ideological resemblance to neo-realist film, Bazin's commentary upon *Paisà* is helpful in articulating an aesthetic strategy underpinning many of Winterbottom's films. This strategy involves the retention of 'concrete parasites of an abstraction', which would normally be dispensed with in order to reproduce a conventionally efficient narrative form and thus generates narratives with an apparently provisional, fragmented quality (ibid.).

Heritage cinema and Jude

One of the most productive ways of situating Winterbottom's films, then, is to understand them as signs of an engagement in a sceptical, contradictory, dialogue with British cinema traditions. The stylistic and structural idiosyncrasies common to many of Winterbottom's films displace certain characteristic features of anonymous genre films such as romantic comedies, but overall they are not radically experimental and consequently retain their generic identity. Just as the films of Kathryn Bigelow and Stanley Kubrick can be plotted as systematic appropriations and re-workings of cinematic genres in the context of mainstream commercial cinema (science fiction, horror, war films, crime dramas, costume dramas and melodramas, erotic thrillers and social problem films), so Winterbottom's films can be understood as re-workings and recombinations of genre films in the more (commercially) minor context of international art cinema. Delimited by a set of tacit and constantly shifting guidelines for filmmakers and viewers, genres constitute flexible spaces for play and innovation. The challenge of producing an engaging genre film is to manage the relationship between repetition and difference and in this respect the production of a genre film becomes an abstract formal exercise in carefully judged manipulation of 'found' or preconstituted elements; if a film reproduces genre predecessors too completely, with too little mediation, it may be boring for a viewer familiar with the genre. If, on the other hand, it is too novel it may frustrate a viewer's expectations of the pleasurable reprise of recognisable characters, narrative, *mise-en-scène*, music, and other elements.

Probably the most internationally visible and critically overdetermined genre of British cinema (in part because it is defined by its production and circulation contexts as a transnational commodity) with which Winterbottom has engaged is that of the costume drama or heritage film, a genre that is engaged with reinventing or constructing a national past. Much academic and popular criticism of costume drama has explored questions of how the contested genre and proliferating sub-genres might be codified and to what extent they can be understood as aesthetically and ideologically conservative, repressive or, in some instances, politically progressive. Hossein Amini, screenwriter of *Jude* (and *Wings of a Dove* (Iain Softley, 1997)), recounted that the intention behind the film was 'destroying the heritage film from within', which clearly indicates a dissatisfaction with the politics of heritage cinema, but it is consistent with the operation of genre that such an approach is invited and accommodated (Wilson 2003: 96). The process of genre filmmaking is precisely that of a continual destruction and reconstruction from within. This is not to argue that the production of a genre film necessitates the dissipation of political refusal or contestation, since, in situating the filmmakers 'within' this commercially and critically prominent field, Amini appears to recognise the currency of the heritage film as a platform. By contrast with the imagined past exemplified by the spectacular *mise-en-scène* of contemporaneous films like *Sense and Sensibility* (Ang Lee, 1995) and *Emma* (Douglas McGrath, 1996), the past depicted in *Jude* is socially divided, misogynistic and violent. As Julianne Pidduck observes in a study of costume cinema in the 1990s, *Jude* is 'exceptional as a relentless tale of defeat and despair' (Pidduck 2004: 124). This is articulated, Emma Wilson suggests, through the defiant adoption of a 'mortuary aesthetic' (as opposed to the 'museum aesthetic' that Richard Dyer has suggested is dominant in the heritage film (Dyer 2004)). This aesthetic is characterised by a self-conscious attention to the spectacular qualities of the cinematic image with occasional references to photography and magic lanterns, and in particular, an allusion to 'the nineteenth-century tradition of post-mortem photographs which were taken of the loved one soon after death' (Wilson 2003: 104). Wilson argues that 'this combination of acknowledgement of death, yet disavowal, seems apt to the contradictory dynamics of Winterbottom's heritage cinema which seems to acknowledge the loss of the past, the impossibility of its cinematic reanimation' (ibid.).

The film's opening scene is presented in black and white, as if in rebuttal of the rich visual spectacle typically associated with heritage cinema, and shows the young

Jude beaten by the farmer

Jude at work scaring crows from a newly ploughed field. When he comes across the bodies of several dead crows hanging on a gibbet, he has a change of heart and begins feeding the birds. He is caught by the farmer and beaten and, with this depiction of brutal child labour, the film foregrounds the working-class labouring bodies and lives that normally remain in the background of heritage films.

Jude returns to the village, Marygreen where he joins the group of primary school pupils who are assembled for a photograph. He then follows the teacher who is leaving the village for Christminster with his possessions on a horse and cart. He tells the boy, 'If you want to do anything in life, Jude, that's where you have to go, even if it means giving up everything else for a while.' With an irony that becomes clear later, and which is the first of the many grim ironies around which this narrative is oriented, he advises him that, 'You can choose your future'. With a shift to colour, the adult Jude (Christopher Eccleston), now a stonemason, is shown working on scaffolding in a church. During his lunch break he sits by the river reading Greek – reading and recitation is a motif used to represent his commitment to self-improvement – when he is interrupted by a young woman, who tosses a raw pig's heart at him. Arabella (Rachel Griffiths), a sexually confident and flirtatious woman who was washing pig's viscera in the river and is closely associated with the animal, goes on to seduce Jude in a pig sty and they subsequently marry when she becomes pregnant. The open-air wedding feast is a brief interval in which the film reproduces the pastoral *mise-en-scène* of flowing dresses, dancing, musicians, flowers and food. However, the abrupt telegraphic narrative structure of the film in which many scenes are reduced almost to vignettes, and the rapid editing mean that we are denied the opportunity for contemplative enjoyment of these images. After the wedding night, where Jude is surprised as Arabella undresses, to find that she wears a fashionable wig, the film shifts to the winter as the two of them are required to slaughter the pig they received as a wedding present. Jude sticks the animal reluctantly and then leaves Arabella to hoist and butcher it. He returns later to find a note pinned to a side of pork. It explains that she had not tricked him into marriage and she had genuinely believed she was pregnant. It announces that she is leaving for Australia and wishes him luck now he is free to travel to Christminster.

The text of the note is read in voice-over as Jude travels by train, a motif used several times in the film. The film is punctuated by train journeys, which function as a transition between stages of the story, but the physical mobility of the characters does not equate with social mobility or progress. As Pidduck notes, 'Exceptionally, in Winterbottom's *Jude* and the 1900 segment of *Orlando*, the steam engine appears as an

Jude (Christopher Eccleston) travelling by train

interruption – a noisy harbinger of the Industrial revolution disrupting the peaceful English countryside' (Pidduck 2004: 97). The recurrent train journeys disrupt the sense that the story takes place in a historically non-specific but distant past. Instead they propel it forwards into a relationship with the present.

In Christminster, Jude is transfixed by a young woman, Sue Bridehead (Kate Winslet), working in the window of a shop selling religious artefacts and stationery. He follows her when she leaves work through the busy streets of the city to a political meeting where she is the only woman listening to a speaker attacking the endemic inequalities of nineteenth-century society:

> Then there's your back-to-back houses, your grubby children hanging off scaffolding. It's the same city; maybe a five-minute walk from Church Street to Scum Street. Why don't we go over? Why don't we go over and knock on their doors? Because they've convinced us that this is the way it is. No change. Why change? They've won their argument. They educate their kind to win that argument.

This brief scene succinctly encapsulates the film's own argument. Counterpointing the naïve idealism of the advice given Jude by his schoolteacher, it outlines the way that inequality is a function of ideology, institutionalised through the apparatus of the education system Jude aspires to belong to, and reproduced through the spatial organisation and architecture of the city and the flow of people through it. The scene also constitutes an explicit critique of the heritage film since the shots of the city that precede it correspond closely to our expectations of costume films – location shots featuring dozens of authentically costumed extras playing their parts in carefully dressed sets. A mobile camera moves briskly through streets and squares bustling with people and horses. We see families, couples, students – some of them wearing mortar boards and reading books – groups of children playing games, and a street market where livestock is being sold.

This sequence is set to an excerpt from *St Matthew's Passion* by J. S. Bach and, alongside the clatter of horses' hooves and the hubbub of voices, it lends the scene an

Sue (Kate Winslet) moves through the bustling streets of Christminster

optimistic, urgent and grandiose register, echoing, perhaps, Jude's excitement at finally reaching Christminster. The political speech, however, invites a more critical, politicised reading of this scene and reminds us that this is a partial view, and that another more abject city exists within or alongside the spectacular urban spaces that characterise many heritage films

By coincidence it transpires that Sue and Jude are cousins and after she seeks him out they strike up a close friendship. Sue is characterised as an independent, sceptical woman who smokes and plays drinking games. She is also a feminist who is at least Jude's intellectual equal and she later declares she is not afraid of any man, describing them as 'the timid sex'. After she loses her job and lodgings, when her landlady discovers ceramic statuettes of classical male nudes she bought at a fairground stall, Jude introduces her to his old schoolteacher, Phillotson, who has failed to get into university. Phillotson employs her, but Jude's application to the university is rejected. The moral economy of this narrative dictates that each achievement or positive incident is accompanied by a depressing setback. The terse rejection letter reaffirms the prohibitive social barriers decried by the speaker earlier: 'Sir, I have read your letter with interest and judging from your description of yourself as a working man, I think you have a much better chance of success in life by sticking to your own trade than by adopting any other course.' This rejection coincides with Jude's discovery that Sue and Phillotson are becoming romantically involved. While Jude is drinking despondently with his colleagues, a student overhears Jude say that he can recite the apostle's creed in Latin and challenges him to do this publicly. Jude stands and recites the text vehemently, before leaving the silenced pub shouting, 'You bloody fools! Which one of you knows if I said it right or not?' He later scrawls a biblical quotation on a city wall: 'I HAVE UNDERSTANDINGS AS WELL AS YOU.'

After Jude returns to his aunt's house in Marygreen – a place he returns to repeatedly as if unable to escape the gravitational pull of his origins – he receives a letter from Sue telling him she has moved with Phillotson to Melchester where she is enrolled at a teacher training college. Jude visits and discovers that Phillotson has proposed to her.

Sue is expelled when she climbs over the wall at night to visit Jude, prompting a rumour that she is having an affair with him. Despite her attraction to Jude, she agrees to marry Phillotson and Jude returns to Marygreen again where his impatient but perceptive aunt, now on her deathbed, asks him, 'Are you crying for me or your precious Sue, you ninny?' After her funeral, Jude travels to Shaston, and ends up lodging awkwardly with the two of them. Sue asks Jude to 'Promise me you'll never stop trying', and Phillotson eventually agrees to let Sue leave with Jude. There is a rare happy passage in which we see them cycling together and playing on the beach before Arabella again makes contact with Jude and leaves him a letter revealing that she had actually given birth to their son, little Jude, after she left for Australia. The boy subsequently arrives from Sydney to live with Jude and Sue. Sue becomes pregnant shortly thereafter and the birth is a bloody spectacle which Jude invites his son to watch. From this point on the narrative becomes progressively bleaker and the two protagonists become increasingly physically bedraggled. They have two more children and become itinerant as Jude is sacked from a job for being unmarried and they move from one lodging to another because of their status, about which they are both unapologetic. They finally return to Christminster where they attend a graduation ceremony and encounter Jude's old colleagues. After finding a room to stay in they are told they can stay for only one night when the owners discover they are unmarried. The following day Jude gets his old job back and Sue and Jude return happily home, excitedly discussing what they can do with the money, to find the three children all dead, an explanatory note pinned to their bedroom door: 'becos we are to many'. The wretchedness of the funeral service as the three little coffins are interred is compounded by the absence of compassion in the oration, which is delivered blankly by the priest:

> Even to this present hour we both hunger and thirst and are naked and are buffeted, and have no certain dwelling place. Being reviled we bless, being persecuted we suffer it, being defamed we entreat. We are made as the filth of the world and are the off-scouring of all things to this day. I write not these things to shame you, but as my beloved sons to warn you.

Their relationship disintegrates as Sue becomes convinced that this is divine punishment for their 'wrong' love. She leaves Jude, whom she says she can no longer look at since his child killed hers. He continues to pursue her as doggedly as before and the film concludes with their meeting at the children's graves at Christmas 1889 – the only instance of a specific date in the film.

The wintry scene is almost monochrome and recalls the film's opening, suggesting that no progress has been made by the character. There is an awkward exchange in which he demands to know whether she still loves him. They kiss before she pulls away and leaves him. He shouts, 'we are man and wife if ever two people were on this earth', and the camera cranes away to leave him standing alone, just as he was in the opening shot.

In one of the most influential and provocative critiques of heritage cinema of the 1980s, 'Rooms without a View', Cairns Craig argues that the heritage film is an ideo-

Jude and Sue in the churchyard at Christmas

logically reactionary form that depicts historical past (as it is mediated through literature) in a way that reinforces conservative conceptions of class and national identity. Just as Orientalist discourses construct the 'Orient' as a historically and geographically homogeneous, undifferentiated space, so, in a predominant focus upon 'the English middle and upper classes at home and abroad', the heritage film represents the past in a highly reductive way as temporally, socially and culturally flat (Craig 1991: 3). Heritage films, Craig argues, present us with a sanitised, commodified, ahistorical view of the past:

> These are films in which the past is treated as though it existed in isolation from all that went before and after it, just as all those objects and possessions exist in isolation from any sense of grubby thing-making. (Who made them? Where? With how much sweat?) It is a cinema focused on a class that could pretend to be insulated from the world outside. In this it is very much in tune with our contemporary consumerist view of the world as a place in which objects exist only in acquisition, not in the labour of their creation. (Craig 1991: 5)

In this context, Winterbottom's film can be understood as a direct critical response to the conventions of heritage cinema. With its focus upon provincial working class characters in one sense it addresses the questions posed by Craig of who made the possessions and objects that comprise the *mise-en-scène* of heritage cinema, where and with how much effort. If the films condemned by Craig are primarily preoccupied with the depiction of life on Church Street, Winterbottom's film is concerned with the marginalised inhabitants of Scum Street, with the material and visceral as opposed to the spiritual, the filthy and profane rather than the pure and idealised.

One of the most shocking and transgressive images in *Jude* is of Sue in the midst of childbirth. She is seen lying on a bed in their terraced house groaning, her legs apart, blood smeared over her thighs, her crotch and the bedsheets, while the crown of the baby's head emerges from her vulva. Jude explains to his son, who is sitting outside the

Sue in labour

door, 'There's nothing to be frightened of', and pushes him into the room to witness this scene. This is an image that offers a frank realism as opposed to the artifice and aestheticised confection of archetypal costume drama and it insists upon the material physicality of the bodies that occupy these historical spaces. The first section of *A Cock and Bull Story* is oriented around the difficult painful birth of Tristram Shandy, and we also see Mariane Pearl screaming in pain during labour in *A Mighty Heart* and Molly undergoing exhausting labour in *Wonderland*. In each of these three films the father is absent, emphasising the solitary, unromantic, trauma of childbirth. Winterbottom's films depict childbirth as a violent rupture rather than as an uncomplicated solidification of a heterosexual relationship, as well as an example of women's work. The bodies of Jude, Arabella and Sue are sexualised and visible and the film is marked out among costume films by the matter-of-fact depictions of sex between Jude and his two partners. As an image of a woman in *labour*, however, it also demonstrates punningly that, beyond the leisured classes, women are not excluded from physical work. All the female characters in this film do paid work in addition to unpaid domestic labour within the family, and, to some extent they are more resourceful and adaptable than Jude who remains preoccupied and hamstrung by his desire to gain access to (and approval from) the University. They acquire agency while Jude impotently bemoans his fate. Sue is acknowledged by Jude to be cleverer than him while Arabella eventually accumulates wealth when she inherits her husband's estate. Jude, on the other hand, despite the humiliations and hardships he has endured, says masochistically of Christminster, 'I love this place, even though I know it looks down on people like me: the self-taught, too-determined. It takes two or three generations to do what I tried to do in one'. He is, as Sue indulgently observes, 'a tragic Don Quixote … a St Stephen, who sees heaven open up even as they're stoning him'.

Craig suggests that a central function of heritage films is their reaffirmation of boundaries between classes, cultures and communities. As he observes of E. M. Forster, whose novels *Room with a View* (1908), *Howard's End* (1910) and *Maurice* (1971) were adapted by Ishmail Merchant and James Ivory and came to typify the costume film of the 1980s and early1990s:

'Only connect' was Forster's theme in *Howard's End*, and his stories are about trying to connect across cultural and class boundaries. But Forster's trite little phrase could only have come to have such weight because of the deep inhibition against communicating with other classes and cultures that had developed in middle-class England in the course of the nineteenth century. (Craig 1991: 5)

In this respect, *Jude* works within the thematic conventions of heritage cinema in its dramatisation of Jude's attempts to acquire a university education and the couple's attempts to live as an unconventional family. Where it differs from a typical heritage film is in its insistence upon the violently unjust consequences of the maintenance of these boundaries. It is made especially plain that when Little Jude kills himself and his siblings it is as a direct result of the prejudice against their unmarried status and their uncompromising refusal to pass themselves off as married. When he asks his parents whether he is the reason that they will have to leave their lodgings on the following day, Sue tells him that it is, 'Because there's too many of us. There isn't enough room'. It is made equally explicit that Jude's class identity precludes him from a university education but, rather than enduring these setbacks stoically, these characters suffer profoundly. The melodramatic register of the film, in which social class is examined through the experience of a small number of intimately connected individuals, means that these points are made in a powerfully affecting way. Craig observes of heritage cinema that:

> The plots of some of these films show characters struggling to cross boundaries (across class in the homosexual relationship in *Maurice*, across cultures in the Italian films). But their effect is precisely the opposite: they situate us firmly in the barricaded room of an English identity from which the outside world is viewed from above and without, not engaged with. They take us back into a world for which 'others' (the Italians, the working class) may seem alluring in their apparent openness, but are always, in the end, proved to be both unstable and untrustworthy. (Ibid.)

Unlike the films Craig refers to, in its concentration upon the experiences of Jude and his family, Winterbottom's film refuses to allow the viewer this secure distance from the milieu of the characters. Despite a sometimes ironic framing of Jude's idealism, there are no perspectives with which to identify beyond his. Nor, in its depiction of a divided, indifferent culture, does it offer a nostalgic depiction of England that might constitute the attractive, secure, inclusive basis for a national or cultural identity with which we might imaginatively identify.

The film's realist style, described by Pidduck as 'quasi-documentary', collapses the 'safe' historical distance that allows us to enjoy the theatre of some heritage films from outside without reflecting on their critical relationship to the present. As the shift from black and white to colour early on in the film indicates, colour signifies immediacy, presence. The colour scheme of the film is muted and it becomes increasingly monochromatic as the narrative progresses. However, it eschews the sepia-tinted or faded colour schemes that are commonly used to depict 'pastness' through pastiche of aged film, photographs, prints or oil paintings as employed in *The Claim*, as well as the rich, vibrant colour schemes that are sometimes used to depict the past as spectacularly staged theatre (as in the Hardy adaptations *Far from the Madding Crowd* (John Schlesinger, 1967) and *Tess* (Roman Polanski, 1979)). Little attention is paid in the production design, the lighting or the framing of shots to the intricate construction of a plausibly authentic past through costumes, vehicles, and the design and arrangement of interiors. The 'quasi-documentary' style means that film is shot and edited as if it were a contemporary drama like *Wonderland* or *9 Songs*; there are very few establishing shots, for example, where the camera can linger on the spectacle of the cinematic staging of the past. The graphically simple *sans serif* white-on-black intertitles that contextualise the action in an economic fashion – 'AT MELCHESTER', 'AT SHASTON', 'AT ALDBRICKHAM AND ELSEWHERE' – have a similarly contemporary effect. As a consequence, Winterbottom's film fails to disguise the paradox that is central to the enjoyment of heritage cinema in which, 'The audience is invited to understand the plot of the film as though we are *contemporary* with the characters, while at the same time indulging our pleasure in a world which is visually compelling precisely because of its *pastness*' (Craig 1991: 4). On the contrary, this anachronistic relationship is made explicit by characters that are out of phase with their context. As Jude says, when they are forced to move after he loses his job because he and Sue are unmarried: 'We'll move somewhere where nobody knows us. If they find out we'll move on again, and again, and again. As long as it takes for the world to change.'

We can understand the exceptional quality of *Jude* as a sign of the flexibility or tenuousness of genre categories as a way of framing and interpreting film. We might argue, for example, that the designation of heritage cinema or costume films covers a broad spectrum of films from a low-budget production like *Jude* to the unprecedentedly costly blockbuster, *Titanic* (James Cameron, 1997), released just over a year later making Kate Winslet a star.[3] We can also understand *Jude* as an interrogation of the common tendencies of heritage cinema, a testing of its boundaries in order, perhaps, to test them to destruction but also, conceivably, to discover what can be articulated through the limited 'lexicon' of the costume film. In this respect, *Jude* might also be understood as an example of what Claire Monk names 'post-heritage' cinema – a distinctive group of costume films that display a 'transgressive sexual politics' through the self-conscious foregrounding of themes of sexuality and gender (Monk 2001: 6). Post-heritage cinema is characterised in particular, by 'an overt concern with … non-dominant gender and sexual identities: feminine, non-masculine, mutable, androgynous, ambiguous' (ibid.). Examples of this are *Orlando* (Sally Potter, 1992), *The Baby of Mâcon* (Peter Greenaway, 1993), *Quills* (Philip Kaufman, 2000) and *The Libertine* (Laurence Dunmore, 2005). With its focus upon the non-standard masculinity of Jude, the assertive, defiant femininity of Sue and the unorthodox family unit comprising unmarried parents and children from different mothers, Winterbottom's film is a good example of this generic reconfiguration.

Post-heritage cinema and The Claim

I have used the terms 'heritage cinema' and 'costume film' interchangeably in this chapter but it is important to recognise their provisional value as comprehensive descriptive terms. As Monk has observed in a reflection upon critical engagement with British heritage films, heritage cinema is more an instrumental critical construction by academics and journalists than the product of the systematic scrutiny of a group of related films:

> 'Heritage films' were identified as a putative grouping in order that they might be collectively denounced, *a priori* of any more disinterested investigation, as 'all too familiar' (to borrow a phrase from Dyer and Vincendeau 1995): the 'far from imaginary work' of 'directors who know perhaps too well their audiences' expectations', in the words of one of their most hostile critics, Cairns Craig. (Monk 2002: 177)

The term heritage cinema was initially coined by Charles Barr to describe a historically and generically broad range of British productions before being taken up to name a small group of films (some of them transnational productions) released during the 1980s. The term quickly developed a critical currency and has been applied much more widely to identify common features and connections between a growing number of films. As a result, Monk suggests that the films taken to exemplify heritage cinema are much more ideologically and aesthetically disparate than is suggested by their characterisation as stylistically conservative, nostalgic, nationalistic and sycophanti-cally preoccupied with wealth and privilege. This heterogeneity is an inevitable feature of any generic classification since genres can be defined by a range of factors beyond the formal or thematic properties of individual films including marketing campaigns and the associations certain actors carry for an audience. As a result, genre definitions are under continual revision and qualification, but the value of genre (as process) as a way of thinking about film lies precisely in this function of facilitating discussion. Debates around heritage cinema are often intensely overdetermined because of a sense that these films are more or less direct commentaries upon contemporary culture and politics, and also that they are making competing claims for definitions of nation. In other words, the discourse around heritage cinema is never solely concerned with film and in some cases the films function primarily as the pretext for politicised exchanges, rather than the object of such discussions. It is a platform through which questions of race, class, gender and sexuality, regional and national identity, commercialisation, public policy and aesthetics can be explored. It is unsurprising, therefore, that some accounts of heritage cinema should frequently involve a misrepresentation of the films themselves. As Monk suggests:

> the contradictory discourse around the films – which caricatures them for their supposed repression and sexlessness while condemning their seductive and ideologically pernicious spectacular excess – suggests that their dismissal has

as much to do with their troublesome resistance as to such imposed binarisms (Monk 2002: 184–5).

The project of atomising or reconfiguring the heritage film begun with *Jude* is resumed and developed further in Winterbottom's next costume drama, *The Claim*, released three years later. Another adaptation of a novel by Thomas Hardy, *The Mayor of Casterbridge* (1886), it retains the broad narrative armature and historical location of the novel but recontextualises or reterritorialises it, displacing the action from a fictionalised approximation of Dorset on the South coast of England to the Sierra Nevada mountains in California in 1867, site of the gold rush of the 1840s. This is not so much a sign of compromised authenticity, as a recognition of the fundamental historical and literary inauthenticity that characterises many costume dramas in which historical 'authenticity' is an effect of cinematic realism rather than a product of scholarly concern for accuracy. Some of the most studied examples of this disregard for authenticity in costume drama are the deliberate anachronisms in the *mise-en-scène* of Derek Jarman's *Jubilee* (1978) and *Caravaggio* (1986) or Peter Greenaway's *The Draughtsman's Contract* (1982). Of course, we might also ask whether stripping away some features of the novel in the course of its adaptation facilitates an even more direct engagement with its core themes and melodramatic focus. However, in its conception of films as complex audio-visual texts, this study of Winterbottom's films is not concerned with tracing the transformative relationship between the films and their literary source material, an approach that can privilege the screenplay or novel, reducing the creative labour of the filmmakers to that of adaptation or illustration, consigning the director to the role of *metteur-en-scène*.

Two narrative lines intersect in *The Claim*, both of which are concerned with the ways in which interpersonal relationships are framed and constrained and determined by economic relationships. The story is set in the town of Kingdom Come which has been established high in the mountains on the site of a successful gold-mining claim. The claim was purchased some years earlier by Irish prospector Daniel Dillon, the town's founder and autocratic patriarch, in exchange for his Polish wife and baby daughter, as is revealed in intermittent flashbacks. The film opens with the arrival by stagecoach of his daughter Hope, who is now a teenager, and his wife, Elena, who is dying from consumption and wants Dillon to take financial responsibility for Hope. Disembarking from the same wagon train is a group of women to be employed in the town's brothel, and the centrality of prostitution to the economy and the town's social fabric highlights the economic foundation of gender relationships and intimate or sexual relationships. There is an obvious irony in the contradiction between the morally pragmatic sexual infrastructure on which the town is founded and the naming of the town. The town's biblical name invites us to read it as allegorical, an embryonic stage of the development of contemporary western society, with a bank, a saloon, a variety of other businesses and an autonomous legal and penal system; anyone entering the town is required by Dillon's men to surrender their guns, and, early on in the film, we see Dillon punish a thief with a public whipping.

Arriving in town at the same time as the wagon train is a party of surveyors employed by the Central Pacific Railroad Company to identify a suitable route for the laying of a trans-continental railway through the mountains. They are charting the territory in order to exploit it commercially and so this second narrative line is concerned literally with the delimitation and 'construction' of the nation. The survey party is initially welcomed but Dillon advises them as they leave the town for their final surveying expedition in the area not to return for their equipment if the railway will not run through Kingdom Come. The town is on the threshold of modernity and is dependent for its survival and growth upon the communication and trade links that would be enabled by the railway.

In an attempt to atone for his abandonment of Hope and Elena, Dillon terminates his relationship with Lucetta, the Portuguese owner of the brothel, and remarries Elena to ensure that Hope will inherit the town and the rest of his wealth. Despite the intervention of a 'doctor' who attempts to cure her with electricity, Elena dies and, shortly thereafter, the town learns that the railway will run along the valley floor. Lucetta responds by closing the brothel and moving down to the valley to oversee the construction of a new town, Lisboa, while a distraught Dillon reacts by setting fire to the now depopulated Kingdom Come. The town is destroyed and Dillon is found by Hope and Dalglish, the chief engineer of the survey party, frozen in the snow outside the town.

By contrast with the 'quasi-documentary' style employed with *Jude*, *The Claim* is a visually spectacular film that exploits the dramatic landscape of Alberta in Canada and Colorado in the US, and depicts intricately constructed sets and interiors.[4] The film's opening shot is of a misty, snow-covered mountain range running away into the distance as a horse-drawn carriage appears over the ridge at the bottom of the frame. A shot of the carriage and its occupants, the nine women arriving to work in the brothel, is followed by an establishing shot of Kingdom Come, a sprawling collection of wooden buildings and canvas tents nestled in a valley against the backdrop of the mountains. The scene is set at dusk and the desaturated blue-grey colour of the shots, achieved partly through the optical combination of colour and black-and-white negatives in the production of the final print, emphasises their evocation of popular landscape photography from the period that depicted the North American landscape as unspoilt and sublimely vast, such as Eadweard Muybridge's delicately detailed mammoth plate photographs of Yosemite and Yellowstone.[5] The two sequences in which the survey party conducts expeditions through the mountains and a third sequence in which they travel by steam train along winding river

Sublime Californian
landscape

Surveyors mapping
the landscape

valleys are built around striking images of this landscape, the epic scale frequently emphasised by the device of extreme long shots taken from a distance in order to show groups of people dwarfed by the scenery. The orchestral score, composed by Michael Nyman, is similarly grand during these sequences, built upon a fast, regular rhythm that echoes the sound of the train. It is clear that the landscape we see in these sequences is fragile and under threat from the railway and the irresistible technically and commercially progressive forces it represents. In a conversation about the beauty of the surroundings between Hope and Dalglish as they trek through a mountain pass, Hope asks, 'How will you get a railroad here? You'd have to knock down the mountain'. Dalglish replies, 'Maybe that's what we'll do. Blast a tunnel through'. The music is used to articulate the destructive threat posed by the railway in a different way since in the two surveying sequences, Nyman's score is silenced by explosions, in the first by dynamite, in the second when a wagon carrying nitro-glycerine across a river explodes killing its driver and the horses. Thus, while the images of a beautiful, empty landscape are a source of visual pleasure, they are also images of a landscape about to be violently domesticated and restructured.

Kingdom Come, the town in which most of the action takes place, represents an initial stage of this commercial exploitation of natural resources. The town (which was constructed for the film) is a complex, weathered assemblage of buildings, walkways and platforms organised around a main street, and includes elaborately ornamented interiors. The saloon, which incorporates a casino and a stage, is an impressively grand and visually rich space, decorated with oil paintings, filigree ironwork, patterned wall-paper and painted wood panelling, mirrors and velvet curtains. It is lit by oil lamps and gilded candelabras, the yellow light of which establishes the dominant colour-scheme of the interior shots in the film. The warm yellow cast of the interiors at night is contrasted throughout with the blue cast of the scenes taking place in daylight and reinforces the picturesque quality of these images that reproduce the earthy ochres, yellows and browns of an ageing oil painting. Shots of the saloon, which is crammed with dozens of people, recall, in particular, Manet's paintings of the Folies Bergère. While the cutting and framing of these sequences means that we rarely have the opportunity to contemplate the spaces in full or at length – the DP, Alwin H. Küchler states, 'I like to concentrate on the faces' – these images nevertheless correspond to a conventional aesthetic of the costume drama in which the authenticity with which the past is rendered is guaranteed by the elaborate and extensive textural detail of the reconstructed spaces and costumes (Oppenheimer 2001: 24).

Lucia sings 'Coimbra Menina e Moça' in the town's saloon

The town looks as if it has grown gradually outwards and is in the process of spreading along the main street and up the lightly forested snow-laden slopes of the mountain. There is a variety of buildings, from large two or three storey residential buildings to small shacks, warehouses and workshops, and they are mostly made from grey, unpainted wood. Many of the buildings are fronted with walkways and platforms raised on stilts and ramps, ladders and steps connect them to the street. Signs painted on the sides of the buildings indicate that there is a range of businesses including a hardware shop, a cigar store, a shop selling hats and caps, a blacksmith's and a hotel, and it is clearly a busy town. Cattle are being herded along the main street, around which are scattered sand-bags, crates, barrels, woodpiles, carts and many people mill around the public spaces. There are no children, few women and the impression is that this cold, colourless, utilitarian environment is a hard, physically uncomfortable place to live.

By contrast, the interior of Dillon's house is even more sumptuous than the saloon, decorated with lace curtains, vases, classical statues, ornate (French-style) furniture and a baby grand piano. The small, rude, makeshift prospector's shack where Dillon sold his family and which bore the sign 'THY KINGDOM COME' still exists outside the town as a reproachful reminder of Dillon's past. He visits the shack by himself, which prompts the flashback to the sale of his family, and takes Elena and Hope there separately in gestures of apology or confession. The co-proximity of the two buildings thus attests to his financial success and the ineradicable traces of his crime – the shack is a physical manifestation of his guilt. The narrative foregrounding of Dillon's incongruous pagoda-shaped house is also a means by which the film displays its cinematic intertextuality. In an absurd, spectacular demonstration of romantic extravagance and of his power within the town, Dillon has his house physically dragged on ropes across the snow to the edge of the town by a team of horses and dozens of men

Kingdom Come

while he stands on the first-floor balcony. He then invites Elena into the house where he proposes remarriage. This sequence appears to be a direct reference to *Fitzcarraldo* (Werner Herzog, 1981) in which the film's eponymous protagonist, an Irish railway engineer called Brian Sweeney Fitzgerald (Klaus Kinski), employs native 'Indians' in the Amazon jungle to haul a steam ship over a hill separating two rivers so that he can reach an unclaimed and otherwise inaccessible area of rubber trees. The casting of Kinski's daughter, Nastassja, as Elena confirms the connection between the two films (although Nastassja also played the eponymous role in *Tess*, an adaptation of Hardy's *Tess of the D'Urbevilles*, emphasising again the self-consciousness with which Winterbottom's film engages with genre). The allusion invites the viewer to recognise an affinity between Winterbottom and Werner Herzog, a director whose often distinctive, narratively unpredictable and generically ambiguous work traces an unstable line between documentary and fiction. However there is a specific thematic logic motivating the citation as it aligns Dillon with Fitzgerald, who renames himself Fitzcarraldo due to the local unpronounceability of his name (and his passion for Italian opera). A European colonist whose cultural arrogance and sense of entitlement (and instability) is demonstrated by his indifference to the deaths of the natives crushed under the ship, Fitzcarraldo's driving desire is not so much to acquire wealth as to reproduce civilised European culture in that most improbable location, by using the profits of this venture to fund the construction of an opera house in the jungle in which Enrico Caruso can sing. The invocation of *Fitzcarraldo* thus frames this story of an internationally mixed assemblage of entrepreneurs and pioneers on the American frontier as a story of colonial occupation.

However, *The Claim* is also a western, a genre that functions like the British costume film as a nationally specific form of heritage cinema within US culture. It is a mythic narrative form that allows the repeated retelling and embellishment of the story of the formation of a nation *ex nihilo*. The western codifies the ideological system that structures the nation, insisting repetitively on the contradictory values of private enterprise, masculine self-determination, loyalty, family and communality, mobility and lack of acquisitiveness, and it places characters within a moral, melodramatic universe. For a variety of reasons, including the international commercial dominance of US cinema from the 1910s onwards, this American genre, has come to constitute a transnational commodity, an adaptable and abstracted, schematic story-form that has been appropriated repeatedly by international audiences and filmmakers. The British director, Shane Meadows, for example, a self-described 'regional filmmaker' employs the narra-

The founding of 'Lisboa'

tive schema of a western in order to tell a story about an act of violent revenge set in contemporary England, *Dead Man's Shoes* (2004), while his previous film, *Once Upon a Time in the Midlands* (2002), makes playful references to Sergio Leone's spaghetti westerns in its account of a family in crisis. Winterbottom's film engages not so much with classic American westerns from the 1920s through to the 1950s, but with those films involved with the revision of the genre. *The Claim*, concludes with a ceremony to mark the foundation of 'Lisboa' on the site where the railway will run. This new town, named after the Portuguese capital, which consists of tents and the wooden frames of uncompleted buildings, is run by Lucetta who, Dalglish predicts, will soon be rich. It is clear that this is a foundation story. The virtual town alludes to the skeletal church in the classic western, *My Darling Clementine* (John Ford, 1946) but this concluding scene also revisits the dénouement of the revisionist western, *Once Upon a Time in the West* (Sergio Leone, 1969), which also recounts a story of the laying of a trans-continental railway and the murderous, sadistic violence with which the railway company employees clear a path for the tracks. The film concludes with the former prostitute, Jill McBain welcoming the railway engineers onto her land where she intends to establish a new town named Sweetwater.

However, the most direct allusion in *The Claim* is to the New Hollywood western, *McCabe and Mrs Miller* (Robert Altman, 1971), an illustration, for Robert Self, of 'the innovative surgery performed on the classical narrative genres by the art cinema appropriation of mass-media forms and consciousness' (Self 2002: 89). Altman's adaptation of the 1959 novel *McCabe* by Edmund Naughton, tells the story of the establishment of a mining town, 'Presbyterian Church', in the muddy hills of the North West Pacific coast. The film opens with the arrival of gambler, John McCabe (Warren Beatty), who builds a saloon and brothel, which becomes the centre of the growing town. He later takes on English prostitute Constance Miller (Julie Christie) as his business partner and they develop a tentative relationship. After refusing an offer by a mining company to buy the town from him, McCabe is shot by a gunman hired by the company and dies alone in the snow. Like *The Claim* the film ends with the solitary death of the town's patriarch.

The *mise-en-scène* of Altman's film closely prefigures that of Winterbottom's. The set is a jumble of tents and wooden buildings, mired in grey mud and under continual construction. It resembles the makeshift army field hospital of Altman's earlier film, *M.A.S.H.* (1970), more than it resembles the traditional setting for a western. The ironically named 'Presbyterian Church' is an emerging community, and so the film depicts the past not as an ossified heritage site, but as a space that is in process. The film records the formation of the town from a small chaotic group of buildings initially through to a complex aggregation of substantial buildings. The climactic burning of the church, which is set alight by the company gunmen as they hunt McCabe through the snow-covered town, asserts the impermanence of this construction. The eponymous central characters are not itinerant cowboys or outlaws, but a self-important, heavy drinking professional gambler (who is helpfully mistaken for a gun-slinger by the town's residents), and an opium-addicted English prostitute. This characterisation undermines any heroic foundation narrative about the formation of the nation on a principle of free enterprise or pioneering independence. The social and economic centrality of prostitution in 'Presbyterian Church', as in 'Kingdom Come', demonstrates that relationships are intrinsically alienated and exploitative, structured in the first instance by exchange value. The film also proposes that individual enterprise quickly gives way to corporate exploitation, which is far more immoral, impersonal and aggressively violent.

The film's influential visual style is consistently unspectacular – the negative was 'flashed' during processing in order to reduce the contrast and desaturate the colour of the final image which simulates a faded sepia-toned photograph – and the colour scheme is dominated by greys, yellows and browns. However, Altman's film is more than a superficial visual reference for Winterbottom and his collaborators; as an example of New Hollywood cinema's critique of classical cinema, it constitutes a revisionist or anti-western – a generic hybrid that challenges some of the dominant cultural narratives articulated through the western.

It depicts the western town as an immigrant community comprising not just Europeans but also Asian inhabitants and presents violence as casually brutal rather than ritualised theatre. While the gunmen hired to murder McCabe are professional killers, they are also deeply vicious; we see the youngest of the three trick an innocuous young cowboy into a stand-off for the sake of target practice.

Alongside Nicolas Roeg, whose allusive, mystical gold-rush drama, *Eureka* (1983), may also be a source, Altman also serves as a helpful point of reference with regard to understanding Winterbottom's work. A filmmaker who has incorporated experimental formal devices into commercial films, Altman worked across a variety of genres and modes, including *film noir*, westerns, fake documentary, costume dramas, romantic comedies, satirical comedies, thrillers, war films and a drama about the Hollywood film industry. Altman's most well-known work is characterised by a naturalistic style of cinematography and editing (telephoto lenses, long takes, low-key and natural light) and sound recording and editing (with shifting spatial relations between foreground and background sounds) that gives films such as *The Long Goodbye* (1973) and *Nashville* (1975) a distinctive authorial style. Like Winterbottom, then, Altman moved between genres, discarding and modifying certain aspects of the formats as he did so.

In relation to his previous costume film, *Jude* and British heritage cinema as a whole, *The Claim*, a hybrid European western, is an ambitious expansion of the vocabulary of the costume film. In its appropriation of the template of the New Hollywood western, among other sources, Winterbottom's film invites us to recognise that like the western,

Dillon razes
Kingdom Come

the British heritage film is a transnational form. By transplanting the story into an unlikely generic framework it demonstrates both the idealised, non-specific character of the costume film, and also the status of the western as costume drama. However, in taking New Hollywood cinema as a model, Winterbottom's film is engaging with a group of films preoccupied with the dismantling and retooling of ideologically objectionable or aesthetically redundant genres and formats. *The Claim* can similarly be understood as a refusal or playful dismantling of the British costume film, a more radical continuation of the project, begun with *Jude*, to destroy the genre from within. It is appropriate that the film concludes with Dillon's destruction of Kingdom Come and the symbolic dismantling of the *mise-en-scène* of the heritage film.

Literary adaptation, cinematic narration and A Cock and Bull Story

A Cock and Bull Story is, on the face of it, another adaptation of a classic novel, Lawrence Sterne's *The Life and Opinions of Tristram Shandy, Gentleman* (1759–67), but very little of the substantial fictional autobiography is transferred to the screen in this complex, slippery and often comic film. This is not so much a recontextualisation of the costume drama, as an atomisation of it that is difficult to situate generically since it has as much in common with fictional and documentary films about filmmaking such as *8 ½* (Federico Fellini, 1963) (whose soundtrack music is borrowed), *Day for Night* (François Truffaut, 1973), *Stardust Memories* (Woody Allen, 1980), *The Player* (Robert Altman, 1992) or *Hearts of Darkness: A Filmmaker's Apocalypse* (Fax Bahr & George Hickenlooper, 1991), as it does with conventional costume films. It is a film *about* the production of a film based on Sterne's novel, exposing the unglamorous realities of shooting on location, and the flirtations and fleeting relationships that form among cast and crew, and it is a reflection upon the compromised, improvisatory process of commercial filmmaking, and the problems of literary adaptation and narrative construction. The boundaries between the 'behind-the-scenes' frame narrative and the film-within-the-film are mobile and unclear replicating the book's meta-narrative, self-referential structure, but the sequences that we do see of the film-within-the–film are partly a parody of the conservative conventions of British costume dramas, and partly (following the model of the source novel) a radical reworking of these conventions incorporating anachronisms, self-reflexive humour and digressive narrative fragmentation.

The film opens, for example, with a short (pre-credits) sequence in which the two lead actors, Rob Brydon and Steve Coogan, are being made up, Coogan having a

Coogan and Brydon
in make-up

prosthetic nose applied in order to play Tristram Shandy. They are playing themselves (the absence of direct address means that this is not coded as documentary footage) and they are discussing, among other things, their comparative status within the film. This is an obsessive concern throughout for Coogan, who is portrayed as narcissistic, philandering, competitive and careerist; Brydon insists he is a 'featured co-lead', while Coogan suggests that Brydon is merely in a 'supporting role'. Thus, the film begins with the demystificatory gesture of laying bare the device, exposing the mechanism by which a (costume) film is produced and thereby undermining its gravity. In the next scene, the introductory scene of the film-within-the-film, Coogan, now in costume as Shandy, strides towards the camera along the gravel drive of a stately home. The shot is framed with perfect symmetry, Coogan in the centre of the image, the house behind him, and this compositional device, which is very rare within Winterbottom's films, immediately situates the film in relation to a tradition of international arthouse *auteur* cinema.

The films of Peter Greenaway and Stanley Kubrick use symmetrical framing so persistently that it is a signature trope of their films. Thus, this shot aligns Winterbottom's film both with Kubrick's costume drama, *Barry Lyndon* (1975), whose soundtrack music is also appropriated, and Greenaway's *A Draughtsman's Contract*, which makes a virtue of stylised 'inauthenticity'. The shot of Coogan is accompanied by an excerpt from Michael Nyman's score for Greenaway's film,[6] punctuated with the crowing of a cockerel in reference to the film's title, but any grandeur of this shot, which seems for a moment to epitomise the urgency and visual splendour of heritage

The ordered aesthetic
of heritage cinema

cinema, is destroyed as Coogan/Shandy pauses and says to the camera, 'Groucho Marx once said that the trouble with writing a book about yourself is you can't fool around. Why not? People fool around with themselves all the time.' The line is followed by the 'moo' of a bull as if groaning at the pun. Coogan continues, 'I'm Tristram Shandy, the main character in this story … the leading role.' The anachronistic, intertextual reference to Marx, and the crude joke, establishes an irreverent, comic attitude towards the costume drama.

This shot is the prologue to a dense, chronologically discontinuous twenty-five minute sequence that dispenses with realist conventions and is assembled from a rapid succession of flashbacks and occasional explanatory digressions. Narrated by Tristram, the sequence introduces key family members and acquaintances, and it tells the story of his conception, birth, naming and circumcision (when, as a boy, a window sash drops on his penis while he urinates out of the window). The sequence also shows his uncle Toby receive an injury 'down there' by cannon-fire at the battle of Namur, which is the basis for a running joke as the sexually innocent Toby (Rob Brydon) repeatedly answers questions about where *exactly* he was injured by pointing out the location on the battlefield. This busy sequence incorporates a range of cinematic devices not normally associated with costume films: split-screen sequences, green-screen shots where Tristram (Coogan) steps in front of scenes in which Coogan plays Tristram's father, Walter, iris-ins, wipes, a digitally animated map of Namur, and archive film of Ivan Pavlov's experiments on salivating dogs incorporated in order for Tristram to illustrate why, due to inadvertent *coitus interruptus*, he was 'cursed from the moment of his conception'.

The sequence ends by returning to the scene in which Tristram is being delivered with the assistance of the disengaged and insensitive Dr Slop (Dylan Moran). Tristram's screaming mother lies pinned to the bed by the midwife and the maid, while Slop, gripping the baby's head with (newly invented) brass forceps, yells, 'Lay her down flat! Flat! I can't work like this! *Flat!*' The camera pans to the left to reveal the director and crew in the same room filming the action.

The director calls a halt to filming and with this shift of perspective we are returned to the frame story of a film crew producing an adaptation of Sterne's novel. Most of the remaining running time of the *A Cock and Bull Story* is given over to depicting the events of the rest of the afternoon and evening until the shooting of Tristram's birth

Coogan as Tristram Shandy
(foreground) and Walter
Shandy (right)

Mark, the director, and crew shooting the birth scene

resumes the next morning. With a few exceptions, the rest of the film is more stylistically restrained and it is largely chronologically linear and naturalistic. The incomplete film-within-a-film, however, proposes a stylistically experimental alternative to the more conventional modes of the costume drama. It can be viewed as a model for a self-consciously cinematic form of costume film that foregrounds its own cinematic structural features, rather than subsuming them within a stylistically and formally unified system in a gesture of subordination towards the source medium. In any case, the convoluted structure of this opening follows the rhizomatic structural principle of Sterne's branching, episodic and unfinished novel more closely than would a film that straightened out the material into a linear narrative.

Beyond this opening sequence, we are given only brief glimpses of what else the finished adaptation might consist of. It exists as a set of possibilities and we are left to imagine what form the completed film might take and what elements of the nine-volume novel will be retained. We see the crew and producers watching rushes of an unimpressive battle sequence later in the evening, and we see a brief scene in which Walter recounts the classical history of circumcision to console his injured son. This illustrative insert is cued by a comment from a 'runner', who suggests to Coogan that the most original, exciting element of the novel is the *Tristapaedia*, the encyclopaedia that Walter compiles for his son during his wife's pregnancy. Thus, it is a conjectural sequence, showing us how the scene might appear had it been included in the screenplay. There is a surreal sequence in which Toby is courted by the widow Wadman, played by Hollywood star Gillian Anderson (associated with costume dramas through her role in *The House of Mirth* (Terence Davies, 2000)). This is dreamt by an anxious Coogan who is worried about being upstaged by Brydon after he learns that Anderson has been cast as Toby's lover with the last-minute addition of this substantial romantic sub-plot.

We are also shown a possible ending to the film when, after a screening of a rough cut of the completed film attended by the cast and crew, an unimpressed producer asks how the book ends. 'The book's got a great ending', replies the screenwriter, which cues a transition to a dinner party attended by the Shandys, Slop and Parson Yorick, played by Stephen Fry, an actor and filmmaker associated with heritage cinema perhaps primarily through his central performance in *Wilde* (Brian Gilbert, 1997). The conversation ranges from sex with the candle lit, to a discussion of Walter's father's bull and its failure to inseminate all the cows in the parish. 'Good Lord, what is this story all about?', asks Elizabeth, to which Yorick replies, 'A cock and a bull story'. Yorick makes clear with a phallic thrust of his fist the double meaning of the phrase, which traditionally refers to a nonsensical or preposterous story. This scene finally offers a self-deprecating explanation for the film's title. It is an absurd and incoherent narrative and it is a story preoccupied with sex and, in particular, with anxiety around cocks – with Coogan's wayward cock, Tristram's injured cock, Walter's misfiring cock and Toby's possibly mutilated or severed cock, not to mention the bull's.

Adaptations and adaptability

A central theme of this film is the failure to produce an adequate adaptation of the novel. Given the nature of Sterne's novel this is, perhaps, inevitable. As Coogan explains when interviewed by TV presenter Tony Wilson (who plays himself here but who was played by Coogan in *24 Hour Party People*), the attraction of the book is that it is said to be 'unfilmable'. It is, he suggests, 'a postmodern classic written before there was a modernism to be "post" about, so it's way ahead of its time'. One of the challenges posed by the novel is that of finding a cinematic equivalent to the digressive, experimental literary style employed by Sterne, and, ironically, *A Cock and Bull Story* repeatedly acknowledges its unfilmability. For example, during a script meeting to consider cheaper alternatives to reshooting the disappointing battle scene, they return to scenes that were discussed when the idea for the film was originally pitched. The screenwriter, Joe, recalls that 'When the good parson Yorick dies, the book has a completely black page.' At this there is a cut to a black screen, but the producer responds, 'I don't know how interesting a black screen's going to be for an audience', and there is a cut back to Joe explaining 'that the original cover for "Anarchy in the UK" was inspired by that page'. The producer's comment is a reminder of the commercial constraints under which independent filmmakers operate (whereas Joe's response – that the shot is justified because of its influence upon a record sleeve – is exquisitely postmodern).

The excerpts from a possible finished film that we see are fascinating, but it is appropriate that it remains fragmentary and incomplete. As is explained in an insert by Patrick (also played by Stephen Fry in another gesture of doubling and identity confusion), the curator of Sterne's home, Shandy Hall:

> The theme of *Tristram Shandy* is a very simple one: life is chaotic, it's amorphous. No matter how hard you try you can't actually make it fit any shape. Tristram, himself, is trying to write his life story, but it escapes him, because life is too full, too rich to be captured by art.

The impossibility of imposing a narrative framework upon lived experience faced by the fictional Tristram Shandy (and also Lawrence Sterne) is doubled with the filmmakers' vain attempt to impose a satisfactory cinematic narrative framework upon the inadequate or fugitive literary narrative. The film suggests then, that cinematic narration is intrinsically limited as a means of articulating experience and in this respect the film can be understood as a critique of conventional film form. As well as experimenting with the form of the costume film, the sequences of the film-within-the-film also propose a different way of depicting lived experience as fragmentary, repetitive, layered and non-linear, continually diverted, sometimes implausible and dishonest, and necessarily incomplete. The 'amorphous' quality of life and non-linear patterns of thought and of memory processes are represented by the intricately structured 'back-and-forth', looping movement of the narrative. *A Cock and Bull Story* is also, therefore, a film about the impossibility of 'faithful' literary adaptation. Sterne's novel is a limit case for the transposition of narrative across media, an example that demonstrates the futility of aspirations to fidelity and the unbreachable media-boundary that makes it impossible to transfer a narrative intact from a novel to the screen. Sterne's novel requires the filmmakers to find a cinematic equivalent to the dense structures and registers of a classic novel and, of course, in this speculative, heterogeneous approach to the problem of rendering the novel on film, the filmmakers are far more faithful in their approach than a filmmaker who chooses simply to treat a film as an illustrated version of a particular book.

The film also satirises the preoccupation with superficial historical 'authenticity' that characterises the spectacular *mise-en-scène* of many costume dramas. The anachronisms and allusive intricacy of the film-within–the-film demonstrate a disregard for accurate reconstruction, while the absurd pedantry of a preoccupation with historical authenticity is personified satirically in the frame story by the figure of the humourless historical consultant, David Ingoldsby.

There is a deceptive lightness to the film in its treatment of these issues. Its formal complexity, allusiveness, and the self-reflexive account of its status as film text and commodity invite the contemplative response of a cineaste. However, through its comic account of the compromised and extemporised decisions taken rapidly and under pressure during a film shoot, the film implicitly ridicules solemn, earnest or humourless responses to the cinema. It problematises any apprehension of authorial intentionality by demonstrating that the film's final form is as much a consequence of uncontrollable contingencies as it is the result of measured creative decisions; the commodity form of the film is only partially determined by aesthetic criteria. For example, the film's backers are unconvinced that reshooting a disappointing battle scene at a cost of £100,000 is warranted and so a script meeting is called in order to consider whether other scenes or sub-plots could replace the battle affordably and at short notice. It is clear that such choices are improvised and externally imposed. The meeting leads to the decision to introduce another character from the novel, Widow Wadman, thereby rendering the film a 'romantic comedy', as the producer observes (to the director's disgust). The business of contemporary cinema is also mocked here as Gillian Anderson is hired to play the widow with laughable ease in a 50-second intercontinental phone call. Her agent explains that 'Gillian's interested in the quality of work, she's not looking for a payday', and Anderson immediately agrees to fly over the following day.

Through an unromantic depiction of filmmaking as a chaotic and provisional collaborative activity (in which the director is shown to have a very marginal role) the

The transnational business of film production – Gillian Anderson (top left) and her agent (bottom left), Mark, his producer (centre) and the screenwriter (bottom right)

film's own authority is undermined. On the one hand there is an explicit acknowledgement of the film's textuality, that it is an object that may be pored over and scrutinised by cineastes and academics. For instance, Coogan's voice-over interrupts the scene in which the actor is being interviewed by Tony Wilson to comment, 'If you want to see the EPK [electronic press kit] interview, it'll be part of the DVD package along with extended versions of many of the scenes, which should act as footnotes to the main film'.[7] At the same time, *A Cock and Bull Story* makes gentle fun of the cinephile's enthusiasm for arthouse cinema and the practice of over-interpretation, through the character of the runner, Jennie. Back at the hotel where the cast and crew are staying, during a conversation comparing battles on film she interjects that the best battle scene of all is that in *Lancelot du Lac* (Robert Bresson, 1974) and offers an impassioned reading (that returns us to the recurrent theme of intimacy within Winterbottom's films):

> It's just these two knights, and they're both encased in armour and they just keep clobbering each other and it goes on forever – hitting and hitting. It's actually like a metaphor for life, you know? It's about the impossibility of actually connecting with another human being, because we're all wearing these carapaces, these casings, this rubbish, really, and the more they hit and hit, actually, the less they impact.

She realises as she continues speaking, that the people gathered around her are frowning and nodding, bemused and nonplussed, and she stumbles to a halt before excusing herself and walking swiftly from the room. Coogan turns to the others after she has left and asks, 'What was that all about?' The scene's humour is derived more from the befuddlement and ignorance of the others rather than from contempt for Jennie's genuine enthusiasm. 'She's a bit of a film nut; you should hear her when she's on about Fassbinder', the producer explains. 'Fassbin-, Fassbinder?', replies a puzzled Coogan clearly none the wiser. This exchange typifies the register of the film. It is characterised by self-deprecating humour and fear of intellectual pretentiousness so that our attention is drawn to the difference between this film and a film by, say, Fassbinder or Fellini. Comedy functions here as a prevarication since at the same time, the humour depends partly for its success upon an informed cine-literate audience and it refrains from closing down entirely a more nuanced reading of the film. For instance, we could take Jennie's reading of Bresson's film as a comment upon the combative relationship between Brydon and Coogan. Like the bickering protagonists of a buddy movie, the relationship is unequal, their friendship marked by physical awkwardness, but it is also touchingly close. The opening and closing scenes, the film´s funniest, are simply of Coogan and Brydon making small talk with one another. Beneath the competition, masculine defensiveness and compulsive joking lies an affectionate coupling, a desire for connection.

It is a mark of the depth of this relationship that Winterbottom returns to it as the basis for *The Trip,* an extensively improvised TV series in which Coogan and Brydon (playing versions of themselves) tour the north of England reviewing restaurants.

Conception, creation and doubles

A Cock and Bull Story explores the culturally unequal relationship between the process of child-birth and maternity and the process of writing and filmmaking. Tristram's birth is the central event in the incomplete film and the film returns repeatedly to the scenes of Elizabeth in labour. Walter insists upon taking control of the birth, removing Elizabeth's agency as far as possible by requiring her to sign a legal contract agreeing to her confinement in the house during pregnancy. He also intervenes during labour by summoning Dr Slop to deliver the baby, due to his faith in the masculine domain of medical science and reason over the feminine knowledge and expertise of the local midwife. Ironically, the inept Slop crushes Tristram's nose with his forceps during the delivery.

The creative act of birth is mirrored absurdly with uncle Toby's sterile, obsessive parody of reproduction in constructing in the vegetable garden a scale model of Namur, the site of the battle where he was injured, perhaps castrated. While Elizabeth is in labour, Toby takes the anxious Walter to examine his fortifications in order to distract him. The film draws a direct contrast between childbirth – the primal event that is of profound explanatory importance for Tristram – and Toby's 'hobbyhorse'. Toby's elaborate castles and battlements are like a little boy's toys, but also recall the miniature models used for special effects sequences in films. Thus, Toby's childish play (which marks and masks his trauma), is also disparagingly likened to filmmaking, recalling Orson Welles's observation, of the RKO studio, 'This is the biggest electric train set a boy ever had!' (Ebrahimian 2004: 99) Filmmaking in Winterbottom's film is a chaotic, self-indulgent, and puerile undertaking. It follows that when Coogan falls asleep while reading Sterne's novel and dreams about the shooting of a scene, he sees himself, suspended inside a prop of a womb – tiny, naked, covered in simulated amniotic fluid.

The frame narrative extends this depiction of film production as a largely male-dominated activity with women consigned to marginal supporting roles as make-up and wardrobe assistants, runners, PAs, actors, financial backers and girlfriends. The indulgence of Coogan, the self-absorbed, self-important centre of the production epitomises this attitude. Like Walter, he has a partner and baby, and his partner has travelled to the shoot with the child in order to spend some time with him. Coogan,

'Womb with a view' –
Coogan's dream

however, is too preoccupied with other things to pay any attention to his partner. He is distracted by meetings with his agent, flirting with the runner, giving interviews, attending script meetings and costume fittings.

A further dimension through which the film reflects upon the process and status of cinematic representations is the trope of doubling. The film is populated with doubles and copies to the extent that the distinction between originals and representations becomes quite blurred. Coogan, Brydon, Anderson, and a number of other actors play doubles of themselves. Coogan's wife Jenny, is doubled by Jennie the runner, both of whom seek his sexual attention, while the grand hotel where the filmmakers stay is a double, of sorts, of Tristram's home. Coogan's character is also doubled through the figure of Walter, of whom Tristram is, in turn, a double. Beyond a prosthetic nose and period costume, Coogan's performance of these two characters is only minimally distinguishable from his performance of himself. He is irritated when other characters repeat the catchphrase of his most famous TV character, Alan Partridge, as if he is being confused with his fictional construction, but *A Cock and Bull Story* constitutes just such a doubling, blurring the distinction between Coogan the actor and 'Coogan' the character. For example, the fictional Coogan and his agent have to work to suppress a newspaper story about his sleeping with a prostitute, a detail that recalls real-life tabloid 'scandals' about the actor.

The film refuses ultimately to resolve uncertainties about the relationship between reality and cinematic simulacrum. Indeed, the final scenes, in which actors and crew watch the rough cut of the Shandy adaptation, confuse the issue further. At the end of the screening, the actors and crew appear to remain in character, discussing the film they have just viewed (and which they are clearly unimpressed by – it remains a failed attempt to transpose the novel). However, a passing exchange between 'Coogan' (Coogan) and his partner Jenny (Kelly MacDonald) disrupts the distinction between naturalistic frame story and the fictional film-within-the-film. Coogan says to MacDonald, 'I thought you were fantastic, by the way, for what it's worth', and kisses her awkwardly, suggesting that the two of them have just watched the same film as us in which they play a couple, rather than the Shandy adaptation that we might assume they have watched *as* a couple within the frame narrative. There is, as a result, no stable spectatorial position from which to distinguish between graduated, infinitely regressing levels of fiction.

The closing credits are accompanied by shots of Brydon and Coogan chatting in the now empty screening room, commenting upon the film (although at this point it is not clear which one) and discussing acting techniques. Reprising the first scene, where the two of them are in make-up, the film is bracketed by short sequences that appear to lay bare the mechanisms of screen performance. However, in this terminal scene their conversation turns to the pertinent issue of impersonation as they compare their impressions of Al Pacino. Brydon explains that he openly models himself on Pacino: 'When I lean against a wall, that's Pacino. When I do a look of shock, that's Pacino.' At this a perplexed Coogan asks him, 'but are you being serious now, or are you joking?' It is as if, by this point, even the lead actor is confused about the mimetic status of this shot/performance/moment, unable to decide whether he is confronted by an authentic Brydon or an act, but, as Brydon's reply suggests, such distinctions are a misapprehension: 'We're in the same business.' In the context of Winterbottom's body of work, this comment is telling, acknowledging that the naturalist style employed in many of the films is as artificial, aestheticised and conventional as any other approach. As Brydon explains to Coogan, veracity in screen acting is a matter not of transparency and immediacy, but of imitation and technique, intertextuality and generic verisimilitude:

> I look for truth and that's why I go to Pacino, and that's why I go to Hopkins. But I go to actresses as well … I regularly go to Streisand. I say, 'what can you give me?', and I look at her body – of work – and say 'I'll have a little bit from *Hello, Dolly!* and I'll take a little bit from *Yentl*', and put 'em together.

The film's transgression of the boundary between the frame narrative and the film-within-the-film, between the fictitious and the real, invites a critical, spectatorial gaze. Partly through its comic exposure of the processes of filmmaking, it directs the viewer to cast a sceptical eye at the costume film, recognising the unfaithfulness of the cinematic adaptation, the formal conservatism of many such films (by contrast with the wild film being made by Coogan and Brydon), and their anachronisms and profound historical inauthenticity. It also directs the viewer to treat Winterbottom's work as a whole with similar scepticism, recognising the artificiality of the realist codes employed throughout his career. It invites us to recognise that Winterbottom's work is characterised by a self-reflexive relationship to the European tradition of realist narrative cinema from which it emerges, and to recognise the processes of mediation, compression and framing involved in the production of sequences of film.

The costume film remixed

The three films discussed above constitute a series of variations upon the costume film. While one could plot across them a progressive dismantling and destruction of the generic model, it is equally arguable that they constructively test and expand the boundaries and configuration of this flexible generic framework, co-opting or appropriating it to tell different stories (and to tell familiar stories differently). In this context, *24 Hour Party People* can be understood as a recodification of the costume drama or heritage film in order to document and celebrate a much more recent past that is localised, regionally specific, structured by social class hierarchies and articulated through music subcultures and popular culture. In place of the aristocratic and bourgeois traditions associated (somewhat inaccurately and reductively) with the costume film, *24 Hour Party People* reconstructs and mythologises the cultural, intellectual and industrial heritage associated with trends in Manchester pop music from the 1970s to the 1990s. The film records an evanescent, disposable past, but one that was no less consuming and transformative for those that experienced it. Through the loose frame of the costume drama, combined with that of the 'bio-pic' – as the story of TV presenter and entrepreneur Tony Wilson provides the film with its narrative armature – *24 Hour Party People* asserts the cultural and aesthetic importance of this music in a manner that is simultaneously sincere, frustratingly incomplete, and knowingly hyperbolic. Whereas *A Cock and Bull Story* establishes an initial distinction between the fictional film adaptation and the frame story of a film shoot in order then to problematise and challenge this separation, *24 Hour Party People* declares from the outset its status as mythic narrative.

The pre-credits scene begins in 1976 with Tony Wilson (Steve Coogan) shooting an item on hang-gliding in the Pennine hills for the regional news programme, *Granada Reports*. The report, which intercuts genuine footage with footage of Coogan, shows Wilson first of all flying, then crashing repeatedly. The scene concludes with Wilson walking away from the shoot and then noticing the camera/viewer. He walks towards it and explains:

> You're going to be seeing a lot more of that sort of thing in the film. Although that actually did happen, obviously it's symbolic. It works on both levels. I don't want to tell you too much. I don't want to spoil the film, but I'll just say, 'Icarus'. If you know what I mean, great. If you don't, it doesn't matter; but you should probably read more.

The scene is set to a historically loaded theme from Richard Wagner's opera, *Die Walküre*, a piece of music famously employed in the score for the epic film of the American Civil War, *Birth of a Nation*, as the Ku Klux Klan assemble their forces for the climactic confrontation with freed slaves. It is also used in *Apocalypse Now* (Francis Ford Coppola, 1979), when US soldiers play a recording from speakers mounted on their helicopters while strafing and bombing a Vietnamese village, providing themselves with their own soundtrack for the slaughter. For Coppola's film this citation draws oblique links between the Vietnam War and the white supremacist ideology that structures Griffith's film – and perhaps with the Nazis who appropriated the composer as an exemplary German artist – and it also demonstrates the contradictorily seductive, thrilling spectacle of the critical war film. In Winterbottom's film, the citation immediately underlines the distance between these epic cinematic precursors which recount pivotal historical intervals, and his film which recounts the founding of an independent record label and the flourishing of several post-punk pop groups. The

'Icarus' – Tony Wilson announces the film's allegorical function

allusion also underscores the pretentiousness of its protagonist, establishing him as a somewhat unreliable, optimistic and self-promotional narrator who imagines or proclaims himself to be at the centre of a historically crucial moment. At the same time, however, the citation prompts reflection on the relative importance of historical moments. Griffith's melodramatic account of the civil war and the post-war reconstruction is in large part historical fantasy, while Coppola's influential account of the Vietnam War is a partially extemporised adaptation of Joseph Conrad's novella about European colonial exploitation of the Congo, *Heart of Darkness* (1902). The allusion to these films might prompt us, then, to ask why certain histories, or certain modes of historical experience are deemed significant, and to what extent history is generated through narration, rather than the documentation of objective events.

Certainly, the film's account of a twenty-year period is selective and of questionable reliability, and a brief synopsis gives a sense of the dense, fragmentary narrative. Following the opening hang-gliding sequence, Wilson and some friends see The Sex Pistols perform in Manchester. Inspired, he and Alan Erasmus go on to establish the 'Factory' evening at the Russell Club in Moss Side, owned by Don Tonay. Wilson meets DJ and manager Rob Gretton and singer Ian Curtis at the club and he sees Curtis's band Warsaw perform there. The band subsequently change their name to Joy Division and Wilson encourages them to sign a contract with him, written in his own blood, which offers them 'total creative freedom'. He then employs eccentric, anti-social recording engineer Martin Hannett, whom he earlier described as one of the two geniuses of the story, to produce a record, which is to be released by the co-operatively owned Factory Records. We see snatches of several Joy Division concerts, one of which descends into violence after the epileptic Ian Curtis has a fit on stage. After being informed by manager Gretton that they are to tour America, Curtis commits suicide. Wilson views Curtis' body at the funeral home and his partner Lindsay announces that she is leaving him. Driving away from Piccadilly train station where he has dropped her off, Wilson announces to camera the beginning of the second act.

The film then introduces Shaun and Paul Ryder – who go on to form the band, Happy Mondays – feeding rat poison to hundreds of pigeons while Wilson expounds his theory of cyclical musical development to the camera. The Haçienda club is opened and Hannett quits the partnership with Erasmus, Gretton, and Wilson in disgust at the expense of the project. New Order, the band formed by the remaining members of Joy Division, begin rehearsing the song, 'Blue Monday', which is then released to great commercial success. The Happy Mondays are shown performing in a battle of the bands at the Haçienda and then playing anarchically in a recording studio. While the Haçienda emerges as a successful venue, we also see the Happy Mondays return to the recording studio, where they are produced by Hannett who is now hugely fat, and embark on a chaotic tour. Wilson becomes derailed by drug addiction during this period, conducting a comically misjudged television interview with a government minister while under the influence, but also meets his future partner, Yvette.

The Haçienda runs into problems both financial and practical, as the burgeoning drug culture means that customers are no longer spending money at the bar while drug-dealing leads to a proliferation of shootings in and around the club. Wilson visits his second wife and child in hospital (whom we were previously unaware of and do not appear again) and then attends Martin Hannett's funeral where the enormous coffin is too large to fit in the grave. The heroin-addicted Happy Mondays travel to Barbados to record a new album (since there is no heroin problem on the island) but once there they become addicted to crack cocaine which is in plentiful supply. On their return their manager, Nathan, tells Wilson, Erasmus and Gretton that Shaun Ryder, the band's singer, is holding the master tapes of the new album for ransom. They meet at a bar where Ryder fires a revolver at the wall and hands over the tapes for £50. Listening to them later they discover that there are no vocals recorded on them.

Wilson's parallel TV career continues alongside his role as the owner of a nightclub and record label, and he is shown presenting the *Wheel of Fortune* TV gameshow. In the editing room he points out the real Tony Wilson (who is playing the show's director) and identifies the other real people who have appeared in the film. Later on Don Tonay, the owner of the Russell Club and a repossession agency, lets Wilson know discreetly that he has a repossession order for the Haçienda. At the same time, (with humiliating irony given Wilson's aggressive regional pride) the head of London Records, Roger Ames, tries to buy Factory Records and the club but Wilson explains that there is nothing to sell as they do not own the rights to the work of any of their bands. He explains to the nonplussed Ames that the company is 'an experiment in human nature', and that, 'My epitaph will be that I never literally nor metaphorically sold out. I've protected myself from ever having to have the dilemma of having to sell out by having nothing to sell out.' The film ends with the last night of the Haçienda. While the bailiffs gather outside, Wilson tells the crowd to loot the building on the way out, instructing them to 'Let a thousand Mancunians bloom'. He then joins Gretton, Erasmus, and Shaun Ryder on the roof of the club as the sun is coming up. He shares a joint with them and then has a vision of God, who looks and sounds exactly like him and tells him, 'You did a good job. Basically you were right.'

Lensed by Robbie Müller, who is best known for his work on the formally restrained films of Wim Wenders and Jim Jarmusch, as well as Sally Potter and Lars von Trier, the film is stylistically heterogeneous, reproducing the aesthetic inconsistency of the music released by Factory Records and the popular cultural shifts covered by the film's time-span. As well as incorporating black and white footage to depict Joy Division on stage, the film includes archive material from TV news programmes and Wilson's show, *So*

God as he appears to
Tony Wilson in the skies
over Manchester

It Goes, an excerpt from the promotional video for the Joy Division song, *Atmosphere*, as well as reconstructions of programmes featuring Wilson (Coogan), a parody of the opening credits of the French TV series, *The Adventures of Robinson Crusoe* (featuring a naked Shaun Ryder perched on a rock in Barbados), comically animated sequences of pigeons and a UFO above Manchester, and a theatrical depiction of God who floats in the air on a heavenly clockwork contraption like an effect from a Georges Méliès film.

(Hi)story-telling

One of the film's central themes is the construction of historical narratives through the synthesis and over-writing of competing claims and partial accounts. This theme is most evident in Tony Wilson's repeated insistence to the viewer, in his capacity as narrator – and also to other characters in the film in his dual role as protagonist – that the events we see are of great moment. Wilson repeatedly draws questionable historical parallels, and makes preposterously excessive claims in order to persuade those around him that they are witnessing crucially important events, that these stories need to be told. For example, after seeing the Sex Pistols perform, Wilson tells his producer at Granada TV, 'I would describe it as history.'

> Charles: History? How can it be history? There were only 42 people at the
>   gig.
> Wilson: Well what difference does that make? How many people were at the
>   Last Supper?
> Charles: Twelve. Thirteen, if you include Jesus, but it's not historically docu-
>   mented.
> Wilson: In other words, not many. How many people were at the murder of
>   Julius Caesar?
> Charles: I don't know, Tony. You tell me.
> Wilson: Five, so shut up then.

When he visits a funeral home to view the body of Ian Curtis, the singer with Joy Division, he ushers in a journalist, explaining to him: 'It's historic [...] That is the musical equivalent of Che Guevara.' In a voice-over he later likens Manchester during the flourishing of rave culture to Renaissance Florence, and he goes on to (mis-)quote Wordsworth's commentary on the enthusiasm at the sense of possibility during early stages of the French Revolution in order to claim that 'Being at the Haçienda was like being at the French Revolution. "Bliss it was that dawn to be alive, but to be young was very heaven!"'

In another sequence, addressing the camera while walking through the Haçienda (as if introducing a news report), Wilson solemnly likens the popular cultural shift documented in the film, in which a youth subculture becomes mainstream, to some of the key technical and industrial developments associated with the city:

> Manchester: birthplace to the railways, the computer, the bouncing bomb. But tonight something equally as epoch-making is taking place. See? They're applauding the DJ. Not the music, not the musician, not the creator, but the medium. This is it: the birth of rave culture, the beatification of the beat, the dance age. This is the moment when even the white man starts dancing. Welcome to Manchester.

And at the point at which the Happy Mondays become commercially successful, he goes as far as to declare that, 'Manchester became the centre of the universe.'

In its concern with rhetoric and historical process, the film proposes a narrative model of history – both cultural history and social history – as perpetual cyclical, dynamic change. As Wilson explains to the viewer: 'The history of popular music is like a double helix. That's two waves that intertwine [...] Basically, when one musical movement's in the descendent, another one's in the ascendant.' A similar model – of individualised historical experience – is expounded by the 6th century Roman philosopher Boëthius (Christopher Eccleston), in a surreal scene when Wilson encounters him sitting under a railway arch. After Wilson has handed some money to a beggar, the man calls after him (in a Manchester accent):

> I'm Boëthius, author of the *Consolation of Philosophy*. It's my belief that history is a wheel. 'Inconstancy is my very essence', says the wheel. 'Rise up on my spokes if you like, but don't complain when you're cast back down into the depths.' Good times pass away but then so do the bad. Mutability is our tragedy, but it's also our hope. The worst of times, like the best, are always passing away.

Given the overall tenor of the film, this concept of history is framed ironically – Wilson later incorporates it into his slick introduction to an episode of the TV gameshow, *Wheel of Fortune*, observing that the wheel has been employed as a fatal metaphor for centuries – but it broadly describes the 'rise-and-fall' movement that the film plots. Indeed, the problem of history, is a problem of narrative structure and, as noted above, one of Wilson's functions as Brechtian commentator, is to describe the film's narrative organisation. After his wife, Lindsay leaves him, Wilson addresses the camera: 'I think it was Scott Fitzgerald who said American lives don't have second acts. Well, this is Manchester. We do things differently here … this *is* the second act.'

Boethius lectures Wilson on the cyclical nature of history

In addition to occupying the distinct roles of character and narrator, Wilson also occasionally steps out of character within scenes to address the audience, offering clarification or direction as to how to interpret the film. In one sequence where he leads the former Miss United Kingdom on a tour of the TV studios, he opens a door for her and then turns back to the camera to admonish the viewer: 'Don't judge. Piety is a very unattractive quality. Flirting is a very natural process. She's aware of it. I'm being postmodern before it was fashionable.' However, while Wilson is presented as the central historian and story-teller, his authority as narrator is also constantly undermined meta-narratively by his comic characterisation as an idealistic, defensive, fashion-conscious pseudo-intellectual who enjoys the minor celebrity of being a public figure.

Thus, the film makes clear that Wilson's account – and the film itself, in so far as it is primarily his version of events – is of dubious veracity. Wilson's insistence that the hang-gliding scene 'actually did happen' alerts us to the likelihood that much of the following film will be inaccurate or apocryphal. For example, in a subsequent scene, events in the film are contested by one of the historical participants. Early in the film Wilson discovers his partner Lindsay having sex in the toilet stall of a nightclub with Howard Devoto, singer with punk band, The Buzzcocks. As Wilson leaves, having retrieved the car keys from her handbag, the camera travels over to a cleaner wiping the sinks in the background, who declares to the viewer, 'I definitely don't remember this happening'.

Over a frozen close-up of the cleaner, Wilson explains on the voice-over:

This is the real Howard Devoto. He and Lindsay insist that we make clear that this never happened. But I agree with John Ford; when you have to choose between the truth and the legend, print the legend.

Typically, this quotation from *The Man who Shot Liberty Valance* (John Ford, 1962) is misremembered,[8] but it is a cautionary acknowledgement of the film's pragmatic attitude towards fact wherein truth has been sacrificed in the interest of popular entertainment and historical reality is displaced by fiction. This displacement is nicely demonstrated by the commingling of real historical figures with the actors that play them, including the real Tony Wilson. Much more so than with *A Cock and Bull Story*, the

Howard Devoto challenges the film's historical accuracy

viewer is encouraged to approach the film with a sceptical eye, recognising that the protagonist is an inveterate self-promoter and the account we are offered here may well be heavily fictionalised.[9]

As an argument for the cultural or aesthetic value of the music, the film's argument is somewhat inadequate. Wilson insists with pretentious humility that 'this is not a film about me. "I am not Prince Hamlet nor was meant to be". I'm a minor character in my own story. This is a film about the music, and the people who made the music: Ian Curtis, Shaun Ryder and Martin Hannett.' However, what we hear of the music does little to support Wilson's repeated claim that Hannett and Ryder are geniuses. We hear excerpts from the recordings on the soundtrack, but the music we see the actors perform in rehearsals, in recording studios and on stage is some distance from the polished, final versions. Instead the film emphasises the musicians' technical and temperamental limitations so that we see the members of Joy Division struggling even to play their instruments. To some extent the depiction of the musicians is thoroughly romantic; they are not self-regarding artists, but often hedonistic, anti-social, self-destructively excessive characters driven to create, with Ryder in particular, depicted as almost an *idiot savant*. Wilson's opinion that, 'Shaun Ryder is on a par with W.B. Yeats – as a poet', is comically hard to reconcile with the figure that we see in the film, a truculent, delinquent addict. When asked by Wilson to give a producer an example of his lyrical brilliance, Ryder obliges with, 'Good good, good. Good good, double good.' The film – which borrows its title from a Happy Mondays song – is clearly not intended to ridicule Wilson's judgement, nor does it give us evidence with which to assess Wilson's claims. It depends upon a readiness to follow an inter-textual relay to the music, or alternatively it requires a foreknowledge of the music, and perhaps nostalgia for the cultural context the music belongs to. Either way, the film is structured by the assumption that it is not necessary to argue for the aesthetic or historic worth of the music.

Bio-pics and monumental cinema

However, despite Wilson's self-effacing protestations, this *is* a film about him and his role in enabling and driving the development of several groups and dynamic subcultural shifts. Thus, the film is concerned with a less conventional model of authorship than is employed in biopics that fetishise the mysterious, solipsistic process of artistic production, and in this respect it is no less a film about filmmaking than *A Cock and Bull* Story, with Wilson occupying the role of director. The film's celebration of the creative role of the recording engineer, Martin Hannett, recognises that producing a record is a laborious, technically complex process involving judicious decision-making. The recording process involves the layered construction of a piece of music designed for a specific medium, rather than the simple documentation of a pre-existing performance, and is an extension of the composition process. This extended creative process is also intrinsically collaborative requiring the participation of multiple authors. Wilson's co-ordinating authorial role is that of a facilitator and collaborator without whom the music may not have been produced or heard in the form that it eventually took. In conjunction with a range of other people, he provides a platform for bands to perform and music to be circulated (at the Factory club, on his TV programme, *So It Goes*, and at the Haçienda club). He is a 'match-maker', introducing people with complementary talents to one another. He also bankrolls their recordings, publishes their music and is an enthusiastic promoter. In the process, Wilson occupies a self-deprecating, tolerant role in which he is subjected to constant abuse and is treated with little respect – on his first encounter with Ian Curtis, the singer calls him a cunt, as does his belligerent business partner, Gretton, while Martin Hannett fires a revolver loaded with blanks in his face. While he enjoys the localised fame, Wilson endures this treatment, and plays the degrading role of TV presenter producing 'human interest' reports on such topics as a shepherd who herds sheep with a goose and a dwarf who works as an elephant cleaner at the zoo, in order to make this music and these generative situations possible.

Control (Anton Corbijn, 2007) offers an instructive point of contrast as a more orthodox and reverent cinematic account of the creative process. Directed by Anton Corbijn, who shot some influential photographs of Joy Division and directed an elegiac promotional video for their song 'Atmosphere' (1988), based on Deborah Curtis's book about her husband and scripted by Matthew Greenhalgh who also wrote the screenplay for *The Look of Love*, the film was co-produced by Curtis and Tony Wilson. It is an account of the last seven years of Ian Curtis's life, following his progression from disengaged teenage schoolboy in Macclesfield through the formation and flourishing of Joy Division and the parallel disintegration of his marriage, to his suicide in 1980. Shot in crisp, cold black and white, with many long takes and a largely static or slow-moving camera, the slow, melancholy film alludes to Corbijn's own atmospheric photographs of the band, but the visual style also functions to historicise the events, stressing their location in the past. The minimal but detailed production design situates the film clearly in an earlier period without reliance on a kitsch, camp overemphasis on contemporaneous popular culture to anchor the action historically, while the absence of colour and the settings of tower blocks, suburbs and Victorian terraces invokes 'kitchen sink' films of the 1950s and 1960s and socially committed BBC TV dramas and 'single plays' of the 1960s. This simple visual style also lends the action a monumental quality.

By contrast with Winterbottom's film renditions of the music are more central to *Control* so that, for instance, when the band first plays on Tony Wilson's

Monumental history and social realist pastiche – Ian Curtis (Sam Riley) in *Control*

programme, *So It Goes,* we see a complete performance of the song, 'Transmission', effectively reproducing the sound of the original recording. In Winterbottom's film the performances of the songs are frequently ramshackle and fragmentary, and are mixed so that they compete for our attention with voice-over and diegetic dialogue, ambient noise and variable acoustics, thereby producing a convincing approximation of a band playing live. In *Control* the performances by Joy Division are note-perfect, presenting the familiar songs as fully formed, rather than experimental, tentative and in process. Sam Riley achieves a very convincing vocal and physical imitation of Curtis, but he has a slightly smoother, stronger voice than Curtis which gives the music a slightly greater coherence and confidence. Winterbottom's film shows (non-)musicians struggling against the frustrating limits of their technical abilities, incorporating accidents in learning how to play new forms of music that draw on the heterogeneous influences of punk, glam pop, disco, funk and European electronic and avant-garde music as well as romantic poetry and underground literature. *Control*, on the other hand, represents a band that appears to know exactly what it is doing.

In its account of Curtis's life, *Control* also establishes a biographical explanation for the songs, inviting us to understand them as a directly confessional or expressive commentary upon Curtis's experience, representing him as a depressive, desperately unhappy individual who is impelled to write and whose performance is also a form of transparent self-exposure. Thus, for example, we see Curtis write the title of the song, 'She's Lost Control' on a note pad after learning of the death of an epileptic client he met while working at the labour exchange, and, as he writes, we hear the song's introduction on the soundtrack. The creative process is depicted as solitary and contemplative, from which band members and collaborators are excised. Similarly, moments after Curtis tells Deborah that he no longer loves her, we hear the opening chords of the song, *Love Will Tear Us Apart*, and, following Curtis's suicide at the end of the film, the song 'Atmosphere', is heard on the soundtrack and continues to play out over the credits. With the film's tragic narrative focus upon Curtis, all the events that take place can be understood to lead to Curtis's death; at one point, after he himself has been diagnosed with epilepsy, we see him studying his face in the bathroom mirror, stroking his neck as if contemplating his eventual suicide. In turn, his death is offered as the explanatory key with which we can read Joy Division's music and its continuing influence.

Control shares with *24 Hour Party People* a number of characters and depicts some of the same events – Tony Wilson signing a record contract with his own blood, a recording session with Martin Hannett, a riot at a Joy Division concert in Bury, Curtis collapsing on stage and later hanging himself – but these are represented from an alternative, inverted perspective, isolated from the messy, colourful and dynamic context in which Winterbottom's film places them. It is a complementary account that adds detail, historical range and an expanded cast of characters to the compressed treatment of this story in Winterbottom's film. However, *24 Hour Party People* employs various strategies to put into question Wilson's claims that the events documented in it are momentous and originary. These range from the casting of a number of comedians familiar from British TV (Steve Coogan, Keith Allen, Rob Brydon, Dave Gorman, Peter Kay, Simon Pegg) to incongruous comic or surreal episodes such as the sequence where, in a parody of a World War 2 film, an unconvincing animated pigeon dive-bombs the Ryder brothers who are poisoning birds on a rooftop. There is no such irony in *Control*, which maintains a solemn, sometimes harrowing tone throughout, as it traces the sequence of progressively unbearable events – including his collapsing marriage, the birth of a daughter, his illness and treatment regime, the physical burden of touring and live performance – that propel the sensitive, vulnerable singer towards suicide. The film elaborates upon *24 Hour Party People*, but also reaffirms a familiar, romantic image of Curtis as a melancholic poet – a Chatterton – that is problematised by Winterbottom's film.

24 Hour Party People also employs the song, 'Atmosphere' to mark Curtis's death, with a short excerpt from Corbijn's lugubrious video inserted after we see Curtis's body in the crematorium. However, just before this scene, Wilson addresses the camera to comment:

> If you listen to Ian's music and you know that he killed himself, you probably imagine some very dark, depressing figure – a prophet of urban decay and alienation – but I have some wonderful memories of him, such as the very last Factory night at the Russell Club.

There follows a gleeful scene in which Curtis is singing and dancing on the cramped stage joining in with other singers and musicians in an anarchic performance of 'Louie Louie' led by John the Postman (Gorman) that has the smiling crowd pogoing, throwing water and singing along.

The central theme of *24 Hour Party People* is just as much the life and opinions of Tony Wilson and his unreliable version of events as it is an account of the music or musicians he was involved with. The narrator and the process of narration are as significant as the film's narrative content. As an account of recent history, then, the film can be understood as a film about the cinematic representation of history and the impossibility of objective truth and accurate recall. When it comes to history, the film seems to say, all we can expect is a partly fictionalised, partly bowdlerised, wholly mediated reconstruction that draws on a heterogeneous variety of sources and models. In this respect the film constitutes a particularly self-conscious form of heritage cinema or costume film in which the past is represented and reconstructed in a highly anachronistic, aestheticised manner. This does not constitute a demolition of the costume film or heritage film but embraces its implausibilities and its pleasures.

Conclusion

Writing about discourses of British cinema, Andrew Higson observes that there is a tension between the two genres most directly associated with a British national cinema, documentary-realism and the heritage film:

> Paradoxically, the two genres most frequently cited in debates about British cinema as a national cinema seem to pull in opposite directions, and to embody different ideological perspectives. Or, if they are not opposed, then the documentary-realist tradition at least tries to modernize and democratize the idea of heritage, by representing the mundane cultural traditions of ordinary people, rather than of the canonical, the acclaimed, or the distinctive. (Higson 1995: 27)

As discussed above, these two apparently opposed genres are brought together in Winterbottom's practice. If there is a paradoxical incompatibility between a localised mode of politically committed realist cinema and British heritage cinema, Winterbottom's films nevertheless traverse this discrepancy repeatedly, opening up ideological contradictions that are sometimes uncomfortable and sometimes (partly as a function of that discomfort) comic. In employing the stylistic codes of documentary realism (in itself an irreducibly paradoxical term) with a concomitant narrative focus upon 'ordinary people', the films discussed in this chapter refuse the spectacular and seductive theatre of wealth and privilege that characterises the archetypal heritage film. They are concerned with practices, cultures and individuals that are socially and historically displaced. The collision of these apparently opposed traditions within Winterbottom's films also invites us to ask whether the divide between documentary-realist cinema and the elaborate, inauthentic artifice of the costume film is really so great. These films remind us that the documentary authenticity of films such as *In This World* and *The Road to Guantánamo* is an artful construction while the elaborate, farcical fabulation of *24 Hour Party People* may be the most historically accurate and revealing means of telling these particular stories.

Notes

1   Electronic press kit interview, 2001 UK DVD.
2   *The Time Out Film Guide, 2010*, 2009, London: Time Out.
3   *Jude*'s budget was approximately $7m, while that of *Titanic* was approximately $200m.
4   Although the Director of Photography on *The Claim*, Alwin Küchler, states that 'The approach was meant to be closer to that of a documentary, rather than planning everything out' (Oppenheimer 2001: 24).
5   See Solnit 2004 for an account of these photographs and Muybridge's relationship to railroad companies.

6   Perhaps by coincidence, Nyman has been working since 1981 on an opera, *Tristram Shandy*, although none of the movements from this unfinished work was used in the score of Winterbottom's film.

7   This is also a recognition of the incomplete state of the 'main film'; it is a non-definitive text (like almost any commercially produced DVD) that is embedded among supplementary texts.

8   The line, which is delivered by a newspaper editor to a reporter, runs, 'When the legend becomes fact, print the legend.'

9   Incidentally, the novelisation of the film by Tony Wilson compounds this uncertainty about where the line between fiction and fact should be drawn. Wilson draws heavily on the screenplay for his account of the events, sometimes reproducing dialogue from the film, appropriating and embellishing lines attributed to him by the screenwriter Frank Cottrell Boyce, and sometimes criticising the film. This passage from a chapter recalling how he met his wife is typically oblique: 'When they made the movie of Wilson's story they planned to put a sex scene in, but probably couldn't manage the truth and gave up [...] The movie people ... left in a post-coital conversation between the lovers which may or may not have taken place, but which advances our story just a little' (Wilson 2002: 216).

CHAPTER FOUR

Borders and Terror

The operation of cameras, not only in the recording and distribution of images of torture, but as part of the very apparatus of bombing, make it clear that media representations have already become modes of military conduct. So there is no way to separate, under present historical conditions, the material reality of war from those representational regimes through which it operates and which rationalise its own operation. (Butler 2009: 29)

The global 'War on Terror'[1] is a densely mediated, expanding and, literally, endless conflict that has generated a vast deluge of coverage – what Jean Baudrillard aptly terms 'the improbable orgy of material' – circulating through major commercial media channels such as newspapers and magazines, TV and radio networks, as well as through minor, alternative or personal media such as activist videos, independent news networks, internet discussion fora, blogs, file-sharing websites, amateur photographs and academic scholarship (Baudrillard 1995: 58). The complex transnational configuration of battles, atrocities, protests, locations, debates, discourses and individuals that constitutes the War on Terror has been characterised by spectacular hypermediation from the outset; it is a 'war' that has been exceptionally (but nevertheless only partially) visible, and of crucial significance for global international relations during the last decade. It is inevitable that such a devastating conflict should have preoccupied filmmakers and audiences since the terrorist attacks in the US in September 2001, and the subsequent retaliatory attacks upon Afghanistan and Iraq, although, as Douglas Kellner observes, American films were already exploring fantasies and anxieties regarding US military imperialism and terrorism in advance of the attacks on the Pentagon and World Trade Center, fictional rehearsals that gave the events themselves an uncannily familiar, cinematic quality:

The transition from the Clinton-Gore era of relative peace and prosperity to the militarist interventionism and multiple crises of the Bush-Cheney administration was anticipated in a series of war films and political thrillers released before and just after 9/11. Films have an anticipatory dimension and can predict and anticipate events of the era. (Kellner 2010: 19)

Of course, this foreshadowing indicates not so much the uncanny prescience of Hollywood filmmakers, as the critical potential of cinema to make visible the ideological formation of the present, to recognise and reframe social narratives that are continually in the process of extemporised performance. This critical facility – the capacity to interrogate value systems and to examine the construction and narration of events by politicians, reporters, military representatives, public relations initiatives, participants and witnesses – remains potential, however, and is partly contingent upon a sceptical or resistant reading to bring it forward. Certainly many of the films and TV programmes to address the War on Terror directly or indirectly, range in tone from critical ambivalence, or melancholic resignation to the inevitability of the conflicts and the violence and moral recalibration it necessitates, through to aggressive, xenophobic militarism and paranoia in which a deeply familiar colonial adventure is framed as a new form of warfare that permits the dehumanisation and suspension of rights of the 'othered' enemy. So, for instance, a film such as *Mission: Impossible III* (J. J. Abrams, 2006) 'features and legitimates torture and murder in fighting evil terrorists and their accomplices', while 'torture in fighting terrorism was also normalized in the TV series *24* (2001–2010), which featured its operatives using more and more extreme methods as terrorist threats intensified' (Kellner 2010: 119).

The three films by Michael Winterbottom to address the War on Terror directly, *In this World*, *The Road to Guantánamo* and *A Mighty Heart* eschew the martial spectacle, seductive carnage and oppositional moral framing of the conventional war film with its focus upon combat and the ideologically and narratively restrictive perspective of the soldier's experience, in order to concentrate upon marginal figures caught up in the blast wave of violence, racism and paranoia that travelled across the globe in the wake of the 2001 attacks and whose pressure waves continue to circulate, justifying the continuing reconfiguration of economies, new rafts of repressive legislation and shifting international relations. Viewed as a trilogy, the films offer different ways of seeing the War on Terror from many of the contemporary films that reproduce the perspectives, ideological frames and experiences of US and European soldiers and their families, contractors and politicians such as *Green Zone* (Paul Greengrass, 2010). In their orientation around marginal figures, Winterbottom's films recognise the impossibility of producing a comprehensive, fully coherent account of the war – especially in the face of the overwhelming volume of images and narratives – and instead they make visible bodies and make audible voices that have been absent from, obliterated by, or indeed terrorised and abjected by, dominant accounts of the war. This act of reframing and recontextualisation is most explicit in *The Shock Doctrine*, the fourth of Winterbottom's films to address the War on Terror, and which offers a constructive framework through which to read the other three. The film is an adaptation of journalist Naomi Klein's history of 'disaster capitalism' and rather than reiterating the claim that the invasions of Afghanistan and Iraq can be understood simply or primarily as unpremeditated retaliation for the terrorist attacks of September 2001 (however misguided), the film proposes that these wars were episodes in a longer history of neo-liberal capitalist interventions in regions undergoing political or economic crises.

War and cinema

Since the first *actualités* produced by the Lumière brothers that included films of soldiers and sailors drilling and training, and early films of restaged battles, such as Mitchell and Kenyon's filmed reconstructions of events from the Second Boer War, warfare has proved an irresistibly attractive subject for filmmakers. The phenomenon of industrialised destruction and non-productive expenditure, and the extravagant display of thousands of rehearsed, costumed and choreographed bodies moving across the 'theatre' of conflict corresponds closely to the emphasis upon the aesthetic non-narrative spectacle of startling, violent, visually arresting scale and excess in mainstream cinema that extends back to the 'cinema of attractions' identified by Tom Gunning and André Gaudreault as a dominant aesthetic characteristic of late nineteenth and early twentieth century films – a disregard for narrative continuity, coherence and an exhibitionist emphasis upon display (see Gunning 2000; Bennett 2007). Furthermore, tracing a technical-industrial history, Paul Virilio has argued that there is a close relationship between the development of cinema technology and military technology from the early twentieth century. The industrialisation of slaughter with the growing use of long-range weapons during the First World War ensuring that killing was increasingly done by remote control, posed a cartographic and optical challenge that 'explains the urgent need that developed for ever more accurate sighting, ever greater magnification, for *filming the war* and photographically reconstructing the battlefield' (Virilio 1992: 70). Thus, the development of military technology, from the late nineteenth century onwards was dependent upon the development of technologies of vision so that:

> By 1967 the US Air Force had the whole of South-East Asia covered, and pilotless aircraft would fly over Laos and send their data back to IBM centres in Thailand or South Vietnam. *Direct vision was now a thing of the past:* in the space of a hundred and fifty years, the target area had become a cinema 'location', the battlefield a film set out of bounds to civilians. (Virilio 1992: 11; emphasis in original)

In this respect a military optics converges with a cinematic optics wherein reality is framed and perceived as a performance space, and this convergence becomes ever tighter with the development of digital technologies of enhancement, modelling and simulation. Taking into account the conscious mobilisation of cinema as a means of instruction or propaganda at various points, we can observe that there is a historically, technically, formally and – consequently – ideologically close relationship between war and cinema. Or, as director Sam Fuller puts it, when quizzed about the ontological nature of cinema in a cameo role in *Pierrot le Fou* (Jean-Luc Godard, 1965), 'a film is like a battleground'.

More than has been the case with previous conflicts, the War on Terror has been marked by a burgeoning of audio-visual representations from multiple (and continually multiplying) perspectives, a phenomenon explored by several films and dramas in their incorporation of mobile phone videos, webpages, broadcast TV footage and a proliferation of screens. One of the clearest examples of this tendency is Brian De Palma's simulated compilation documentary, *Redacted* (2007), a fictionalised reimagining of a genuine incident of rape and murder by US soldiers stationed in Iraq. *Redacted* appears to be composed entirely of found footage from a variety of sources and is described by Douglas Kellner as a 'strongly anti-war statement' and, somewhat generously given its confused liberalism, 'an avant-garde interrogation of media technology and the politics of representation' (Kellner 2010: 222; see also Bennett 2010).

The documentary turn

As De Palma's film demonstrates, one of the primary ways Anglo-American filmmakers have responded critically to this global explosion of violence, and its mediation – the corresponding global explosion of images – is through a turn to the production of documentaries, docudramas and dramatised documentaries, and 'activist cinema', although, notably, there is an increasing movement towards comic accounts of the war evident in such films as *Harold & Kumar Escape from Guantanamo Bay* (Jon Hurwitz & Hayden Schlossberg, 2008), *In the Loop* (Armando Iannucci, 2009) and *Four Lions* (Christopher Morris, 2010), or the UK TV sitcoms, *Gary: Tank Commander* (2009–12) and *Bluestone 42* (2013). Documentary is a potentially inexpensive form, not reliant upon stars, large crews, complex special effects or elaborate sets. The production and post-production schedules for documentary-style films can therefore be much shorter than for a fictional feature, allowing a film to enter circulation in rapid response to current events.[2] A documentary may also marshal greater rhetorical force than conventional fiction due to an abiding impression of indexicality or immediacy, and in different ways this connotation of immediacy and authenticity underpins the plethora of 'War on Terror' documentaries and fictional dramas from *Fahrenheit 9/11* (Michael Moore, 2004), *Ahlaam* (Mohamed Al Daradji, 2006), *Iraq in Fragments* (James Longley, 2006), *Heavy Metal in Baghdad* (Suroosh Alvi & Eddy Moretti, 2007), *Taxi to the Dark Side* (Alex Gibney, 2007), *The Hurt Locker* (Kathryn Bigelow, 2009), *Green Zone*, *Restrepo* (Tim Hetherington & Sebastian Junger, 2010) and *Route Irish* (Ken Loach, 2010), to the TV series, *Generation Kill* (2008) and *Occupation* (2009). Perhaps the clearest, most disturbing exemplification of documentary's status as objective record is *The Al Qaeda Plan* (Evan Kohlmann, 2008), a feature-length history of the terrorist organisation produced as evidence for the prosecution in the trial of Salim Ahmed Hamdan, Osama Bin Laden's former driver, at a Guantánamo Bay Military Tribunal.[3]

Docudrama, 'contingent truths' and a politics of aesthetics

The most interesting films produced during this period are those texts that acknowledge and examine the uncertain relations between actuality and fiction and Winterbottom's films exemplify this tendency. The imbrication of documentary and drama is a particularly appropriate device for the exploration of some of the specific questions raised by the War on Terror with regard to visibility, representation and mediation, because of the ethically/ontologically/generically problematic status of the dramatised documentary. Winterbottom has stated (echoing ethnographic filmmaker Jean Rouch)[4] that, 'I don't think there's a border between fiction and reality'.[5] While the delineation of this boundary in cinema may be unclear or mobile, nevertheless it is certainly the case that a number of his films are preoccupied with this border, crossing and re-crossing it repeatedly to varying effects.

Film theorist Bill Nichols suggests that films that mix documentary footage with filmed reconstructions in the interests of spectatorial engagement, or in order to compensate for the absence of useable or extant material, inevitably 'trade documentary authenticity for fictional identification' (Nichols 1991: 250). He argues that this practice involves filmmakers in ethical and political compromises that also risk undermining a film's 'credibility' since the result of such a collocation of actuality and staged sequences is that:

> the special indexical bond between image and historical referent is ruptured. In a re-enactment, the bond is still between the image and something that occurred in front of the camera but what occurred occurred *for* the camera. (Nichols 1991: 21)

Nichols recognises that 'historical indexicality' can never be guaranteed since 'one person's historical evidence is another person's fiction'; nevertheless, he insists that documentary and fiction are distinguished fundamentally by their referential function (Nichols 1991: 161). As he explains, 'Documentary shares the properties of a text with other fictions … but it addresses the world in which we live rather than worlds in which we may imagine living' (Nichols 1991: 112). Responding to this position, Derek Paget argues that this apparently clear distinction is untenable in relation to the dramatised documentary, a form that provocatively posits the equivalence of documentary and fiction, but that nevertheless remains directed towards lived reality:

> From its 'moment of presentation' in fictional, dramatic form dramadoc/ docudrama points beyond the realm of fiction to a realm of non-fiction that is always already lived. In one sense, all drama aspires to this condition, but this kind of drama, by pointing at an explicit rather than implicit reality, 'indexes' that explicit reality in ways that are difficult to ignore even if we deny them. (Paget 1998: 136)

In this respect, for Paget an insistence upon the irreducible distinction between drama and documentary is unhelpful in its disregard for the historical realities that dramatised documentaries both represent and trouble. While stating that 'some form of truth is the always receding goal of documentary film', Linda Williams contends that the political value of such films lies not in a demystificatory capacity to lay bare to us the truth of contemporary/historical reality behind a false perception, but in their particular capacity to intervene in the mediated public sphere (Williams 1998: 393). Williams acknowledges that the specific cultural context in which films are viewed will necessarily frame their meaning and so the truths represented or embodied by a particularly film are inevitably relative and partial, though not necessarily insignificant or ineffective. However, in the strategic deployment of staged scenes and reconstructions, documentary films can articulate 'contingent' truths that function to counter dangerous or destructive fictions. Thus for Williams:

> The choice is not between two entirely separate regimes of truth and fiction. The choice, rather, is in strategies of fiction for the approach to relative truths. Documentary is not fiction and should not be conflated with it. But documentary can and should use all the strategies of fictional construction to get at truths. (Williams 1998: 393–4)

In other words, the relative truth-value of documentaries is that they can work to challenge, qualify or affirm univocal truth claims already in circulation; they are texts that can interfere with the contexts through which they move, generating alternative or multiple perspectives. In bringing together different orders of material in this way, straddling the border fence between fiction and reality, Winterbottom's films constitute a potentially troubling, playful intervention amid the proliferation of justificatory, belligerent or putatively 'even-handed', liberal representations of the War on Terror.

In a film such as *The Road to Guantánamo*, the authenticity of those shots and scenes that appear to be unstaged gives a greater impact to those moments that are apparently dramatised, a quality Vivian Sobchack describes as the 'charge of the real' (Sobchack 2004). Writing on the interplay between represented reality and irreality in fiction films that incorporate documentary elements – such as real historical figures or star couples who play fictional couples – Sobchack argues that the distinction between these supposedly different elements of a film turns as much on the extra-textual knowledge and expectations with which films are viewed, as it does on any indexical properties or textual qualities of the film image. In this sense, the distinction between documentary and fiction film is more a distinction between different modes of spectatorship or consciousness, than a distinction between irreducibly different sequences of film. Moreover, Sobchack observes that our mode of spectatorial engagement is mobile or distracted, so that we typically move between these different modes of consciousness in the course of viewing a film. When, for example, we watch a scene with an actor playing a fictional character on a crowded city street we may find our attention wanders to fall on the people in the surrounding crowd as we reflect on whether they know they are in a film:

As we scrutinize their faces for signs of possible awareness of the camera filming them or of what suddenly becomes not the character but the actress acting in their midst, they no longer are generalized in status, no longer merely quasi characters necessary to the verisimilitude of the realist mise-en-scène. Rather, they become for us real people, ambiguous existential ciphers. (Sobchack 2004: 275)

Many scenes in Winterbottom's films are shot guerrilla-style with the actors required to improvise as they move through public spaces, and the scenario described by Sobchack characterises well the experience of watching many passages in his work. They pose the question not whether or not this is documentary – a question that is attendant on viewing any film or TV documentary and which is, in any case, unanswerable – but to what *degree* a particular scene may be considered to be documentary. As Sobchack suggests, this question is as likely to be posed by a fiction film since a shift of perspective, in which we recognise that what we are watching is a filmed record of a staged event, is a common experience of film-viewing. Indeed, we could ask whether this layered, distracted mode of spectatorship, a double perspective of a different order, always characterises film-viewing. For example, the success of a star performance is dependent upon our recognition that it is, precisely, a performance, no matter how unmediated, before a camera – a condition described by Graham Thompson as 'a mode of assessment of the "textual/character/actor" interaction', wherein the performance is not an objective profilmic event but subsists in the spectator's individualised reading of the performance as a set of mobile relations (Drake 2003: 187). Watching Angelina Jolie in the film, *Beyond Borders* (Martin Campbell, 2003), for example, we are presented with the character, Sarah Jordan, an international aid worker, and at the same time we understand that this is a performance and so we assess this as a more or less skilful technical construction by an actor. Since Jolie is a star, we are probably aware of other prominent roles she has played, such as fantasy action figures, which may colour our reading of this character and our knowledge of her celebrity identity as adoptive mother, political campaigner and UNESCO 'goodwill ambassador' will also frame our reading of the film with intertextual references. In addition to these three layers of meaning or performance Jolie may also be compared with other female performers to whom she is similar or from whom she is different. For Sobchack, such a process of interpretation rests on the 'compossibility' of documentary and fictional consciousness:

For a moment, then, in the midst of a fiction, we find ourselves in a documentary. This quite common experience demonstrates that although documentary and fictional consciousness are *incommensurable*, they are *compossible* in any given film. Furthermore, it demonstrates that documentary and verisimilar fictional space are constituted from the same worldly 'stuff' – the former giving existential ballast to the 'realism' of the latter even as its specificity is usually bracketed and put out of play and on the sidelines of our consciousness. (Sobchack 2004: 275)

The worldly 'stuff' of docudrama

The Road to Guantánamo, more clearly, perhaps, than any of Winterbottom's other films, is a heterogeneous aggregate of this 'worldly "stuff"'. Rather than carefully brackets eting the documentary material, pushing it safely to the margins, on the contrary Winterbottom's films often put it into play with the fictional components so that it is frequently unclear whether we are watching actuality or drama. The effect of this complex double perspective is that the dramatic reconstructions and conjectured sequences are given a 'charge of reality' from the documentary material (rather than being 'exposed' by this juxtaposition as fictional), while the distance between the documentary and reconstruction is largely maintained and made visible. At the same time, however, since the dramatised elements of the films are at times indistinguishable from documentary due to the use of improvisation, hand-held cameras, non-actors, and shooting on location with hidden microphones, the reliability of the documentary sequences is, in turn, put into question.

Take, for instance, a scene from *The Road to Guantánamo* in which the protagonists cross the border into Afghanistan. This opens with the caption, 'PAKISTAN-AFGHANISTAN BORDER 13 OCTOBER 2001', superimposed on what appears to be an excerpt from a contemporaneous British TV news report or documentary accompanied as it is by this fragmentary voice-over: 'Border trade continues unimpeded. Among those crossing are brave Afghan aid workers. The people rely on them for food and healthcare and to explain their needs to the outside world.' A montage of shots of shifting crowds of people, soldiers, motorbikes and trucks, is intercut with shots of the actors making their way across the border on foot or riding pillion on motorcycles. Shots in which Asif Iqbal and Ruhel Ahmed, the real individuals represented by two of the actors, recall their experience of crossing into Afghanistan are inserted into this sequence, and they are also heard speaking in voice-over during the montage. The rhythmic, non-diegetic music that plays quietly throughout this sequence helps to 'smooth over' the multiple cuts, making it difficult to identify the precise points of transition between the different elements.

This uncertainty – what Sobchack terms an 'unsettling epistemological ambiguity' and one newspaper review of the film describes as 'a kind of vertigo in the viewer, an almost philosophical confusion about the literalness of the filmed image' – has varying affects in Winterbottom's films, but I would suggest it is rarely experienced as radically disruptive or unsettling by the spectator (Scott 2006). One of the main reasons for this is that this montage of different orders of material is a very familiar televisual aesthetic. A huge number of TV programmes combine dramatic reconstructions with other types of material in a casual and sometimes indifferent fashion that Raymond Williams' characterisation of broadcast TV output as non-linear, discontinuous, heterogeneous 'flow' identifies as the general organising principle underlying the medium, but is perhaps better described by John Ellis who describes television's formal characteristic as 'segmentation' (Williams 1975: 86; Ellis 1990:116).

Thus, Winterbottom's segmented films draw on the expectations and cognitive aptitudes of the television viewer adept at reading across different types of material and so, for example, expository voice-over commentary is intermittent (except where the film incorporates excerpts from news programmes) and there are no captions to indicate when we are watching a reconstruction with actors or even that the film tells a 'true story'. The deployment of a televisual aesthetic with *The Road to Guantánamo* can be explained in part by the film's financing by a TV company (a feature of much recent film production in Europe), as well as by Winterbottom's background in directing TV drama. It could also be understood as an effect/acknowledgement of the increasing convergence of film and television – a movement that is suggested by the decision to adopt the new business model pioneered with this film of releasing a film in several media formats simultaneously.[6]

In addition to its rhetorical force, docudrama is a form that also allows filmmakers to overcome practical restrictions of documentary such as the scarcity or non-existence of compelling material. According to Winterbottom, the dramatised sequences were 'all improvised', and the improvisations based on the transcripts of interviews with Iqbal, Ahmed and Rasul by co-director Mat Whitecross (Anon. 2006a: 11). While there remains a large degree of conjecture in the dramatisation of the accounts of the three men, the function of these sequences is primarily illustrative; they show us, more or less, what happened to these men and, in doing so, offer an account of the war in Afghanistan and the management of the Guantánamo Bay prison that is unavailable from the perspective of western news and entertainment media. They make visible what is hidden from view and in this respect dramatised documentary is simply an expedient form that enables the filmmakers to show what is practically unfilmable. As TV producer Ian McBride puts it, the format allows filmmakers to 'take the camera where the camera couldn't go, loosen wooden tongues, rehearse the evidence when the witnesses were all dead or too dutifully mute to testify' (McBride 2005: 488). It comprises an exchange in which documentary devices lend enhanced authenticity or plausibility to the fictional elements establishing the implicit compact with a spectator that dialogue, characters and events are broadly historically accurate. In turn, the fictional trappings bring with them the dynamics of drama and narrative cogency. The boundaries where historical record folds into speculative fiction are usually intentionally unclear, so that the spectator is undistracted by the divergence between what he or she knows or assumes about a historical moment and its depiction. Managing the relationship between conjectural or invented passages and dramatic reconstructions or archival footage is a formal problem on one level, but is also a point of ethical and political tension. As a form, docudrama can have a particularly complex, supple relationship to questions of veracity and a sophisticated relationship with audiences increasingly skilled at interpreting different representational orders of material, given that 'the presumed border between the real and the fabricated in the world of mass-mediated representation, never so intact, is currently in serious disrepair' (Renov 1999: 318). In this context, the documentarist's ethical responsibility to minimise editorial manipulation, or to retain visible traces of manipulation, while relying upon the rhetorical and affective power of visible evidence to carry an argument, weighs just as heavily upon the docudrama director. It is no surprise that a number of directors have returned to docudrama as an appropriate format for contemporary political cinema –

in Michael Shapiro's terms, a counteractant cinematic 'politics of aesthetics' – but this comes with risks (Shapiro 2007: 311).

Reframing the War on Terror: alternative histories and The Shock Doctrine

As a body of work, Winterbottom's films explore various configurations of fictional, imagined or conjectured material and actuality footage, which render the boundaries between fiction and document unclear, inconsistent and mobile. Documentary thus remains a productively unstable term that invites us to consider its general adequacy as a framing approach and thereby also to reflect upon the ways in which the War on Terror has been framed. Commissioned by the UKTV channel, More4, but also screened internationally in cinemas and on television, *The Shock Doctrine*[7] (co-directed with Mat Whitecross[8]) is a comparatively conventional documentary, eschewing overt self-reflexivity and formal experimentation in a polemical abridgement of Naomi Klein's book of the same name. The film is a densely compressed, fast-moving aggregation of a great deal of archival film, television clips and interviews, interwoven with footage of Klein lecturing in the US and conducting field-work in Baghdad, Chile and Sri Lanka, and animated graphic visualisations that summarise statistics and illustrate passages from the CIA's 'KUBARK Counter-intelligence Interrogation' manual. Some of the archival footage appears to have had synchronous sound effects such as gunfire, explosions and crowd noise added while elsewhere the sound has been amplified, and varied background music (including a Michael Nyman music cue from *A Zed and Two Noughts*) is used discreetly throughout to produce a dynamic, affectively engaging text. This material is colligated through an expository non-diegetic 'voice-of-God' narration delivered by Kieran O'Brien in his fourth collaboration with Winterbottom. This is a significant choice of narrator, signalling the status of the film as a multiply authored reinterpretation of the book, rather than a neutral transcoding of the narrative from one medium to another. As Klein, who has no credit in the film, observed in response to UK newspaper reports that she had disowned the project:

> the original idea was for me to write and narrate the film. For that to have worked out, however, there would have needed to be complete agreement between the directors and myself about the content, tone and structure of the film. As often happens in collaborations, we had different ideas about how to tell this story and build the argument. (Klein 2009)

As a result, she explained, 'we all – Michael, the producers, and I – came up with a compromise: that someone other than me would narrate and that it would be clear in all materials that this was not my film but rather Michael and Mat's adaptation of my book' (ibid.).

The Shock Doctrine opens with film of Klein delivering a lecture at Loyola University in which she proposes, 'A state of shock is what happens to us when we lose our narrative – when we lose our story'. The film is thus presented as an attempt to produce a compensatory narrative that can reorient an audience stunned and confused by a period of global instability marked by natural disasters, the War on Terror and recession. The story told is that of the emergence of a fundamentalist ideology of free-market capitalism, developed by monetarist economist Milton Friedman at the Chicago School of Economics, and the consequences of the application of this rational economic theory to the management of real economies. The narrative begins by recounting the enthusiastic use of experimental electro-shock therapy and sensory deprivation by psychiatrist Ewen Cameron at McGill University in the early 1950s as a means of 'de-patterning' or erasing his patients' identities in order to allow him to rebuild their personalities from scratch, and the adaptation of this research by the CIA as the basis for techniques of interrogation and torture that were detailed in the 1963 KUBARK manual. A parallel is then drawn between the deployment of catastrophic shock in order to dismantle and rebuild an individual's personality and Friedman's conviction that drastic social and political crises offered the opportunity to rebuild an economy and, by extension, a society, around free market principles, or what Klein terms, 'disaster capitalism'. As the film makes clear, the relationship between torture and the disassembly and reconstruction of economies is not merely a suggestive analogy, since the CIA directly supported the imposition of free market legislation in several key instances while torture was liberally employed by these repressive new regimes often following the CIA's counter-insurgency guidelines as taught at the US Defense Department's 'School of the Americas'. The film traces a succession of crises in which Friedman-trained economists, the 'Chicago Boys', intervened to rebuild economies in the wake of social upheavals in order to put Friedman's theory into practice and test the validity of the model. These include the military coup in Chile on 11th September 1973 (a date invested with ominous irony in the context of this narrative of US-sponsored trans-national violence), the military coup in Argentina in 1976, the dissolution of the Soviet Union, the Falklands war, the terrorist attacks of 11th September 2001 and the subsequent wars in Afghanistan and Iraq, the Sri Lankan tsunami in 2004, the devastation of New Orleans by hurricane in 2005 and the global financial crisis that took hold in 2008. In each case, economists, diplomats, politicians and military forces moved very quickly to exploit these intervals of uncertainty in order to introduce radical economic legislation that included slashing or abolishing the minimum wage, removing price controls, selling nationalised industries, dismantling the welfare system and putting public services out to tender, deregulating the financial system and removing protectionist barriers to the international flow of capital. As the film observes, the effects of these economic transformations were often disastrous, causing acute civil unrest, mass unemployment and plunging countries into deep recessions – in Russia the number living in poverty increased by 72 million during the 1990s. Therefore, in order for such policies to be irreversibly embedded and to begin to take effect, in each case it was necessary for inevitable popular resistance to be contained. From the destruction of the National Union of Miners in Britain in the 1980s to the 'disappearing' of critics of the Argentinian military dictatorship in the 1970s, it is argued by the film that free market policies could only be imposed by anti-democratic force, crushing resistance and silencing dissent – ironically the freeing of the market depends upon the suspension by decree of many literal freedoms. Thus, the 'shock doctrine' of disaster capitalism consists of three successive mutually rein-forcing shocks– the initial shock, such as the bombing and occupation of Iraq, that permits the introduction of new economic policy, the shock that is induced by these policies, such as rapid inflation and economic collapse, and the protracted shock that is required to enforce the policies. The effect of the shock doctrine, Klein explains, with reference to the forced internal displacement of coastal dwellers to clear space for hotels and luxury accommodation in the aftermath of the Sri Lankan tsunami, is 'the systematic raiding of the public sphere in the aftermath of a disaster when people are too focused on the emergency, on their daily concerns, to protect their interests'.

Situated in this history of the brutal effects of free market capitalism, the War on Terror is framed not as a singular, unprecedented event but as a further oppor-tunity for the application of these policies in the reorganisation of a real economy. Harlan Ullman who conceived 'Shock and Awe', the strategy of opening an assault with a sustained, overwhelming and spectacularly catastrophic bombardment that was employed against Baghdad in 2002, explains it in the film as a means of softening up the opponent through collective sensory deprivation. The film makes clear the relationship between Cameron's medical treatments and this form of military shock therapy, but what distinguishes the War on Terror from other episodes of disaster capitalism recounted in the film is that it is also depicted as the clearest instance of self-interested economic imperialism as well as a superpower's triumphal display of military dominance. As the narrator observes over a montage of images of protesting crowds, a missile-launch, and shots of Pakistani President Pervez Musharraf making a speech:

> There were many justifications given for the invasion of Iraq, but if the US had really wanted to attack a country where the leaders of Al Qaeda were thought to be hiding, which had nuclear weapons, and was selling nuclear technology to other countries, then Pakistan would have been the obvious choice.[9] It had close connections to the Taliban, and was being run by a military dictator. Instead, George Bush chose to target Iraq, a country with the third largest oil reserves in the world.

In telling the story of the dissemination of a particularly destructive form of capitalism and its consequences, *The Shock Doctrine* has an explicitly polemical agenda, and in this respect is a conventional campaigning documentary, intending to expose the anti-democratic, violent condition of neo-liberal or 'free-market' capitalism. However, it is also stressed repeatedly that it is engaged with the construction of a narrative, and this understanding of history as a nexus of narratives rather than a sequence of objective events – that history is always already mediated – is exemplified by the film's heavy reliance upon found footage. It is acknowledged in the film that the assertive power of the documentary rests on its capacity to tell a coherent, convincing story.

The film offers a reinterpretation of recent history through a recombination of historical texts from various sources including other documentary films, amateur footage, news reportage, propaganda material, photography and official documents.

Stock footage – the mediation of history (troops suppressing dissent in Chile; Margaret Thatcher speaking at a Conservative Party conference)

Moreover, in its selective examination of the previous eighty years of world history (extending back to Roosevelt's New Deal), the film may be seen as a reflection upon the rhetoric of historiography and the way that competing historical narratives structure our comprehension of historical events and constitute the basis for decisions and understanding in the present. For example, Klein is shown explaining during a public lecture, 'What I'm trying to do in *The Shock Doctrine* is tell an alternative history of how this savage stream of pure capitalism that we've been living – capitalism unrestrained – came to dominate the world.' It is proposed in the film that the success of this form of unbound capitalism is due partly to the shattering dominance of a particular narrative that insists repeatedly that there is no alternative to unregulated capitalism as a means of social and economic organisation. This world-view, one that refuses to recognise as rational any alternative positions (much less the fundamental irrationality of capitalism in its systemic tendency towards waste and over-production) and understands the dissolution of the Soviet Union as evidence of the inevitable triumph of the market, is described elsewhere by Mark Fisher as capitalist realism: 'the widespread sense that not only is capitalism the only viable political and economic system, but also that it is now impossible even to *imagine* a coherent alternative to it' (Fisher 2009: 2).

In the face of the 'grand narrative' of capitalist realism, the film counters with a demystifying alternative story, erecting a protective shield to insulate the informed viewer from the shock effect of the neo-liberal narrative. As Klein explains to an audience towards the end of the film:

Naomi Klein lecturing on
Milton Friedman at the
University of Chicago

The shock doctrine as a strategy relies on us not knowing about it for it to
work, and what I find most hopeful about the current crisis is that this tactic is
getting tired, because that element of surprise is no longer there. We are on to
them and it's not working. We are becoming shock-resistant.

Perhaps because of its genesis in compromise, the film has a somewhat uncertain status
in relation to the book. The sequences in which Klein delivers public lectures function
as exegetic narration – her voice is sometimes over-laid upon montage sequences and
accompanied by incidental music – but since in these sequences she is not addressing
the camera, but the audience in front of her, she occupies an ambivalent role as both
narrator and co-author of the film, and also its subject matter. When she refers to
The Shock Doctrine, for example, it seems that she is referring to the book she wrote,
rather than to the film in which she is participating. Klein is an engaging, confident
and lucid speaker, but in some respects an awkward presence in the film as she appears
only intermittently, and the sequences in which she is shown doing field-work or
conducting an on-camera interview with one of Cameron's former patients, are redundant in terms of the film's argument. Brief shots of Klein sporting a hijab on the streets
of Baghdad in 2004 – or visiting a former torture site in Chile with the widow of
Orlando Letelier, a member of the Allende socialist government ousted by the Pinochet
coup, tortured and later assassinated in Washington DC – do nothing to substantiate
the film's argument, but rather suggest an underlying uncertainty about whether the
film is a commentary upon the book and its high-profile author, illustrated lecture, or

Klein doing field work in
post-tsunami Sri Lanka

adaptation. The cartoonish animations resembling the illustrative graphics employed on TV news programmes, interstitials and adverts are also superfluous interruptions, used only occasionally in the film. Appropriated from a short 2007 promotional film for the book made by Klein, Alfonso Cuarón and Jonás Cuarón, they resemble book illustrations coming to life and stencilled graffiti moving across concrete walls, but since the graphic aesthetic of the rest of the film is comparatively simple, with white captions and white-on-black intertitles, these insertions emphasise a conceptual uncertainty about Winterbottom's film, and perhaps indicate the film Klein would like to have made.

Perhaps also as a result of compromise, the heterogeneous film is at points variously incoherent and simplistic. It is inconsistent in its construction of a spectatorial position, since certain passages of the film seem to assume minimal fore-knowledge on the part of the spectator, whereas other sequences require a deeper familiarity with the historical background to the events recounted. At some points the narrative voice-over resorts to sound-bites, observing of Russia's economic restructuring under President Yeltsin, for instance, that, 'It was all shock, no therapy', while at another point the narration presupposes a more sophisticated knowledge of the background to the events narrated: the voice-over describes the sacking of half a million Iraqi state workers by the Coalition Provisional Authority as an act of 'De-Ba'athification', without explaining the term or the policy of dismantling the Iraqi branch of the pan-Arab socialist party. Elsewhere, in a sequence on the Guantánamo Bay prison, the film briefly introduces the three British men that are the subject of *The Road to Guantánamo*. Rather arbitrarily, they are shown playing football in a park,[10] and this is followed by a fifteen-second clip of Shafiq Rasul recalling the experience of confinement, but there is no mention of the particular circumstances of their arrest (while on holiday) or the physical trials they endured. Presumably, they are introduced into the film as a form of proof – witnesses to the bankruptcy of the prison – but the compressed structure of the film gives them almost no space to speak. Broader criticisms that might be levelled at the film are that it fails to examine the ideological and intellectual basis for Friedman's thought, or to detail the mechanisms, such as the central roles of the World Bank and the International Monetary Fund, by which these ideas were transmitted globally, and, perhaps, that it over-states the significance of macro-economic policy in effecting social change.

The adaptation of a book to a (79-minute) film always necessitates acts of selection, condensation, embellishment, expansion and substitution. However, Klein's symptomatic presence in the film as a contributing author is an indication that Whitecross and Winterbottom (like the filmmakers in *A Cock and Bull Story*) have failed to resolve the process of cinematic or televisual adaptation, which typically requires not fidelity or respect for an original, but the displacement and symbolic eradication of the source literary text by the film in order for it to have an independent status. With this film, Klein's book remains under erasure but visible, the film acting both as a relay to the book and as a supplement. There remains a tension between Klein's emancipatory project and the tendency of Whitecross and Winterbottom's film to acknowledge that the project consists of competing stories, but it is apt that a film concerned with the problem of history retains the narrative traces of its own development within its structure.

The Shock Doctrine stands apart from Winterbottom's other films due to its focus upon a complex field of events and individuals. The contrary melodramatic tendency underlying most of Winterbottom's films and dramas is to structure a narrative around the interactions of a couple or a small group of individuals that can serve as the basis for the navigation and mapping of broader social relationships, networks and historical structures of feeling. Whereas this means that complexity emerges from an apparently simple narrative premise, such as the close scrutiny of localised events within a household, or between family members as in *Wonderland* or *Everyday*, one of the distinctive features of *The Shock Doctrine* is a reductive insistence upon narrative coherence in the face of a complex scenario. Rather than searching for complexity in simplicity, the film identifies simple patterns in complex historical formations. More than Winterbottom's other films, this is structured as an argument and so linearity, repetition and redundancy are crucial components here, whereas linearity is far less evident in the 'network narrative' (see Bordwell 2007) of *Wonderland*, for example, or the fractured structure of *9 Songs*. *The Shock Doctrine* is a provocation that depends for its effect upon its comprehensibility, but it also provides a conceptual schema through which to view recent history by taking an apparently unrelated series of events and identifying the underlying continuity. The film comprises a corrective lens through which to view recent history and in doing so it is crucial that it is readily assimilable. It is an instrumental film, a tool, rather than a finished work, that also provides a critical context for other War on Terror films – including Winterbottom's – in its refusal of the idea that the War on Terror is a discrete campaign that is motivated or explainable solely by the 11th September terrorist attacks on New York and Washington DC, events that have become over-determined or fetishised as radically new and radically transformative.

The comedy of terror

The War on Terror has constituted a very significant backdrop to Winterbottom's filmmaking practice. He had also intended to direct a fifth film addressing the topic, adapted from *Murder in Samarkand* (2007), former British Ambassador Craig Murray's account of his diplomatic posting to Uzbekistan from 2002 to 2004. This memoir recounts Murray's increasingly frustrated attempts to alert an indifferent British government to the use of torture and other human rights abuses by the repressive Uzbekistan regime under the rule of autocratic president, Islam Karimov, which culminated in Murray's removal from the post of ambassador in 2004 and subsequent dismissal. Winterbottom describes the book, in which Murray depicts himself as a flawed character vainly trying to do an impossible job, hold on to his marriage and family back in the UK while conducting an affair with an Uzbek woman, as 'a very funny version of a Graham Greene novel',[11] and it is possible to imagine the comic film that might have emerged with comedian Steve Coogan having agreed to play Murray. Uzbekistan was regarded by Britain and the US as an ally in the War on Terror, since it co-operated with 'extraordinary rendition' operations, and, as Murray discovered, it was therefore effectively exempt from international accountability for the human rights violations he exposed. Thus the book addresses the moral shifts characterising the state of exception enabled by the War on Terror. For instance, as Murray observes, the British government was itself building a legal case during this period for the use of intelligence gained through torture: 'In October 2005 ... they argued for a threefold use of this intelligence: to guide security operations, to detain without trial, and as evidence in a court of law [...] Thus, the British government is quite shameless in its desire to obtain and use the fruits of torture, and remains a great customer for the products of the torture chambers of dictators like Karimov worldwide' (Murray 2007: 365). Winterbottom's production company, Revolution Films, purchased an option to adapt the book and playwright David Hare was commissioned by Paramount to write the screenplay, but for several reasons, including Hare's decision to write a non-comic script, the film was never realised. As Winterbottom explained in 2010:

> When we got David Hare's script, it was totally not what we were talking about. That was a bit awkward. We tried to carry on. We went looking for places to film. But you can't film in Uzbekistan and that, combined with the idea of a black comedy about torture... well, maybe the moment has gone. (Cooke 2010)[12]

Passing reference to the conflict is also made in the comic film about filmmaking, *A Cock and Bull Story*, as a BBC radio news bulletin is heard on the soundtrack while one of the protagonists is being driven to the film set for the day's shoot. The news reader announces the headlines, 'the Americans have conceded that the insurgents in Iraq are as strong now as they were a year ago, more foreign terror suspects are expected to be freed on bail today as time runs out for the existing powers under which they are detained, and, what Churchill thought of India, and what India thought of Churchill'. The images accompanying this report are of a misty, pastoral English landscape at dawn, an oak tree in a wheat-field in the pink light of the low sun, a rural church surrounded by trees, and cows grazing in a field. This juxtaposition demonstrates with great economy that the War on Terror has become an insistent, intimate part of the political and cultural landscape during the last decade. These romantic images epitomising timeless, complacent nationhood are framed by the voice-over that insists upon the irrepressible reality of the devastating war Britain is participating in, and which is not just taking place 'over there', but returns to haunt even the most idyllic spaces. This apparently peaceful landscape, the calm, institutional voice reminds us, is simultaneously a violently repressive terrain of paranoia, Islamophobia and indefinite detention. The invocation of Churchill further implies that the War on Terror is not a historically isolated event, but is embedded within a history of imperialist violence that extends back through the British government's responsibility for the creation and violent administration of Iraq after World War One and the dissolution of the Ottoman Empire, and Churchill's recommendation in 1919, as Secretary for War and Air, that poison gas be used to suppress a revolt by Iraqi Kurds.

The fact that the filmmakers in *A Cock and Bull Story* are occupied with the technical and logistical challenges of staging a convincingly spectacular reconstruction of a battle for the cameras (which in turn is based on a comic fictional character's unreliable recall of a real event in which he supposedly participated) has an added irony at a historical moment in which the reality of war has become indistinguishable from its hallucinatory representations when viewed from a distance and through multiple levels of mediation. As Jean Baudrillard observed during the first Gulf war, a crucial shortfall in debates around the highly stage-managed war was a disregard for the ontological problem of representations of the war – to what extent can the reality of the war (or any contemporary war) be distinguished from representations of it:

> There is no interrogation into the event itself or its reality: or into the fraudulence of this war, the programmed and always delayed illusion of battle: or into the machination of this war and its amplification by information, not to mention the improbable orgy of material, the systematic manipulation of data, the artificial dramatisation. (Baudrillard 1995: 58)

As a result of this critical incapacity, Baudrillard cautions, 'the day there is a real war you will not even be able to tell the difference. The real victory of the simulators of war is to have drawn everyone into this rotten simulation' (Baudrillard 1995: 58–9). This collapse of reality into simulation is the object of satire in *A Cock and Bull Story*, and in different ways, *In this World*, *The Road to Guantánamo* and *A Mighty Heart* problematise and exploit this collapse, exposing the permeability of the borders between reality and representation, an issue that takes on a much greater urgency when, as Judith Butler suggests, 'there is no way to separate, under present historical conditions, the material reality of war from those representational regimes through which it operates and which rationalize its own operation' (Butler 2009: 29). Winterbottom's films are engaged with making these representational regimes visible.

As with *The Shock Doctrine*, Winterbottom's War on Terror trilogy is engaged with the political project of recounting alternative histories that counteract the dominant construction and interpretation of recent history, repeated with minor variations through a variety of media iterations, which asserts that the story of the War on Terror is the story of the more or less unjustified invasion of Iraq and Afghanistan in retaliation for the terrorist attacks in September 2001. Rather than return again to this problematic narrative, Winterbottom's films tell the stories of a selection of border-crossers and observers – refugees, tourists and a pregnant journalist – individuals with varying agency, cultural and political capital, whose lives are catastrophically transformed by the conflict. Instead of framing the War on Terror in tragic terms as an epic ideological struggle, as an abstracted sequence of political and military strategic decisions and misjudgements by an élite, or as the thrillingly disorienting experience of navigating through a warzone, the films depict the banal, crushing experience of living in a state of terror. That is, they are concerned with quotidian horrors, with the violence, frustrating impotence and humiliations of living with the War on Terror. Terror in these films is not spectacularised as a series of grand events (whose redundancy through repetitive *re*-presentation robs them of any explanatory power), but rather it constitutes a new regime, a state of exception whose protracted, unstable affective experience is that of anguish, panic, uncertainty and distrust, alienation and incommunicability, loneliness, fleeting sociality, optimism and despair. Terror is depicted in these films not as the paralysing fear of an external force, but as an immanent component of mundane reality, a structuring principle underlying social relations and intimate encounters, the policing of borders, legislation and policy-making that the characters in these stories have to endure and adapt to in the hope of eventual relief and home-coming. What the protagonists of these films have in common (with each other and with protagonists of other films by the director) is that they find themselves stranded far from home in a hostile environment, and so the affective experience of the War on Terror depicted in these films is crystallised in this experience of dislocation, impotence and limited comprehension.

The following sections of this chapter discuss the three films of the War on Terror trilogy in detail, examining their depiction of a range of experiences of the War on Terror. They are not examined following the sequence in which they were released, but instead are organised in relation to the narrative centrality of the War on Terror, from the most indirect to the most direct.

In This World: border cinema and political affect

Border anxiety currently dominates the political rhetoric of Western governments and has been dutifully amplified by the corporate news media, and with growing intensity in the wake of 2001. In the US, Australia and Europe ever-tighter national and international border controls have accompanied the implementation of harsh and punitive asylum, immigration and terror laws and the establishment and normalisation of paranoid surveillance cultures. A significant body of 'border theory' has emerged during the last decade in response to the new politics of the border, exposing the ways in which the geo-political landscape impacts unequally on the movement and flow of people, objects and images (Ahmed 2000: 115).[13] In bringing feminist concerns with the 'micro-political' to bear upon critiques of global capital, transnational feminist theory has produced some of the most vital accounts of the border politics of the present.[14] What is important about this scholarship is that it theorises the asymmetrical relations of power *and* knowledge that characterise international borders through a focus on the complex border zones of racial, sexual and economic exploitation – social, political and intimate spaces of encounter with which a number of Winterbottom's films are concerned, from California in the 1860s (*The Claim*) to Northern Ireland in the 1980s and 1990s (*Love Lies Bleeding, With or Without You*), India in the present (*Trishna*) and Shanghai in the future (*Code 46*).

The border has become a central theme within a range of international films that might be categorised as 'the cinema of borders' due to their central preoccupation with border-crossing. Hamid Naficy suggests that 'border films' are characterised formally by fragmentation, multilingualism and liminal characters, and explore themes that 'involve journeying, historicity, identity, and displacement' (Naficy 2001: 4, see also

Bennett and Tyler 2007). Far from depicting the world as a borderless global village, border films depict the underside of cosmopolitanism, a world of barriers, fences, checkpoints, exploitation and death. This is a cinema concerned with what Judith Butler describes as 'those "unlivable" and "uninhabitable" zones of social life' that are nevertheless 'densely populated by those who do not enjoy the status of the subject' (Butler 1993: 3). However, the risk of any relatively mainstream film about borders is that both the filmmakers, and the film's audiences, become border tourists. Focusing on an analysis of the ways in which immigrants and refugees are made visible and knowable within this highly acclaimed 'British' border film, this discussion probes the extent to which this film problematises the hegemonic politics of the border.

In This World is a highly affecting account of the attempt of two Afghan refugees, the teenage Jamal (Jamal Udin Torabi) and his older cousin, Enayatullah (Enayatullah Jumaudin), to travel illegally to Britain from the massive Shamshatoo refugee camp near Peshawar in Pakistan in search of a liveable life.[15] Thus, although the film is not directly concerned with the War on Terror, it addresses the heightened anxieties about border security and immigration that have been a significant component of the representational regime of this war, and, like *The Shock Doctrine* and the other films in the trilogy, it implicitly identifies Pakistan rather than Iraq or the US as the flashpoint.

In November 2001, very soon after the bombing of Afghanistan began, Winterbottom and screenwriter Tony Grisoni travelled to Pakistan on tourist visas where they visited refugee camps, including Shamshatoo, which is home to 70,000 Pashtun Afghan refugees. They then embarked on the journey from Peshawar to London, tracing the people-smuggling route that was to be taken by the film's central characters. In December 2001, casting director Wendy Brazington flew to Pakistan to identify two Afghan refugees to play the principal roles. She found Enayatullah in a chance encounter in one of Peshawar's Afghan markets, and came across Jamal (born in the Shamshatoo camp) in a school where she held auditions. Filming began early in 2002, and the story was shot like a documentary with small, hand-held DV cameras. The final 88-minute cut was edited from over 200 hours of footage shot as the three-person crew (Winterbottom, cinematographer Marcel Zyskind and sound recordist, Stuart Wilson) travelled with the two non-professional actors along a route through Pakistan, Iran, Turkey, Italy and France to the UK.

Enayat (Enayatullah) and
Jamal (Jamal Udin Torabi)
detained at the Pakistan/
Iran border in *In This World*

The differential power relations involved in cross-border mobility were evident from the outset in the difficulty faced by the production team in acquiring visas for Jamal and Enayatullah. As Afghan refugees in Pakistan they had precarious citizenship status, and since they were recognised as neither Afghanis nor Pakistani nationals, it was almost impossible to acquire travel documents for them. The problems faced in gaining official permission for these two actors to travel across borders encapsulates the issue of unequal access to mobility at the heart of the film; the filmmakers, as (white) European citizens, were able to cross national borders with little difficulty, while the actors found their movement endlessly and forcibly curtailed. Even with tourist visas, Jamal and Enayatullah's bodies simply did not fit the available 'touristic' subject position.

The difficulties encountered in cross-border travel during production leak into and shape the meaning of the finished film in a number of ways. Like Steve Coogan and Rob Brydon elsewhere, the actors play characters who share their names, emphasising the way actuality bleeds into fiction, and, furthermore, the difficulty in getting permission to shoot the film resulted in more improvisation than originally intended. The filmmakers resorted to shooting without permits, recording sound with discreet radio microphones hidden in the actors' clothes. Indeed, it was only when the extemporised dialogue between Jamal and Enayatullah – who spoke Farsi – was translated during post-production that the filmmakers discovered what the two actors had been saying.[16] Although this blurring of the boundary between 'fiction' and 'reality' is partly an effect of the contingencies of low-budget film production, it effectively amplifies the film's attention to the politics of border crossing and its affective power.

The film opens with few credits and no incidental music. An expository voice-over (in English) provides background information about the Shamshattoo camp to accompany the initial montage of shots of the camp and its occupants. This opening sequence introduces the central character, Jamal, who is shown manufacturing bricks with a group of other children. The voice-over informs us that Jamal, an orphan, faces a life stranded in the refugee camp earning less than one dollar a day. Born in the camp, Jamal cannot leave it for Afghanistan, nor can he legitimately travel across other national borders. If Jamal belongs anywhere, it is within this densely populated interzone. Jamal's cousin, Enayatullah (or Enayat) lives with many other Afghan refugees in nearby Peshawar and when Jamal learns that Enayat's uncle has decided to pay people-smugglers to take him to London, Jamal introduces them to a man who can arrange this. Faced with no future in the refugee camp, Jamal, who can speak English, persuades Enayat to accept him as a travelling companion and interpreter, and in February 2002 they embark on their search for a liveable life.

The narrative follows Jamal and Enayat's arduous, disorienting and increasingly desperate 4,000-mile journey, in which they travel variously in pick-ups, buses, trucks, shipping containers, ferries, trains and on foot. Periods of frustrating, tedious immobility are interspersed with intervals of frantic movement in which they try to evade border patrols and negotiate checkpoints. The film's most harrowing sequence depicts the journey from Istanbul to Trieste, when, along with a number of other refugees, Jamal and Enayat are sealed inside an air-tight metal box, hidden on a container truck that then boards a ferry for Italy. During this two-day trip all of the passengers suffocate, except for Jamal and Mehti, the infant child of a couple they had befriended earlier in their journey. The screen is almost entirely black during this brief scene, the only illumination the weak light of a torch, and all we can see are glimpses of faces in the darkness, accompanied by the travellers' voices. The scene takes us from the initial friendly small-talk between the travellers to their angry, panic-stricken shouts for help as they pound on the walls and demand to be let out, until finally only Jamal's desperate voice can be heard, trying to elicit a response from his unconscious cousin. The fragmentary editing of the sequence powerfully conveys the disorientation and growing panic of the refugees, giving us little sense of how much time has passed. The short scene does not linger on the awful experience – a cutaway to an image of an animated map showing the ferry's route and the caption, '40 HOURS LATER', spare us much of the horror – but it is no less upsetting because of this elision. Although we can see almost nothing, the dark images invite us to imagine what it must feel like for Jamal and the other refugees (and also the fifty-eight Chinese illegal immigrants who died in identical circumstances travelling to the UK from Belgium in 2000).[17]

Towards the end of the film, Jamal finally arrives at the Sangatte refugee centre in Calais on the north-west coast of France. He makes the last stage of his journey from France to Britain by stowing away underneath a truck. The final scene depicts an enervated, world-weary Jamal washing dishes in a London café months after setting out on his hellish journey. Jamal phones Peshawar from the café to report that he has arrived, and to tell Enayat's father that his son is no longer 'in this world'. The phone call is followed by a montage sequence showing young children in the Shamshattoo camp peering at the camera, posing and playing in front of it, before the film concludes with shots of Jamal walking on his own through London and arriving at a mosque to pray. The sentimental shots of the children in Pakistan, richly coloured with yellow filters make a striking contrast with the grey, wintry light of London, accompanied by plaintive music, emphasise what Jamal has lost in making his horrific journey: his family – especially his younger brother to whom he is shown saying goodbye at the beginning – and his childhood. Another upsetting implication of this sequence is that the trajectories traced by Jamal and Enayat represent the only lines of flight available to the children left behind at Shamshattoo: trauma and/or death. With regard to the

Shamshattoo refugee camp

Jamal in London

question of which life is more liveable for a refugee, the border-lands of Shamshattoo or an 'illegal' life in London among strangers, the ending is decidedly ambiguous.

Political affect, the child refugee and blurred boundaries

In This World concludes with a series of intertitles explaining that after being refused asylum in Britain in 2002, Jamal was granted 'exceptional leave' to stay but is due to be expelled from Britain on the day before his eighteenth birthday. What remains unclear from this epilogue is that this information pertains to the real Jamal, who returned to London by himself after the filming was completed, following a similar route to that taken by the film crew (while, ironically, Enayatullah used his earnings to buy a truck to haul goods across the border between Kabul and Peshawar). This raises disturbing questions about the extent to which the filmmakers intervened in the course of Jamal's life. Writing about the film, Winterbottom notes:

> In one sense, the film is not his story – we set up that journey, after all, and who knows if he would have made it on his own steam. But I like the confusion that exists now between Jamal the character and Jamal the person. (Winterbottom 2003)

Winterbottom's decision to use this extra-diegetic information in order to add affective weight to his film is revealing. He has made clear in interviews and press releases that he set out to make the film as a direct response to the overwhelmingly negative representations of asylum-seekers by politicians and in the British news media. *In This World* aims explicitly to inspire empathy in an imagined European audience for the economic migrants and refugees pushing toward European ports and checkpoints. Although xenophobic discourses within the news media consistently depict refugees as a dehumanised, undifferentiated foreign mass pressing against and breaching national borders, *In This World* asks its audience to recognise 'the human face' of specific, individual refugees, aiming to demonstrate reassuringly that, 'close-up', they are 'just like us'. The aim to inspire empathy through identification is a favoured device of Western humanitarian literature on refugees, which draws on photographic close-ups of refugees' faces, and documentaries that employ first-person accounts of refugee experiences to provoke sympathetic responses in first world audiences. The intimate rhetoric of the close-up is intended to move audiences in ways that will enable 'us' to identify with the victims of repressive asylum laws and border controls (see Tyler 2006). *In This World* mixes these humanitarian devices with the generic conventions of melodrama to create a highly emotive film – one that moves its audience to tears.

In This World generates its political affect through the central figure of Jamal, the refugee child. Two of Winterbottom's other films, *Welcome to Sarajevo* and *I Want You*, also represent the refugee experience through the figure of the child – and, more particularly, the orphan. The figure of the abandoned child is an especially powerful rhetorical device because it connotes innocence and victimhood. The child represents the lack of agency and self-determination associated with the refugee in ways that enable powerlessness to be valorised as morally good. In terms of cinematic conventions, figuring the refugee as an orphan child opens up a possibility of narrative resolution for (liberal) European audiences in which they can imagine themselves as benevolent saviours, the potential adoptive parents of these border children. It is Jamal and the infant who survive suffocation in the freight container, after all, and through the figure of the orphan, the refugee is universalised as one we can choose to 'embrace' and welcome into our 'home'. An inevitable consequence of employing this orphan figure is that *In This World* infantilises the groups it seeks to represent. This limited frame of visibility arguably reproduces the displacement of refugees and the sense that they are not authorised to speak for themselves. Although Jamal and Enayat *do* speak, they are subtitled, edited, directed and packaged for consumption (Jamal's image appearing on the film's poster) within a particular humanitarian frame of visibility. The role of the intermittent voice over, which is male, middle-class and English-accented, is particularly significant in this regard, bestowing the film with authority from a particular and problematic English perspective.

Within mainstream Western representations, the refugee is most often represented either, in humanitarian literature, as a child-like, solitary, destitute and helpless figure or, in hostile news media and political rhetoric, as a mute, threatening, and undifferentiated mass of men pressing at the border. In focusing almost exclusively on the experience of young male refugees the film repeats the over-determined humanitarian representation of the refugee as a helpless, infantilised and feminised male figure. Our identification with the figure of Jamal is crucially dependent upon the absence of women and, most notably, a mother figure. Indeed, through its focus on the patriarchal social, familial and economic relations of Afghani culture, refugee women are marginalised throughout *In This World*. All the significant relationships depicted in the film are between men, despite the fact that, in reality, the vast majority of refugees at Shamshatoo are women and their children. Bans on Afghani women working outside the home, and restrictions on education for girls have compounded the dire situation facing women and female children in these border camps. This situation, contrary to Western media reports, has not changed since the US-backed war on the Taliban.[18] The social mobility of adult women in these camps is extremely limited. They are largely confined to the cramped spaces of make-shift homes and tents, while in public spaces they are often compelled to be fully veiled. The ways in which women are veiled from sight, both within the public spaces of the camp and again through their elision from the film, implies a spectral layer of (in)visibility that the film is unable to address. If a particular set of social and cultural regulatory codes marginalises women in these camps, within the film another set of Western heteronormative imperatives and cinematic conventions work together to reinforce the marginalisation of these women by enabling some identifications while foreclosing and/or disavowing others (see Butler 1993: 3). So, insofar as *In This World* sets out to elicit Western compassion for refugees, it does so through a silent complicity with the patriarchal and economic oppression of female refugees within this violent interzone, as though a focus on the oppression of women might complicate the sympathy that the film elicits through the figure of the orphaned protagonist Jamal.

Accompanied by Dario Marianelli's swelling, melancholic score, *In This World* exploits the emotional conventions of cinematic melodrama and the most sentimental conventions of humanitarianist discourse in order to communicate with emotional power something of the unliveable lives of male refugees. This film offers no solutions or, indeed, even factual insight into the refugee crisis that engulfs this region. It does not operate at the level, then, of political effect but works within a register of political *affect* – a register that is decidedly more ambiguous. Its central aim is to move its audience to recognise the enormous inequalities that divide 'them' from 'us'. However, not only is the frame of visibility that circumscribes this film limited and gender-specific, it also fails to address the larger complicity of Western governments, and by extension the film's audience, in creating and enabling the conditions it depicts. As noted above, the danger of a film like *In This World* is that the filmmakers and the film's Western audience become border tourists. In this process, 'brief forays are made into non-Euro-American Cultures' in ways that elicit cathartic spectatorial experiences of compassion without radically challenging the forms of visibility that frame contemporary border politics, and without fundamentally upsetting the audience's expectations of easy mobility (Mohanty 2003: 518).

A Mighty Heart: the limits of representation and political affect

As the title implies, *A Mighty Heart*, is also concerned with affect – with emotions, repression and courage. It explores the turbulent, complex affect of terror as the characters are confronted with kidnapping and loss, violence, murder and child-birth, paranoia, confinement and isolation, vindictiveness and compassion. In particular, this is explored through the emotional repression and self-possession of the protagonist Mariane Pearl, but whereas *In This World* is powerfully emotionally engaging, *A Mighty Heart* is more cautious in its affective address and refrains from exploiting fully the melodramatic emotional potential of the story. While Mariane Pearl is very much a victim, as a professional journalist and European (albeit of mixed race), married to an American she has a great deal of mobility and transnational institutional support when compared with Jamal and Enayat or the British-Asian tourists of *The Road to Guantánamo*, demonstrating again that cross-border mobility is provisional and unequally distributed along the lines of race and class, and the film demonstrates the catastrophic limits and hazards of that mobility. She also has a corresponding visibility, as is demonstrated by the TV interviews she participates in (as well as the extra-textual fact that the $16m film was based on her co-written book, and was co-produced by Hollywood star Brad Pitt's production company).

A Mighty Heart is derived from Pearl's account of the abduction and murder of her husband in Karachi while he was researching a story for the *Wall Street Journal* on 'shoe bomber' Richard Reid's links to Al Qaeda. The body of the film depicts efforts to find Daniel during the five weeks before a video-tape of his beheading was issued.[19] It is the third film by Michael Winterbottom (in order of production) to address the consequences of the War on Terror for specific individuals, and as in the earlier film, the pivotal location is Pakistan rather than the US or Iraq, although, as with *The Road to Guantánamo*, the focus here is primarily upon Western protagonists. The film is also the third of Winterbottom's films centred on a journalist and it is concerned with the mechanisms and ethics of reportage and news media, as well as with cinema's relationship to journalism as an adjunct to, and a considered critique of news media. *A Mighty Heart* explores questions of representability, accuracy and the epistemological adequacy of images, questions that are crystallised in a direct, emotive fashion around the narrative's central event and/or document, which remains tantalisingly unseen: the video of Daniel Pearl's execution by Islamist terrorists.

Pearl is abducted early in the film after travelling to a last interview before returning to the US. Following his kidnapping, the Pakistani police and military intelligence begin the search for Pearl, while Mariane and friends conduct a parallel investigation from her home. US intelligence personnel and diplomats join the hunt and several *Wall Street Journal* staff arrive in Karachi to support Mariane. Pakistani intelligence services arrest and torture a computer technician who was somehow implicated in the kidnapping and they learn that he received instructions from Sheikh Omar. Omar turns himself in, is interrogated and tried, and announces at the trial he had asked the kidnappers to release Pearl but by then it was too late. The tape of Pearl's murder is handed to *WSJ* journalists at their hotel and, after viewing it, they inform Mariane, who refuses to watch the tape. After a final TV interview, Mariane travels to Paris. We see her in painful labour – a frequent motif in Winterbottom's cinema – and the final shot is of Mariane walking along the street with her son.

Shot and edited in a characteristic manner typically described by critics as 'documentary-style', the film displays variable image quality, a loose narrative structure and extensive hand-held camera-work (Johnson 2007). Unusually, it was filmed almost entirely in continuity with actors only introduced into the shoot as their characters appear in the screenplay, encouraging actors to adopt an 'experiential' mode of performance.[20] Shooting on high-definition digital video enabled longer takes than is possible with film and actors were encouraged to improvise, with rehearsals filmed as well as 'proper takes'. Thus, as with observational documentaries where filmmakers attempt to record unscripted action, camera operators were unable to anticipate how actors would move and behave and so camera movements are correspondingly unchoreographed and speculative as the operator pans and reframes to catch significant actions. The resulting footage is cut and assembled in a highly compressed, fragmentary way, giving the impression that we are being shown only glimpses of what took place, and that a quite different film could have been assembled from the available material. Visually, and narratively, the film offers a partial, provisional account of events. It is deliberately unsatisfactory, a quality which, I argue, serves to give the film an ethical depth.

Characteristically for Winterbottom, many of the exterior shots were filmed guerrilla-style in public spaces rather than closed-off streets. While one effect of this approach is a certain textural authenticity, it is an aesthetic increasingly shared by Hollywood action cinema. Films such as *The Bourne Ultimatum* (Paul Greengrass, 2007), *Quantum of Solace* (Marc Forster, 2008), and *Body of Lies* (Ridley Scott, 2008) use similar techniques, albeit with multiple cameras and extensive staging, to produce a naturalistic effect of spectatorial immersion and disorienting movement. Although naturalism functions differently in those films, operating to disguise the implausibility of character and scenario, many of the visual and narrative codes of such transnational political techno-thrillers are present in *A Mighty Heart*: a technically accomplished Hollywood star, exotic locations (for Western audiences), a diplomatic incident involving international security services, a police investigation under a looming narrative deadline, a preoccupation with communications technology, split screens and on-screen captions. Significantly, it refuses fully to satisfy our expectation of lucid exposition and narrative closure, but while the inconclusiveness of *A Mighty Heart* might constitute a critique of genre cinema through a refusal of ideological resolution, its proximity to a Hollywood thriller also highlights some of its limitations. In emphasising the feeling of lived experience, a sense of 'being there', it shares the immersive aesthetic of an action film. However, just as the aesthetic of a film like *Body of Lies*, which explores the moral dilemmas negotiated by an undercover CIA agent as he moves freely about the Middle East, fails to map the 'violent cartographies' (Shapiro 2007) of the region, so the affective, exhilarating evocation of Pakistani spaces in *A Mighty Heart* does not necessarily render the geopolitical landscape of this zone of conflict clearly.

We see comparatively little of Daniel Pearl (Dan Futterman) who appears briefly in the opening scenes as he arranges and travels to a meeting with a contact. This activity is intercut with scenes showing Mariane's (Angelina Jolie) growing concern over his whereabouts as she packs for their flight back to America the following day. The story is told primarily, though inconsistently, from her perspective and, consequently, we see nothing of Pearl's kidnapping and imprisonment. Apart from several trophy images of the captive journalist circulated by his kidnappers with demands for the release of Pakistani prisoners from Guantánamo Bay prison, and an excerpt from the final video, he is mostly shown in flashback as Mariane periodically remembers details from their past. We also learn little about the kidnappers, 'The National Movement for the Restoration of Sovereignty to Pakistan', who remain entirely off-screen. The restless narrative focus directs our attention back and forth between the aggressive Pakistani police investigation and Mariane's enforced passivity. Aside from TV interviews, she is confined mostly to the house and its grounds. The secure, feminine space of the house is contrasted with the chaotic, almost wholly masculine spaces of courtrooms, prison cells, police stations and newspaper offices. Mariane's pregnant body is a striking visual metaphor for the fragile and unstable borders between interior and exterior, private and public spheres, and life and death that tremble and collapse throughout the film and the way that geo-political borders extend across and mark the body.

The film opens with a montage sequence intercutting news footage of fighter planes, bombings, Taliban soldiers, refugees in Peshawar, the mountains of Afghanistan and mass demonstrations with interpolated shots of Futterman and Jolie as Daniel and Mariane (blending actuality with reconstruction). Accompanied by pulsing, tense music, Mariane's voice-over explains that she and her husband headed for Islamabad on 12th September, along with thousands of other journalists, and she concludes a brief summary of subsequent events with the observation that many in Pakistan perceived America to be the enemy and the Taliban their Muslim brothers. While we learn more about her relationship with Daniel as the film progresses, little contextual information is provided beyond this minimal introduction. The reasons behind Daniel's kidnapping remain unclear and ultimately arbitrary. It is speculated that he was kidnapped because he was mistaken for a CIA agent (an automatic assumption about US journalists in Pakistan, understandable here since it is revealed that the *Wall Street Journal* had passed intelligence to the CIA), or a Mossad agent (because he was Jewish), but the final suggestion by Sheikh Omar (Alyy Khan), who admitted responsibility for the murder, is that it was simply because Pearl was American. This lack of exposition or commentary is consistent with a realist aesthetic wherein the narrative begins *in medias res* giving the impression that we are observing fragments of events and action indifferent to our spectatorial presence. It is also an acknowledgement of the media context in which the film exists, which has covered this murder so extensively that, 'few events of the recent years have materialized their potential to become media events to such a staggering extent' (Banita 2008: 58). *A Mighty Heart* is thus a minor, incomplete, supplementary text that invites an informed spectator to read it in relation to the many other accounts of Pearl's death and also to recognise the War on Terror's fundamental identity as media event.

This incompleteness is redoubled through the motif of visual confusion, which in turn conveys the bemusement, disorganisation and ineffectuality of the security services. Every shot of the bustling streets of Karachi, the frame jammed with vehicles and people, reminds us of the impossibility of their task. The film's visual and aural clutter, with its discontinuous montage of images and constantly blaring car horns, represents this space as impenetrably dense, populous, watchful, and unknowable. Aligning us

The urban chaos of Karachi

Direct address – 'cutaway' in which bystanders return the camera's gaze

with Mariane, the police, and the intelligence services, the film risks reproducing an anxious, paranoid, Orientalist gaze in rendering the city as a press of bodies, vehicles and architecture. As Indian critic Ananya Vajpeyi proposes, in an otherwise largely positive review of the film, 'the city is depicted as a frightening and incomprehensible palimpsest of urban chaos, poverty and Islamic terrorism, teeming with Muslim men who are scarily numerous, devoutly religious and horrendously violent (Vajpeyi 2007: 38–9).

A further consequence of shooting in public spaces is that in numerous exterior shots people stare at the camera or the spectacle of a film-shoot taking place in front of them. Inserted at regular intervals, these eschew the convention of indirect address supposedly crucial to the plausibility of classical cinema, refusing the spectator the comfort of voyeuristic invisibility and mobility. These disruptive shots estrange us from the film's *mise-en-scène*, reminding us of the reality and inaccessibility of these spaces.

A second visual figure for the inscrutability of Karachi and the terrorist networks and cells scattered through it are the whiteboards used by Mariane and her friend Asra (Archie Panjabi) to map the inter-relationship of people and organisations linked to Pearl's kidnapping. This is another palimpsest recalling the pinboards used by detectives in TV crime dramas to profile victims and suspects, and the schematic map a writer might use to plot the story structure of a novel or screenplay. Detection is figured here as narration, the retrospective reconstruction of a sequence of events or a plot. As the film progresses, more information is added, with dates, terms, names and contact details circled for emphasis and linked by lines and arrows, but it clarifies nothing either for the investigators, or the viewer. No communication or command networks or inter-relationships become visible. Rather, the whiteboards are a depressing visual record of the protagonists' ignorance about the kidnappers and their motivation. They reflect the impossibility of seeing patterns and vectors illuminated within the mass of

Mariane (Angelina Jolie) documents the investigation

data. As Banita suggests, 'the essential fragmentariness of Islamic terrorism … inevitably results in an interstitial existence[21] that does not allow for the construction of a narrative, and cannot be perceived in its entirety, but only at the nodes of utmost tension' (Banita 2008: 63). The whiteboards thus document the 'failure' of both the filmmakers and the protagonists to organize this resistant material into a linear, fully coherent plot. They are a self-reflexive comment upon the difficulties of placing a narrative frame around formless reality. The reductive template of a 'police procedural' is only partially adequate. At the same time that this might be a narrative problem for filmmakers, it represents a broader thematic problem of visibility with regard to representations of the War on Terror: the whiteboards attest to the intrinsic invisibility or elusiveness of terrorist networks.

The over-written whiteboards also suggest the equivalence of investigative journalism and criminal detection. These are presented as parallel, complementary processes of information-gathering and interpretation although, in fact, the journalists unwittingly identify the key figure responsible for the kidnapping early on in the film when they are emailed a newspaper article naming Sheikh Omar as responsible for kidnapping a series of Westerners in Afghanistan. At the time they are preoccupied with tracking down Sheikh Gilani, the man whom Daniel Pearl had supposedly arranged to meet (but who, it turns out, was simply used as bait to lure the reporter to a rendezvous) and, consequently, they ignore this lead. While research is conducted by Mariane and her friends and colleagues largely remotely and from their house through reading faxes, web pages and emails, the police intelligence investigations take place cathartically on the streets of Karachi. The journalistic investigation is a feminised process, taking place within the home, the domestic activities of cooking, cleaning and bathing continuing as normal. Meanwhile, to the delight of the accompanying US diplomat, the police investigation moves rapidly and violently through public spaces as doors are kicked down, gun battles are fought, and suspects arrested and tortured.

The spectacle of death

The video-recording of Pearl's murder released by the terrorists – what Banita calls, 'the single unmentionable detail' – is not reproduced in the film. In one respect its restaging is simply unnecessary since the video clip was distributed widely on the internet, one of the 'small media' that play an important role in extending the impact of terrorist activities and spectacles (see Lentini & Bakshmar 2007: 312). It is doubtless easily retrievable and the refusal to show it acknowledges the modest status of Winterbottom's film as partial media text; it cannot show us everything and has no special heuristic status.

Beheading videos are a means of disseminating political and criminal violence through independent and mainstream media circuits. Furthermore, they constitute a highly visible documentary micro-genre, employing particular conventions of staging and performance, cinematography and narrative structure and prompting inevitable speculation about their provenance and authenticity.[22] In an article entitled 'The Terrorist as Auteur', Michael Ignatieff proposes provocatively that, with these videos, 'We now have the terrorist as filmmaker' (Ignatieff 2004). Such videos test the limits of critical language inviting us to ask whether they can be discussed, like any other film, in terms of style, meaning and affect, or whether such an approach is obscenely indifferent since they belong to a different category of (non-textual) object. They also test the representative capacity of film and the spectatorial relationship with the image. As Vivian Sobchack writes on documentary representations of death, 'the event of death as it is perceived in our present culture points to and interrogates the very limits of representation in all its forms – including, of course, the cinematic and the televisual' (Sobchack 2004: 232). Thus, in withholding the beheading video, *A Mighty Heart* indicates what a film can meaningfully show, a representational limit of cinema.

The way in which *A Mighty Heart* treats this sequence is decisive. As Sobchack observes, 'whereas death is generally experienced in fiction films as representable and often excessively visible, in nonfiction or documentary films it is experienced as confounding representation and exceeding visibility' (Sobchack 2004: 235). There is a risk that to show the video would immediately render it banal: an unremarkable, generic image in a hyper-mediated culture. In its repetition (as representation) and narrativising it becomes merely one undifferentiated instance among others. Equally problematically, it may gratify a scopophilic desire to see/discover what had happened to Pearl, as well as providing relief from growing suspense as the investigation progresses and the narrative deadline moves closer. As Elizabeth Cowie argues, visual curiosity is underpinned by a complex range of motivations and certain genres of documentary cinema have traditionally responded to this ambivalent fascination by offering shocking views: 'In documentary films the unfamiliar of the seen has been associated with its sensationalism, as a "cinema of attractions," presenting the exotic and the horrific, as well as the bizarre and unusual, including the erotics of the sexually strange of other cultures and peoples' (Cowie 1999: 28). In leaving Pearl's death off-screen, Winterbottom's docudrama frustrates the pleasurable fantasy of mastery that relies upon an illusion of unrestricted visibility. In circling around Pearl's death it also maintains a consistent formal and ethical simulation of documentary, mimicking the tendency 'to observe the social taboos surrounding real death and generally avoid explicit (that is, visible) screen reference to it' (Sobchack 2004: 231).

These are all plausible reasons, beyond simple sensitivity, why the filmmakers might have chosen not to reconstruct the beheading sequence but there is another possible reason, which is that its screening might attribute too great a significance to Pearl's death, obscuring its historical and political context. As Mariane observes in a television interview towards the end of the film, ten other men – Pakistanis – were kidnapped and killed in the same month. A restricted focus upon one Western death might reproduce this blindness and indifference. Moreover, showing Pearl's murder potentially reinforces a general fetishistic preoccupation with beheading as a sign of absolute barbarity, reinforcing also a casual equation of decapitation with Islamist violence when, in reality, 'jihadists have utilised beheadings infrequently' (Lentini & Bakshmar 2007: 317). To conclude with Pearl's death would inevitably imply an evaluative scale by which one death is more important than numerous unseen others, what Judith Butler terms, 'the differential distribution of grievability', and the film's visual and narrative strategy is perhaps an uncertain response to this moral problem (Butler 2009: 24). Given that the film is about Pearl and his wife, his death carries an exceptional affective force, but this lacuna means that its impact is contained or dispersed as our attention is diverted to the context.

A Mighty Heart occupies an intractable position in which the demands of narrative economy and coherence are irreconcilable with a liberal concern with the complexities, ambiguities and multiple perspectives intrinsic to the story (or any story). Consequently, it has been read by some commentators as politically non-committal (see Pearl 2007 and Jacobson 2007). Of course, it is precisely the staging of a Manichean clash between civilisations that the film is designed to avoid. Georgiana Banita suggests that any equivocation is a visual failure, a matter of deficient style and narrative organisation:

> The paradox of moral equivalence might have been tempered by a clearer visual focus both on the crime itself and its consequences on the family, and the media that disseminated and translated the facts into moralistic jargon. (Banita 2008: 61)

Winterbottom's solution to the problem of how to visualise this complex of events with clarity is to show instead the emotional impact of witnessing the video. We see the tape delivered to Daniel's colleagues at the Sheraton, and the silent reactions of the journalists, diplomats and security service-men who watch it. In the following scene, we observe Mariane's anguish when she learns of Daniel's death, and that they

The Pakistani ISI 'Captain' (Irrfan Khan) watches Pearl's beheading

have seen this video. 'You watched that?' she asks in frantic disbelief. Mariane refuses to view the video, telling the subdued group of men who arrive at her house to inform her of Daniel's death, 'I never, *never,* want to see it!' The film's dominant narrative perspective is hers; her voice-over bookends the film, while occasional flashbacks give access to her memories. As spectators we are positioned accordingly, identifying with her structurally, albeit with a minimal sense of how she feels and thus, except for a fragmentary insert at the end of the film in which Daniel (Futterman) addresses the camera defiantly, we never see the video recording either. Insofar as the spectator is aligned with the camera (operator), viewing a beheading video would place us in a complicit position since the murder is staged for (and, implicitly, by) us.

In *A Mighty Heart* the spectacle of spectatorship displaces the spectacle of death, obstructing identification, and holding us at a distance. We witness rather than empathise with Mariane's desperate howls of grief in one of the 'hyperdramatic moments' that characterise Angelina Jolie's performance in this film (Alleva 2007: 21). In no way is it unaccomplished, but it is a performance of intense emotion, rather than an intensely affecting performance. Affect adheres to the actor rather than the character and we cannot forget that we are watching a star. Jolie is appropriately cast since the filmmakers exploit the alienating effect of her star status, and in this respect the film conforms to the well-established register of political cinema wherein pleasurable identification with individualised and psychologically rounded characters is eschewed in favour of more dispassionate intellectual engagement with the narrative; as Michael Renov observes, Bertolt Brecht called for a form of political theatre in which foreground and background are transposed, effecting a 'radical shifting of figure and ground so that character and dramatic emplotment lose their primacy of place in the refocusing on the broader social horizon' and much political cinema has been concerned with achieving a similar shift of focus (Renov 2004: 32–3). A problematic consequence of employing a hypervisible figure like Jolie, however, is that she tends to remain foregrounded, leaving the geopolitical background obscured and out of focus. This oscillating relationship between figure and context is something the film wrestles with throughout, and it marks the unstable fault line between documentary and fiction. John Corner suggests that docudrama might be defined in relation to 'the *prox-emics* of dramatisation' (Corner 1996: 35); where conventional documentary maintains a critical distance from its object, docudrama can '"bring us close" to the local human detail within the larger themes and sphere of action being addressed' (ibid.). This proximity is illustrated most clearly by a cut from a shot of Mariane soaking in the bath, hands resting on her swollen stomach, to a shot of an ultra-sound foetal scan. The film's focus slides between the turmoil of terrorist and counter-terror activity, and this extremely intimate, sub-visible detail.

Regardless of the framing of the story with reference to its historical context, the narrative is oriented around Pearl/Jolie to such an extent that a scene in which the Pakistani ISI torture a man thought to know the whereabouts of the kidnappers, seems, if not acceptable, then at least completely understandable. We are caught up in her urgency to find Daniel and the film's reticent, unspectacular aesthetic means that this sequence appears as merely another pragmatic, compressed stage of the frustrating investigative process. We see only the aftermath as the 'Captain' (Irrfan Khan) questions the exhausted, sweating suspect almost tenderly, as the man hangs by his wrists. The narrow, censorious dimension of this fragmentary structure is evident here in so far as the torture of this suspect remains unseen and inferred.

As Judith Butler argues, at the same time that the War on Terror is fought through conventional and unconventional means, it is conducted through and constituted by ubiquitous mediated representations of the conflict. Insofar as the War on Terror derives legitimacy and substance from the circulation of media discourses, in visualising the imagined, obscure, unwatchable realities of the war, a film may inadvertently affirm the reality it challenges or presumes to negate. Given the long-standing relationship between Hollywood filmmaking technology and military surveillance and simulation technology (see Virilio 1992; Shapiro 2007), a film that engages politically with the War on Terror must necessarily display caution about the validity, effect and origins of the images it generates and relays. A critical cinematic account of the conflict requires filmmakers to address the blurring of actuality with simulacrum that attends all stages of war. Directors must also resist a cynical or nihilistic postmodern affirmation that the over-presence of a simulated reality of pure (in-)difference empties images of significance rendering politically resistant positions impossible. It is important to recognise that in the face of the hyper-visibility of the war, the transnational infrastructure of dark prisons, black sites, and invisible rendition flights ensures that some of the most disturbing aspects of the War on Terror remain beneath the threshold of visibility and out of sight of recording equipment (see Paglen and Thompson 2007).[23] One of the most interesting features of *A Mighty Heart* is that the film demonstrates an awareness of the ways in which the mediation of the War on Terror is critically disabling for representational systems, and its cautious aesthetic response is a strategy of restricted visibility.

The tagline of the US poster for *A Mighty Heart* promises, 'This is the story you haven't heard', a promotional claim asserting a distinct function for narrative cinema in the context of a global 'media event', as well as docudrama's potential to reframe familiar events, representing them from counter-perspectives. *A Mighty Heart*, like Mariane's whiteboard, assembles an incomplete set of data, narrative fragments that require further organisation into a complete picture or schema. Watching a film, this implies, is akin to the processes of conjecture and interpretation undertaken by the protagonists. It effectively incorporates instructions on how to read the film, but also directs our gaze elsewhere in order to flesh out the narrative, follow leads and make the missing connections. Its elision of the beheading video is an acknowledgement of the limitations of what it can show (and that to show Pearl's murder would be to reveal nothing meaningful). The docudramatic political aesthetic adopted is characterised by incompleteness, granting the film an ethical depth in its refusal to resolve and foreclose this narrative and its themes, and in its refusal to reorganise and simplify these events into a melodramatic narrative. Although far from formally transgressive or radically experimental, *A Mighty Heart* traces and makes visible the limits of cinematic representation, and of documentary realism, in relation to critical accounts of the War on Terror.

The Road to Guantánamo: 'double perspectives' on the War on Terror

The trilogy of films under discussion here all synthesise documentary material with fictional material, but with *The Road to Guantánamo* the borders between fiction and the real remain visible. As a result, more than with the others, this film's structure – composed from heterogeneous elements and the distinct narrative perspectives of the three subjects of the film, as well as the film's own meta-narrative frame – remains visible. As with *The Shock Doctrine*, this film invites us to recognise that with such an account we are presented not with a window onto unmediated reality but with a narrative construction.

The film (co-directed by Mat Whitecross) complements *In This World* and *A Mighty Heart*. It returns us to the same global crisis-point, the troubled border-zone between Afghanistan and Pakistan, at the same historical moment: the early stages of the bombing of Afghanistan by US and British forces. However, it has a broader chronological range tracking the characters from 2001 through to 2005. A similar formal strategy of blending actuality with dramatised passages in a configuration characteristic of television documentary is employed, in order to tell the 'true' story of three British-Asian men, Asif Iqbal, Shafiq Rasul and Ruhel Ahmed (named 'The Tipton Three' by the British press). Apprehended in Afghanistan in 2001 by the Afghan Northern Alliance (United Islamic Front for the Salvation of Afghanistan) and then imprisoned and tortured in the US detention centre at Guantánamo Bay in Cuba, they were finally released without charge in 2004.

The cinematic borderlands

Like *In This World*, *Code 46* and *The Shock Doctrine*, *The Road to Guantánamo* is a film about the uncertainty of being in the borderlands – those exceptional geo-political zones where citizenship, sovereignty and law have minimal purchase. As Butler notes, 'the prisoners indefinitely detained in Guantánamo Bay are not considered "subjects" protected by international law… the humans who are imprisoned in Guantánamo do not count as human… they are not subjects in any legal normative sense' (Butler 2004: xv–xvi). The layers of dehumanisation integral to Guantánamo are countered in *The Road to Guantánamo* in several ways. It refuses Guantánamo's existence as 'out of place', 'out of time', and outside the legal strictures of international law, by telling us how these particular individuals arrived at the specific time/place that is Guantánamo, how easily one can become identified as an 'enemy combatant', and how difficult it is to protest one's innocence. The film counters the supposedly extraordinary legal status of Guantánamo, situated 'outside' any legal or accountable domain, an invisible and practically inaccessible utopia; literally, *no place*. Moreover, by telling the story of Guantánamo through the experiences of English-speaking, British citizens, *The Road to Guantánamo* reveals much more about multi-cultural Britain than the happy face of multiculturalism promoted within the British film industry, through films such as the hugely successful *Bend It Like Beckham* (Gurinder Chadha 2002).[24] Rather than reproducing commodified national stereotypes for international consumption,

The Road to Guantánamo forces us to recognise Britishness and the tentative right to recognition as a British citizen – even for native Britons like the Tipton Three – as a matter of struggle, violent repression and resistance that is at once shocking and banal.

By foregrounding the experience of non-white British citizens, the film adopts a perspective on border politics and border crossings that differs from the more conventional touristic and humanitarian perspectives of *In This World* and *A Mighty Heart*, problematising the tendency (exemplified by many 'second cinema' films) towards a (singular) Eurocentric or Western gaze. To differing degrees the other two films depend upon a conventional affective relationship with a spectator who is moved to distress, whereas *The Road to Guantánamo* maintains a consistently dispassionate critical distance from the events reconstructed within the film, which obstructs uncomplicated identification with the protagonists but also refrains from a reductive objectification or othering of them by giving them a voice.

The Road to Guantánamo interweaves interviews with archival news footage and a dramatised reconstruction of the journey of Asif Iqbal, Shafiq Rasul and Ruhel Ahmed to the nightmarish interstitial destination of the US Naval Base on the island of Cuba, and their subsequent detention there. The narrative begins in September 2001 with 19-year old Asif's trip to Pakistan to meet a possible bride in the Punjab. He decides to get married and invites his friends Ruhel (Farhad Harun), Shafiq (Riz Ahmed), and Monir (Waqar Siddiqui), to fly out and attend the wedding. The four men meet in Karachi and enjoy a sightseeing trip, going to the beach, shopping, and visiting a local mosque with Shafiq's Pakistani cousin, Zahid. After hearing a preacher at the mosque calling for volunteers to help the Afghani people, the five men decide, partly for 'the experience' and partly for the 'big naans', to visit Afghanistan. They make their way across the Pakistan/Afghanistan border and after a few days reach Kabul, where US bombs have begun to fall. The men spend their time wandering around the city, 'not doing anything' and struggling to communicate – for the British visitors, Urdu is a third language and none of them speaks Pashtu or Dari. As the bombing continues in the nearby mountains, they grow anxious to return south to Pakistan but, in error, take a minibus north to Kunduz province where they are stranded with an international group of soldiers on the frontline between Taliban forces and the anti-Taliban Northern Alliance. Afghanistan is descending into chaos under heavy bombardment by the US forces, which are supporting the Northern Alliance against the Taliban and in the chaotic evacuation of Kunduz, they lose Monir (now presumed dead). They are captured by the Northern Alliance who take them for pro-Taliban fighters, and are searched, robbed, marched through the mountains at gunpoint with scores of other foreign fighters and Afghans, and then herded into container trucks. Asif (Afran Usman) only avoids suffocation when the soldiers strafe the metal trailer he is held in with machine guns, peppering it with bullet holes and killing most of the occupants. The men are then transferred to a rudimentary over-crowded Northern Alliance prison in Sheberghan, before being handed over to the custody of US troops. Again, suspected of being foreign pro-Taliban fighters, they undergo weeks of physical abuse and interrogation by British and American soldiers at a US detention camp in

Kandahar, before being flown in January 2002 to Camp X-Ray, the makeshift detention centre at the US Naval base in Guantánamo Bay. Several months later they are transferred to the purpose-built prison, Camp Delta, where they are interrogated by US and MI5 inquisitors, and tortured for hundreds of hours, only to be released without charge in March 2004. The film's second half is given over to recounting the conditions of imprisonment and isolation and the crushingly repetitive processes of interrogation and physical abuse suffered by the three men. In a gesture towards conventional narrative resolution, the film concludes with Shafiq and Ruhel (rather than the actors who play them) returning to Pakistan in June 2005 for Asif's wedding to the (anonymous) Pakistani bride chosen by his parents, an event that is uncritically presented in wholly affirmative terms.

Michael Winterbottom describes *The Road to Guantánamo* as 'part-road movie, part-war film, part-prison movie' and while this is a broadly accurate outline of the tri-partite sequence of events within the film and is a typical example of the reconfiguration and fusion of genres in many of his films, it is also somewhat disingenuous since the film has little in common with the melodrama and eroticised fascination with masculinity and homosociality that is often intrinsic to these genres (Anon. 2006a: 11). It is not a film about heroic resistance and endurance, and, unlike many examples of the genres Winterbottom cites, the film's matter-of-fact style does not invite us to read it as allegory or myth. However, the description of the film as an unlikely assemblage of disparate generic elements does suggest the film's hybrid structure, combining different orders of representational material without privileging one over another. Almost casual in its synthesis of fiction and documentary *The Road to Guantánamo* does not highlight the distinctions between archive footage, interviews with the three men, and documentary reconstruction with the actors who play them, and moves between different types of material with striking economy. Like other works by the director, this inter-generic film distances itself from the transparency sought by cinematic naturalism, but nevertheless draws on the 'authentic' charge of documentary footage – the shock of the real.

'Double perspective', the touristic gaze and direct address

The War on Terror trilogy provides a counterpoint to the accounts of reporters and camera crews 'embedded' with US and UK troops, and the paraphrased press releases that have dominated coverage of the conflict in Afghanistan and the subsequent invasion of Iraq. Interviewed during the production of the film, Winterbottom suggested that *The Road to Guantánamo* adopts a 'double perspective' from the point of view of Western spectators (Anon 2006a: 11). That is to say, we are shown events from a different angle of vision, that of marginal or excluded figures, revealing aspects of events that would otherwise have remained hidden from sight, from the mediated gaze of the Western spectator.

The film seems to have been conceived as an intervention in the transnational media spectacle of the War on Terror in a very precise, partial way, as a contestatory narrative. Winterbottom's comment acknowledges the limited possibilities open to

Double perspective –
stock news footage of
United Front soldiers
preparing to assault the
Taliban in Kunduz (top) is
intercut with dramatised
re-enactment of the arrival
of Ahmed, Iqbal, Rasul
and Monir Ali in Kunduz

(arthouse) filmmakers or commentators in challenging or responding critically to the homogeneous and ubiquitous representations of the war within carefully managed Western news media. At the same time, he recognises a distance between the activist, agitatory capacity of the film and that of news reportage which, as film theorist Bill Nichols observes, 'urges us to look but not care, see but not act, know but not change. The news exists less to orient us toward action than to perpetuate itself as commodity, something to be fetishized and consumed' (Nichols 1991: 194). Winterbottom's comment also acknowledges the limitations of any individual account of the war, accepting that a single film can only ever offer a provisional, questionable narrative, rather than a true and definitive account of any set of events. Following Winterbottom, we can regard *The Road to Guantánamo* not as a comprehensive historical account, but rather as a complicating account that qualifies or puts into play other accounts of the war and that, in turn, will inevitably be read in relation to them.

The term, 'double perspective', describes the film's status as it circulates around the screens of Western Europe and the US and in discourses about the War on Terror. It also describes the political/textual strategies employed by the film. The film is structured around a double perspective in its visible blending of documentary actuality with dramatised re-enactment and one of the consequences of the film's assemblage from this 'material' is that its hybrid composition and unstable textual status remains subtly visible. The double perspective is incorporated into the film, to produce multiple perspectives. Rather than a clear view of events, the film induces a *double vision* of the various activities grouped and legitimated under the name of 'warfare'.

A similar strategy of internal doubling (and implicit engagement with media contexts) is found recurrently in Winterbottom's work. In an essay on transnational films concerned with immigration, Yosefa Loshitzky has argued that Winterbottom's earlier film, *In This World*, employs a similar structural device of double perspectives, suggesting that it refuses to resolve the image by privileging one perspective over the other. Instead, the film maintains a tension between the spectator's touristic gaze, and that of the refugees, Jamal and Enayat, producing a complex 'dialectics of gazes':

> The spectator's gaze (mimicking the tourist's gaze) is negated by the refugee's gaze. One contradicts the other. While one gaze is in search of pleasure (even an involuntary one), the other seeks survival [...] The spectator's gaze ... oscillates between the two gazes, the pleasure-seeking gaze of the tourist and the refuge-seeking refugee's gaze. This oscillation between tourism and 'poorism' as used in *In This World* has a distanciation effect, resulting in a Brechtian drama of alienation. (Loshitzky 2006: 753)

However, the distanciation effect of *The Road to Guantánamo* is quite different since the central figures are British and also, crucially, adults, which results in a subtler play of perspectives. On the one hand, the spectator's pleasure-seeking touristic gaze is frustrated since the film eschews the rich use of colour and striking images of landscape that characterise *In This World* in favour of a muted colour scheme (punctuated by the bright orange of the clothing worn by the inmates at Guantánamo) and a claustrophobic emphasis on the interiors of vehicles, rooms, internment camps and prison cells. On the other hand, the film collapses an opposition between the gaze of the spectator and that of the main characters who quite literally embody the touristic gaze. However, this alignment of gazes has the potential to produce a different sort of discomfort since, while Iqbal, Ahmed and Rasul set out from Britain as tourists at the beginning of the film, as British-Asians their non-white bodies do not correspond to the image of a Western traveller and this, we can infer, is the main reason for the subsequent repeated misrecognition of them as Islamist fighters or terrorists. This incompatibility may well also be the source of an uncomfortable identificatory relationship for white viewers, interfering with a conventional desire to identify with a (white) narrative protagonist since, although they are not 'other' in the same sense as the refugees of *In This World*, their hyphenated ethnic identities and bodies mark them as visibly different.

However, it adopts a quite distinct representational strategy from *In This World* as its protagonists are British citizens and not foreign others in relation either to other characters in the film or to the film's primary intended audience. The juxtaposition of documentary footage and dramatised material is a means by which the Tipton Three can tell their story publicly and so the film's hybrid form is determined partly by the ethical and political imperative to foreground these men. They appear to speak for themselves (insofar as they are permitted to by scripting and editing) as well as through their dramatic avatars. Also, they speak English, so their statements are not mediated through subtitled translations and the fact that they are British-Asian means also that the film does not invite the spectator to identify with the oppressed or subaltern subjects of those countries in a condescendingly liberal or colonialist gesture towards common experience. Instead, the film tells a story of Western tourists who get into trouble while on holiday abroad and much of the film's black humour is derived from the disparity between the ordinariness of the three young men and the absurdity of their imprisonment as they are arrested, interrogated and tortured for months as if they were hardened guerrilla fighters.

The decision to represent the War on Terror through the experiences of these men means that the film offers a provisional and narrowly selective account. It also foregoes explicit commentary or exposition telling us little about the occupation of Afghanistan, and the expansion of the War on Terror with the subsequent invasion of Iraq, and little about the debates around extraordinary rendition, the US's rejection of international law in the treatment and renaming of prisoners of war with the complicity of the 'coalition of the willing'. It tells us little too about the debates around the circumstances in which torture might be legitimate and ethically justified and whether information extracted under torture should be used by Western governments. The narrative focus throughout is on Asif, Ruhel and Shafiq and their exclusion from the public sphere through their misrecognition as Al Qaeda, Al Majaroun terrorists or Taliban soldiers. Apart from the news clips, there are no scenes that do not feature at least one of the three men, whether they are addressing the camera or impersonated by actors.

This cannot pretend to be a comprehensive historical record, although the incorporation of TV news footage and captions indicating dates and locations connotes historical accuracy. Instead, the film makes its argument about the incompetence, ignorance, and racist Islamophobic violence of the British and American military operation through the misrecognition of these men as soldiers or terrorists. Television news accounts are juxtaposed with interviews and dramatised footage in order to highlight the 'contrast between their experiences on the ground as three individuals caught up in it compared to us watching it from the outside' (Winterbottom 2006). The visually neutral style of the interviews (connoting minimal mediation) is unvarying throughout the film,[25] as they address the camera directly (with any prompts or questions from an interviewer having been edited out) and are shot in medium close-up against a mottled beige background with high-key lighting.

Visual neutrality –
Shafiq Rasul

The mechanics of abuse –
Shafiq Rasul (Riz Ahmed)
shackled to the floor

This formal minimalism serves to neutralise the emotional impact of the interviews so that emphasis is placed on the factual details of the men's incarceration, rather than an evocation of the psychological consequences of their experiences, allowing us to reach our own conclusions about their account. In contrast to *In This World* and *A Mighty Heart*, *The Road to Guantánamo* does not draw extensively on melodramatic devices for its political affect. Indeed, despite depicting extreme acts of violence and torture, it deliberately distances the spectator from the emotional impact of the events it evokes. As they tell their story, their delivery is at times cheerful, at times deadpan (when, for instance, they coolly downplay the effects of the abusive treatment they received) and at others, reflective and despondent.

For example, a sequence towards the end of the film recounts the experiences undergone by Shafiq and Ruhel when transferred to isolation cells in 2003. The actors are shown in the steel-walled punishment cells, and there is a cut to Ruhel who explains, 'It was a whole different story for us there: we was getting punished. I was in "iso" for ages. I was there for two or three months'. This is followed by a jarring cut to an almost black room in which one of the actors is chained to the floor in a stress position while thrash metal plays very loudly.

There is a cut to Shafiq who calmly explains that he was shackled to the hook on the floor. The image then cuts back and forth between Shafiq's explanation of the mechanics of abuse – that he might be held there for six hours, and left to soil himself – and brief sequences showing the manacled actor screaming, being berated

Ruhel Ahmed (Farhad
Harun) in his isolation cell

and manhandled by a military policeman, and subjected to strobe lights while the music continues. The sequence finishes by returning to shots of the actors slumped in the isolation cells.

What is notable here is that although the sequence exploits the startling effect of parallel editing – inter-cutting Shafiq's calm account with extreme music that sounds like an expression of sheer desperation or rage – this disjunctive editing is not employed to make us feel what it was like for Shafiq and Ruhel as they underwent this shattering abuse. It is difficult to see the face of the manacled figure or hear his voice; the cues for spectator-identification are absent from these brief bursts of sound and image. Moreover, the dispassionate delivery of Shafiq and Ruhel as they recount their experiences betrays no traces of the trauma they suffered. They are not impassioned, distressed or defensive as they speak, but, rather, remain composed and seem to be variously reflective, cynical, amused and optimistic. The film thus eschews the conventional shot in which a subject breaks down on camera while relating a particularly upsetting episode to the interviewer. This shot typically acts as a guarantee both of the veracity of the subject's account and the incisiveness of the filmmakers' investigative reporting, and in refusing it the film also refuses to offer the spectator the emotional drama and the voyeuristic/sadistic pleasure s/he expects and desires. Affect is conveyed not through gratifying spectacular and emotive representational devices, nor through a humanitarian appeal to empathy, but by provoking in the spectator a residual sense of bemusement and politicised anger at the injustice of Guantánamo and the wider War on Terror represented synecdochically by this abusive confinement. In other words, what the film foregoes is political *affect*, in its concern with political effects. *The Road to Guantánamo* does not move us through empathy and identification, inviting us to share the experiences of these three men as they are incarcerated and relentlessly questioned, taunted and screamed at, held in isolation, beaten, shackled to the floor.

The promotional website for the film's US release functions both as a marketing tool and a tool for political agitation with a page entitled 'Get Active', containing links to Amnesty International, the American Civil Liberties Union, and other anti-Guantánamo humanitarian organisations. It also includes '*The Road to Guantánamo*: Action Guide', containing extensive details of the three men's detention and advice on how to organise protests against the prison. This supplementary material underscores the film's explicit aim – *to move people to action* (rather than to tears).

Invisibility, intimacy, and the unfilmable

In foregrounding Western perspectives of the border, the War on Terror trilogy exemplifies a mode of transnational cinema in its concern with border politics and with the correlative politics of racial and ethnic visibility. This is evident in the graphic and structural properties of the films, as well as in their resistance to ideological and narrative resolution – each of them ending abruptly and inconclusively. The films are marked by a heterogeneous graphic style and fragmentary, elliptical editing. However, Judith Butler's emphasis on the constitutive role of (in)visibility draws attention to the processes of filtering that take place in making abject border zones and those who inhabit them palatable for Western audiences. There is always another 'outside', which is beyond the frame of even the most politically self-conscious cinematic gaze. These three films perhaps prompt us to consider what and who remain outside, marginal and unrepresented, which borders and which 'border lives' remain unrepresentable or screened from view. Certainly the absence and marginality of women within *In This World* and *The Road to Guantánamo*, and the failure to interrogate the status of the nameless mass of non–European victims of war and torture in the latter film, is evidence of the cinematic and ideological limits that constrain how the displaced, the imprisoned and tortured materialise in Western border cinema. At some points these films rely upon the production of 'desirable' and 'undesirable' others in ways that uneasily replicate the exclusionary governance of immigration and 'security' in the West, but their fragmentation and inconclusiveness also remind us that they are bound by representational limits. They work to make unrepresentability or invisibility visible.

As Gloria Anzaldúa suggests, some of the most 'uncrossable borders' are deline-ated not by national geographies, but by economic class, gender, ethnic and/or reli-gious differences *within* the borders of nation states (Anzaldúa 1987). One challenge for Western filmmakers is to represent the 'intimate others of globalization' in ways that can attend to the specificity and materiality of lived experiences of borders and problematise, rather than reinforce, dominant Western tropes of visibility (Chang and Ling 2000). Here the films of Swiss feminist video artist Ursula Biemann are notable for what Imre Szeman describes as their 'sustained and thorough investigations of the complex intersection of new technologies, gender, the body, and labor in the context of the numerous border zones generated by the rapacious economy of global neolib-eralism' (Szeman 2002: 92). Of course peripheral feminist border cinemas such as Biemann's have a limited circulation, while mainstream films such as Winterbottom's can utilise the infrastructures of the global entertainment industry and as a conse-quence garner audiences of many millions. This raises further questions about the poli-tics of mobility, and reminds us that border cinema is not only *about* border-crossings, as border films are themselves sucked into the image flow that characterises global corporate capitalism. In other words, the cinema of borders is forced to negotiate some of the same processes of unequal immobility and unequal distribution that they describe. Despite its limitations, the War on Terror trilogy offers provocative examples of the ways in which mainstream border cinema might negotiate the boundaries that too often segregate political films from mass audiences, offering us, as Western border tourists, a glimpse of the abject 'unlivability' of life at the border (Naficy 2001: 31).

In their exclusion from public spaces, from contact with friends, family (and, for much of their time in captivity, fellow inmates), and from due legal treatment through their designation as 'enemy combatants', the men were excluded from sight. Therefore, much of the film is given over to a depiction of what took place inside the Guantánamo Bay prison, but while the experience of the inmates is shown to be degrading and brutal, the film retains a certain ambivalence or detachment of tone throughout these scenes. Thus, rather than inciting either outrage or impassioned empathy with the three men, the film draws attention to the increasingly bizarre, Kafkaesque way in which they are treated during their detention. Watching the film one has the growing sense that the primary function of the prison is not practical – to hold dangerous or useful people captive before trying and/or punishing them – but that it is an unregulated, interstitial space, a Sadeian border-zone in which one group of people has been given licence to inflict physical and psychological violence upon another group.

In this respect the Guantánamo Bay prison is a *heterotopia*, the counter-site that Michel Foucault argued could be found in every culture and in which 'all the other real sites that can be found within the culture, are simultaneously represented, contested, and inverted' (Foucault 1967). Heterotopic sites, Foucault suggests, are not 'freely accessible like a public space', but, like rest homes and psychiatric hospitals, are isolated and restrictive: 'Either the entry is compulsory, like a barracks or a prison, or else the individual has to submit to rites and purifications' (ibid.). Situated at a distance from the US mainland, on a Navy base, putatively outside international law, the Guantánamo Bay prison is the epitome of a paradoxical heterotopic site – visible but hidden, highly regulated but unrestrained. The sequences in which the men are taunted with pornographic magazines or shackled to an iron ring in the floor, and tormented with flashing strobe lights and deafeningly loud black metal music are an indication of the way in which this heterotopic space exists as an inversion of normative culture. Heterotopias 'reflect and speak about' the societies they are inversions of, Foucault suggests, and in the case of Camp X-ray, the trappings of US consumer culture become means of torture rather than gratification (Foucault 1967).

The Road to Guantánamo makes this obscure, partially veiled space visible from the perspective of three of its occupants. The decision to adhere to the three men's accounts nevertheless imposes some tight formal restrictions on the film. A consequence of this restricted narrative perspective is that we learn next to nothing about the other occupants – guards or captives – of the prisons they find themselves in. As Winterbottom explains, the filmmakers wanted to avoid 'too much drama about the relations between the characters – we wanted to just tell the simple story of what happened to them. It's more about their experiences as opposed to creating a separate drama about what's going on in their heads' (Anon. 2006a: 11). The film is thus unconcerned with the motivations and exculpation of Iqbal, Ahmed and Rasul. Writing on the film's release, journalist Deborah Orr suggested that this omission constituted a 'gaping hole', since:

> only hints were given about their lives before their trip, and the sort of young men they were. They had been in some trouble with the law, so it's reasonable to infer that they were rebellious or thrill-seeking. Perhaps they wanted to take advantage of the chaos in Afghanistan, and felt there might be opportunities to make some money. Or maybe their support for their friend in his wish to marry a village girl from Pakistan suggests difficulties with the freedom and independence of Western women. (Orr 2006)

This criticism is repeated by Ali Jaafar in stronger terms, as he suggests that, 'Winterbottom's stated desire to remain objective is less convincing in relation to *The Road to Guantánamo*, however, where he allows explanations by the Tipton Three of their presence in Afghanistan to go unchallenged' (Jaafar 2007: 25–6). The unstated implication of these speculations about the three men – that Iqbal, Ahmed and Rasul are somehow responsible for having been arrested and tortured – is all too predictable. In their demands for the clear psychological characterisation of mainstream cinema, or, effectively, for further interrogation of the three, both writers betray a desire for reassurance that the global War on Terror is in fact being waged with impartiality and precision. On the contrary, a strength of the film is its comparative indifference to these three men except in so far as they are useful illustrations of a process of misrecognition.

Rather, the film is about the political and legal processes, ideologies, infrastructures and communications systems that are unable to recognise these men as anything other than dangerous people or 'enemy combatants'. Jaafar suggests that 'A major weakness of the film is that it posits the three's innocence as the major plank of its argument against them, leaving unasked the more demanding question of whether their imprisonment would have been justified even had they been guilty' (Jaafar 2007: 26). However, the question of whether or not they *are* 'guilty' is largely irrelevant given that, as the film stresses, they were liable to be recognised as guilty from the moment they were captured (and, indeed, there is no clear consistent sense of what they might have been guilty of). It is ironic and revealing that the responses of Orr and Jaafar to the film repeat – however circumspectly – this (mis)recognition.

The film's title refers to the journey taken by Iqbal, Ahmed and Rasul – the series of events that led to their imprisonment – but also, and more importantly, it refers to the transformations that have led to a political sea change in which, for example, Tony Blair felt able to dismiss the continuing existence of the prison and the several hundred inmates held without charge at a news conference in February 2006, as 'an anomaly' that 'sooner or later has to be dealt with' (Anon. 2006).[26] As Winterbottom's comment on the film's embodiment of a 'double perspective' suggests, the *Road to Guantánamo* is not a self-contained narrative but a partial and limited account of one particular sequence of events, and an account that is one element of an intertextual, multi-media assemblage of narratives. It is not a discursive foreclosure but a prising open of a set of debates. The film presupposes, in this mode of address, a knowledgeable spectator, and assumes that it is a contribution to a context in which debates about Guantánamo are ongoing, inviting us to infer connections between this film and other texts. Rather than a failure or a sign of incompetence, the refusal to offer a closed narrative is strategic and knowing, just as its refusal to interrogate or 'excuse' the three is deliberate and consistent with an ethical decision not to speak on their behalf.

As with *In This World*, events outside the film bleed into and shape the questions it raises regarding who counts fully as a citizen, and who can and cannot move freely across borders. The film has become implicated in the history it recounts partly through the speed with which it entered into circulation and also through the way in which the public sphere in which the film circulates is so thoroughly mediated that the slippage between fiction and document extends beyond the boundaries of the film. In February

2006, along with the actors and film crew, Iqbal, Ahmed and Shafiq Rasul attended the film's premiere at the Berlin International Film Festival where Winterbottom and Whitecross won the Best Director prize. On their arrival back in the UK, Ahmed and Rasul as well as the actors who played them in the film – Rizwan Ahmed and Farhad Harun – were detained by police at Luton airport for questioning under counter-terror legislation. In an absurd and alarming episode, Riz Ahmed, who played Rasul, claims he was asked about his views on the Iraq war, whether he became an actor to further the cause of Islam, whether he intended to make any more 'political' films, and whether he was prepared to become a police informant (Grimmer 2006). This shocking epilogue to the film, which undermines the film's optimistic coda, reveals the pivotal role of visible ethnic difference in forming contemporary Islamophobic border politics in the West.

Conclusion: Making public(s)

Thus, *The Road to Guantánamo* engages with a specific public – an activist public – or, more accurately it aims to activate or generate an activist public. While this aim underlies the other films by Winterbottom that address the new political order of the global War on Terror, this film is the most direct, exploiting developments in media technology and consumer expectations to do this. As well as a means of distribution of the film, the internet also provides a framing context through the film's promotional website, to guide our interpretation and exhorts us to follow intertextual relays to other accounts and interventions.

The film's low budget, small crew, rapid production schedule with its reliance upon improvisation, and the simultaneous release of the film in different media formats also facilitate the film's address to a public, allowing the film to intervene in ongoing debates. The film is concerned with a history that is still very much present for its audience (even though the events and heterotopic locations of the film are largely invisible to most of us) and so – potentially at least – in its spectatorial immediacy the film can suggest the possibility of political action to its audience. Where a film such as George Clooney's historical allegory about reporter Ed Murrow, *Good Night and Good Luck*, which was released six months earlier and depicts politically scandalous events from a safe historic distance can offer us the masochistic pleasures of outrage, empathy and disapproval, *The Road to Guantánamo* refuses to allow us this comfortably disempowering historical distance or delay.[27] As Michael Warner has noted, the potential for texts and discourses to agitate and activate a public is directly linked to the speed of circulation of those texts and discourses:

> A public can only act in the temporality of the circulation that gives it existence. The more punctual and abbreviated the circulation, and the more discourse indexes the punctuality of its own circulation, the closer a public stands to its politics. At longer rhythms or more continuous flows, action becomes harder to imagine. That is the fate of academic publics, a fact very little understood when academics claim by intention or proclamation to be doing politics. In moder-

nity, politics takes much of its character from the temporality of the headline, not the archive. (Warner 2002: 96–7)

The form of *The Road to Guantánamo*, the circumstances of its production and its unprecedented distribution strategy are all determined by the imperative of a rapid response. In this sense the Stakhanovite work rate maintained by Winterbottom throughout his career corresponds perfectly to the requirements of the story being told. Shot and edited digitally and released on 14th March 2006 in multiple formats simultaneously, the film was able to address its audience with an urgency that would be dissipated through the delays of the conventional circuits of distribution.[28] Consequently, the film circulated within the temporality of the headline, rather than that of the archive, or the standard platform-release schedules of the film industry. In this respect, Winterbottom's observation, 'I see my role … as similar to that of a journalist', reflects both the changing patterns of film production, distribution and consumption, and also the sense that (some of) his films are equivalent in function, cultural status and ephemerality as media objects, to a news report (Jaafar 2007: 25).

In conclusion, what makes *The Road to Guantánamo* both an exemplary model of political cinema situated at the margins of mainstream film and television, and the exemplification of Winterbottom's aesthetic, is its articulation of a sophisticated 'double perspective'. The film is conceived as a text or object that circulates within a crowded multi-media context and it functions as an intervention in the interwoven circuits of news and entertainment media, a polemical and partial account. It also incorporates a doubled perspective into its internal structural organisation in several ways, including, most significantly, its blending of documentary and fiction in a self-conscious acknowledgement of the uncertain status of mediated representations. It avoids adopting naïve naturalism in its account of the removal of certain individuals – border subjects – from public spaces and from visibility. In making visible the experiences of these three men, as a text and a commodity the film engages with audiences in a highly self-conscious way both through its differentiation from other media accounts and through its simultaneous release in different formats. In making public the story of the Tipton Three, this film attempts to activate or make *publics*, by inciting them to protest.

Notes

1   The term 'War on Terror', coined by US president George Bush addressing congress in September 2001, is problematic both in framing counter-terrorist or imperialist violence as morally righteous bi-lateral 'warfare', and also in its association with US foreign policy. Clearly, it also describes an endless, quixotic conflict, and, since March 2009, the US government has abandoned the term. The term is used here to describe this particular, historically local framing of political violence, rather than as an accurate description of events.
2   For example, it took only nine months from the initial idea for *Redacted* to be released into cinemas (Burdeau 2008: 16).

3 A montage of footage from the TV news and other sources, and commissioned by the prosecution from 'terrorism expert' Evan Kohlmann, the film's title cites *The Nazi Plan* (George Stevens, 1945) which was produced for the Nuremberg International Military Tribunal. The defence attorney objected to the screening of the film in court, protesting that 'They're trying to terrorize the members [of the tribunal]' (Anon. 2008). See Mills 2008 for a sceptical account of Kohlmann's career.

4 As Rouch writes, aligning cinema with doubled perspectives: 'As a filmmaker and ethnographer, I see virtually no boundary between documentary film and fiction film. As the art of the double, cinema is inherently a transition from the world of the real to the world of the imagination, and ethnography, as the science of other peoples' thought systems, is a permanent crossing over from one conceptual universe to another, a form of acrobatic gymnastics where losing one's footing is the least of the risks one runs' (Rouch 1981).

5 *Michael Winterbottom: Profile of a Filmmaker* (Floriane Charles, 2002) – documentary short included on the 2003 UK 2-disc DVD release.

6 It is common for European arthouse directors to move between media for a range of reasons, both practical and political. Alongside Winterbottom we might cite such border-crossers as Ken Loach, Jean-Luc Godard, Werner Herzog, Krzysztof Kieslowski, Lars von Trier, Ingmar Bergman and Rainer Werner Fassbinder.

7 Tx, More4, 1/11/09.

8 Although Mat Whitecross, who has been employed by Michael Winterbottom's production company, Revolution Films, in a range of roles from runner to editor, is credited as co-director, this chapter discusses the film primarily in relation to other films directed by Winterbottom. This is not to imply that Whitecross, who has directed two feature films and several TV dramas, made no significant creative or authorial contribution to the film. Rather, analysing this film in relation to Winterbottom's other work makes visible the way this film develops and explores certain themes and formal relations.

9 It is notable that the head of Al Qaeda, Osama Bin Laden, who was assassinated by US special forces in May 2011, was indeed found to be hiding in Pakistan.

10 Impromptu football games recur throughout Winterbottom's films, but the politically diversionary complicity of international football is a marginal theme in this film, which notes, for example, the role of the Argentina World Cup in legitimising the regime and includes news footage of Margaret Thatcher posing with the England team, and kissed by two star players, one a miner's son.

11 Quote on the book jacket.

12 The screenplay was subsequently revised into a BBC radio play, broadcast in 2010, and a film adaptation is in preproduction with Steve Coogan's production company, Baby Cow.

13 This writing exists primarily at the margins of cultural studies, ethnic studies, multicultural studies, and anthropology. Feminist examples include, Anzaldúa 1987, Behar 1993, and Castillo & Córdoba 2002.

14 Noteworthy transnational feminist texts include Grewal and Kaplan 1994, Shohat and Stam 1994, and Mohanty 2003.

15 With 70,000 Pashtun-Afghan refugees, Shamshatoo is one of the largest refugee camps in the world. Another million Afghan refugees live in and around Peshawar. While the film was being made there were widespread anti-US demonstrations against the bombing of Afghanistan in this region, and new refugees were arriving daily from the nearby border with Afghanistan.

16 For details see the *In This World* Electronic Press Kit, 2002, Anon. (*In This World* UK DVD).

17 For an account of the significance of this event for the filmmakers, see the production notes, http://www.milestonefilms.com/pdf/InThisWorld.pdf.

18 See Revolutionary Association of the Women of Afghanistan (RAWA) at http://www.rawa.org for reports on the current status of women in this region.

19 There is a curious thematic continuity between the beheading of Pearl and the mythical Judith – the object of Eunice's obsession in *Butterfly Kiss* – who decapitated the Assyrian general Holofernes to protect the Middle Eastern town of Bethulia.

20 *Journey of Passion: The Making of A Mighty Heart* (Michael Strout, 2007) – US DVD special feature.

21 Incidentally, this term describes well the condition of life under the regime of the War on Terror, not just the position of the Islamist terrorist.

22 For example, numerous websites and threads devote themselves to apparent inconsistencies in the video of the murder of Nick Berg, an American businessman kidnapped in Iraq in 2004. See http://www.topplerummy.org/berg/ for a sceptical analysis of the film.

23 One challenge is to visualise what happens inside the perimeter fences of Guantánamo bay prison (*The Road to Guantánamo*), Abu Ghraib prison (*Taxi to the Dark Side*) or a CIA-sponsored subterranean torture cell in Morocco (*Rendition*) (Hood 2007).

24 See Ahmed 2008.

25 Notably, these shots are visually similar and have a similarly expository function to the repeated shots of Mi employed in Winterbottom's first feature film, *Butterfly Kiss*.

26 There is no doubt also a strategic dimension to this apparently careless comment since it also carefully implies that Guantánamo is an exceptional space, rather than a space that is representative of a general policy of the systematic abuse of prisoners and suspects that is deemed legitimate under the 'War on Terror'.

27 Although it is an account of US TV journalism in the early 1950s, director and co-writer Clooney has suggested that *Good Night and Good Luck* is a cautionary comment upon the political function of present-day media representations: 'I thought it was a good time to raise the idea of using fear to stifle political debate' (Brooks 2005).

28 This was the first film ever to be released simultaneously in cinemas, on broadcast television, on DVD and over the internet for streaming or downloading. This

adoption of a 'day-date' release schedule by the film's British distributor is also a sign that, as a consequence of shifts in film-viewing practices, the cinema screen is no longer the first choice of platform for audiences. Releasing a film in several media formats simultaneously cuts the distribution costs (reducing the number of prints that need to be struck, and reducing the advertising costs, since the film only needs to be marketed once), and makes the distribution of such low-budget films as this £1.45m production viable. In one respect this innovation 'represents the emergence of new business models in film that seek to capitalize on the economics of consumer demand to access content when, and where, they want it' while also pre-empting 'piracy' (Davies and Withers 2006: 61). At the same time, it exploits the technical developments that facilitate this commercial shift in order to reach large international audiences quickly.

CONCLUSION

An initial impression of Michael Winterbottom's work might suggest that he is an opportunistic filmmaker whose enthusiasms lead him capriciously from one idiosyncratic project to the next, giving the appearance, as one journalist proposed sardonically in a review of *9 Songs*, that 'Michael Winterbottom picks his films with the consistency of a blind man at a car-boot sale' (Brown 2004: 6). However, what I have sought to demonstrate in this volume is precisely the stylistic, thematic and intellectual consistency that runs through this body of work from the early television dramas (that he now disowns as jobs that were taken due to financial necessity) to transnational co-productions featuring Hollywood stars. As discussed in the introduction, Winterbottom is disparaging with regard to the critical concept of the *auteur* in interview, but what emerges in a close analysis of his work is a distinctive and very carefully crafted body of work shot through with continuities that function almost as stylistic signatures but are also always crucial to a fuller understanding of the narrative and never gratuitous. For example, there is a picture of the Sphinx visible on Lou Ford's bedroom wall in *The Killer Inside Me*, which alludes to the corporation at the centre of *Code*

The riddle of the sphinx:
Amy (Kate Hudson) in
Lou Ford's bedroom in
The Killer Inside Me

Self-referentiality and
cosmopolitan futures –
performer in the Shanghai
karaoke bar in *Code 46*

46. However, this small detail of the *mise-en-scène* is also a subtle clue to the Oedipal complex that may be a contributing factor to Ford's psychosis. In the background of a scene set in a Shanghai karaoke bar in *Code 46* an Asian woman sings 'Coimbra Menina e Moça' ('Coimbra, girl and young woman'), the 'Fado' song which is sung yearningly by the Portuguese prostitute, Lucetta in *The Claim*. Its inclusion in *Code 46* is a gesture of authorial self-reference, and it also emphasises the cosmopolitan and historically heterogeneous character of this future city. However, for the immigrant Lucetta, the song is an exile's expression of nostalgia and the pain of displacement which is the permanent condition of many inhabitants of the dystopian near-future of *Code 46*. One of the minor characters in the neo-noir thriller, *I Want You*, is a Yugoslavian refugee Smokey, who lives in a rough shack on the beach with her adolescent brother Honda. This character is comparatively insignificant in relation to the machinery of the mystery narrative that propels the film, but she is an allusion to Winterbottom's previous film, *Welcome to Sarajevo*, and a recalcitrant reminder that the aftershocks from that catastrophic conflict continue to resonate and that immigration and displacement is an intrinsic element of the fabric of contemporary globalised society and nationhood.

Whatever the intentions behind these choices, it is a sign of the complexity of Winterbottom's cinema, even within the more generically straightforward films and TV dramas, that we are continually invited to search for significance in minor details. It is an example, too, of the way in which reading these stories alongside one another brings into view a subtle intertextuality that might otherwise go unnoticed. Considering these films as a body of work also demonstrates the dogged way in which certain ideas, images and narrative scenarios are worked over and reworked repeatedly within the sprawling range of films as if to explore and exhaust all their possible permutations.

Trishna and the 'Cinema of Borders'

This practice of reworking is very clear in the film, *Trishna*, which reconfigures or remixes elements that are evident in many of the other films. As a Swedish-British co-production, shot in India with an international cast and crew, a score comprising music by Indian composer Amit Trivedi and Japanese composer Shigeru Umebayashi as well as British and Pakistani songs, the film exemplifies transnational cinema in terms of its production history, its blending of distinct cultural traditions, and its thematic concern with a country marked by colonialism and whose economy is organised around tourism and global trade. Winterbottom's third adaptation of a novel by Thomas Hardy (and the first of these on which he has the sole screenwriting credit), the film tells the story of a relationship between Trishna, a young woman from an impoverished rural family and Jay Singh, the British-educated son of a wealthy businessman.

Set in present-day India, the film begins as Jay (Riz Ahmed, who appeared in *The Road to Guantánamo*) and three friends are lounging on the roof of a hotel at the end of a holiday, smoking dope and reminiscing about the places they visited on the trip: the tourist destinations of Darjeeling, Amritsar, Varanasi, Kerala and Goa. Before Jay's friends return to Britain they visit 'the oldest temple in India' and see a traditional dance performance where Jay's eye is caught by Trishna (Freida Pinto, star of *Slumdog Millionaire* (Danny Boyle, 2008)), one of the waitresses. Trishna, who also works with her father delivering vegetables, is injured when he falls asleep at the wheel one morning and crashes his truck into an oncoming bus. Jay tracks Trishna down and, discovering that she and her father are injured and their jeep is wrecked, persuades his own father to offer her a job at the hotel he owns. She travels from the countryside to the big city of Jaipur where Jay meets her and escorts her on his motorbike to the hotel he manages for his father. He enrols her on a part-time college course in hotel management and romance blossoms. However, after they have sex on the way back from the city one evening, Jay having rescued her from two men who were following her through the streets, she suddenly returns home to her family. Morning sickness and missed periods indicate she is pregnant and so her parents take her to an abortion clinic before sending her to live with her ailing Aunt Gomti. Her life, which now consists of caring for her aunt and working in a food-packing plant, seems oppressive and so when Jay arrives at the factory and asks her to come to Bombay (Mumbai) with him, she agrees immediately. Trishna travels with Jay to the city where she moves into his comparatively luxurious sea-front flat.

Jay is trying to establish himself as a Bollywood film producer and introduces Trishna to several figures involved with the film industry. Trishna meanwhile attends dance lessons and we see the two of them shopping and cooking together, walking on the beach and having sex. Jay learns that his father has had a stroke in London, and before leaving to visit him, Jay tells Trishna it's important not to have secrets and confesses to having slept with two women before she moved to Mumbai. Trishna responds by telling him about her abortion but Jay reacts with anger, accusing her of failing to trust him and asking, 'Do you think maybe I had a right to know?' While Jay is in London, she is forced to vacate the flat when the lease lapses and resorts to sleeping on her friends' floor. On his return Jay is required by his father to leave Mumbai for Rajasthan to resume managing a hotel and, after making contact with her again, he offers Trishna work there. Once again she works as a maid and shares a room with other domestic workers, but now, as well as serving his food, she regularly has sex with Jay who is bored, complacent and increasingly contemptuous towards her, making her dance for him and telling her what to wear. She is clearly very unhappy at this treatment and finally stabs him with a large kitchen knife. She then packs her bags and returns once more to her family home where she gets a cold reception from her father who now owns a new jeep but resents the fact that 'Everyone knows I'm living off you'. She escorts her young brother and sister to school and while they recite the Lord's Prayer, in an echo of the

The final shot in the film – a freeze-frame of Trishna's suicide

The road to Rajasthan – Jay escorts Trishna through the countryside to his hotel

final scene of *Code 46* she walks up a dirt road into the countryside and stabs herself in the stomach with the knife she used to kill Jay.

Lensed by Marcel Zyskind, this is perhaps the most picturesque of all Winterbottom's films and presents a visually rich image of contemporary Indian cities and the surrounding countryside. Winterbottom's work is traversed continually by travellers and, as with other films by the director, there is a powerful sense here of the particularity of place, of moving through this landscape and of being in the desert or in crumbling palaces, factories, bus terminals and crowded streets, city apartments, cosmopolitan bars, and rural shacks. The film's scenography sometimes resembles the seductive, colourful settings of *The Best Exotic Marigold Hotel* (John Madden, 2011), a bitter-sweet comedy about British pensioners immigrating to India to retire, that was released in the UK a fortnight earlier. One of the pleasures of that film is the comic spectacle of the British visitors' discomfort at being in an unfamiliar culture. This allows the spectator to laugh at, and thereby distance herself from, the racist, condescending and culturally restricted worldview of the elderly British characters. By contrast Winterbottom's much harsher film reminds us from the beginning that we too are viewing this cinematic landscape with a reductive 'tourist's gaze', and that there is an uncrossable distance between us and the protagonist, Trishna, who remains diffi-

Holiday-maker Sandeep (Neet Mohan) lounges on the hotel roof

cult to read and hence difficult to identify with (Urry & Larsen 2011). Instead, *Trishna* aligns us with the four friends whose complacent relationship to India is epitomised in the opening scene in which we see them lazing on a rooftop, looking down on the surrounding town.

This complacency is compounded in the following scene in which they are chauffeured into the arid countryside in a jeep. Singing along to the swaggering song, 'Shoot the Runner' (2006) by British rock band Kasabian they instruct the driver to go off-road whereupon, to their amusement, the vehicle becomes stuck in a sand-dune. These young men, yelling the song's refrain, 'I'm a king and she's my queen, bitch!', are living out a privileged fantasy of masculinity, arrogant entitlement and colonialist power. Moreover, rather than gaining access to an 'authentic' India, instead they encounter, along with other international travellers, a 'heritage' culture of palaces, hotels, and traditional dance, following a well-travelled tourist trail. Indeed, it appears that Jay's wealth is built upon his father's business managing hotels that cater for foreign visitors, and ironically, although Trishna catches Jay's eye while performing a traditional dance in front of hotel guests, her ambition seems to lie in dancing to contemporary pop; it is when she is dancing with her friends and siblings to music videos and Bollywood 'item numbers' on the TV, or when she is rehearsing street-dance routines that she seems happiest. So, in relocating Thomas Hardy's late nineteenth-century English novel *Tess of the d'Urbervilles* to early twenty-first-century India, the film eschews the reactionary heritage culture and nostalgia for empire with which British cinema is associated. It reminds us (both as spectators of the film and, possibly, as Western subjects) that we are tourists in a reconstruction of the past that is staged for us. Thus *Trishna* extends the project of destroying the heritage film from within, that was initiated with *Jude*.

The cross-class romance at the centre of this melodrama demonstrates that class antagonism and social inequality is not a thing of the past, but continues to structure social relations, regardless of the fact that Jay may be oblivious to the complexities of caste. Having been educated abroad (and therefore, significantly, unable to speak Hindi), Jay belongs, like William Geld in *Code 46*, to a globalised cosmopolitan elite class who can cross national and class boundaries freely. By contrast, Trishna is a bi-lingual manual labourer who has had a limited education and her relationship with Jay offers her unprecedented mobility – she had never seen the sea before moving to Mumbai with Jay – but only a brief, precarious respite from this restricted life. She has little agency, as is demonstrated by the reticence of her taciturn character, and this lack of power is emphasised visually when Jay returns to England, leaving Trishna in the flat, and we see a series of shots of Mumbai through the bars on the apartment windows. This reprises an earlier symbolic sequence in which we see Trishna inside the aviary in the grounds of Jay's father's hotel while Jay talks to her from outside the cage. This motif of imprisonment resonates back through Winterbottom's cinema and indicates that this is, once again, an example of border cinema, a group of films that, for Hamid Naficy, 'involve journeying, historicity, identity, and displacement' (Naficy 2001: 4). As discussed in chapter 4, Winterbottom's films present us with a series of characters caught in the complex border-zones of racial, sexual and economic exploitation and this is dramatised through narratives that follow their attempts to

Social inequality – Trishna studies the view of Mumbai through her bedroom window

The impossibility of intimacy – Jay teaches Trishna how to whistle to the birds in the aviary

plot a course through fraught spaces that are transected by physical and symbolic borders. As a film about the violent boundaries of social class, national borders, and the relationship between past and present, *Trishna* exemplifies Winterbottom's cinema of borders.

In this respect, Indian cinema is a particularly appropriate frame through which to explore the questions of identity, mobility and history with which *Trishna* is engaged. As noted above, this film is tangentially concerned with Bollywood, the Hindi-language film industry based in the megacity, Mumbai, and while film and media production in general is a recurrent theme in Winterbottom's work, Indian cinema in particular has a well-established preoccupation with questions of cultural identity that relate to those explored in the director's films. 'Swadeshi' ('own country') or cultural independence was the influential goal of the first major Indian director, Dhundiraj Govind Phalke, who was determined, despite working in the context of a colonial country, to make films that consisted of 'Indian images' rather than a pastiche of European or American cinema (Rajadhyaksha 2008: 217). Thus, the question of what constitutes a national cinema is addressed by Indian filmmakers from the early 1900s onwards. As an adaptation of a liberal nineteenth-century novel with a thematic focus upon the social status of women, and a melodramatic romance narrative Winterbottom's film has much in

Trishna visits a film set in Mumbai

common with the characteristics of classic Indian cinema from the 1920s through to the 1940s. For example, *Devdas* (P. C. Barua, 1935), one of the most famous films from this period which has been remade repeatedly but is now lost, tells the story of an unrequited romance between Devdas, an upper-class young man and Paro, his childhood sweetheart from a lower caste. This is an archetypal narrative in Indian cinema that is shared by *Trishna*. In many Indian films made after the country became independent in 1948, questions of cultural independence are reframed through an examination of the social effects of modernisation, industrialisation and unrestrained capitalism, which was often depicted through a symbolic opposition between the city (which stands for modernity and the present) and countryside (which signifies tradition and the past) that *Trishna* also reiterates (Rajadhyaksha 1997: 681).

Whether or not Winterbottom knows these films, *Trishna*'s references to Indian TV and the Bollywood film industry invite us to think about the relationship between this European director's work and postcolonial global cinema, situating it beyond the restrictive frame of national cinema. The geographical and historical relocation of this narrative from the centre of the Empire to its former colonial territory is a judicious deterritorialising move. The fact that Jay is culturally British ensures that this film by a British director is not an unreflective, patronising critique of Indian society, so much as it is a self-reflexive critique of an enduring imperial arrogance; Jay's initial fascination with Trishna and his subsequent exploitation of her can be read, should we choose to, as an allegory of colonisation. Despite the exotic scenography *Trishna* is a film about Britain and its troubled, violent history as a global power.

As a film about the dynamics of a couple's relationship, *Trishna* is also a film about the impossibility of intimacy. It is a counterpart to *Jude*, *9 Songs* and *Code 46* since the film tracks the rise and inevitable decay of a relationship between characters from different countries or cultures, but the absence of a subjective voice-over means that although Trishna is present in almost every scene, we are also refused intimate access to her character. The intimacy they share briefly in Jay's Mumbai flat gives way to first of all isolation, then abusive exploitation, and finally violence at the relationship's catastrophic conclusion. What makes intimacy impossible is the impossibility of equality between the couple. Class inequality is compounded by sexual inequality and misogyny so that in this patriarchal culture Trishna is consigned to hard manual labour and feminised domestic labour in equal measure, and of course domestic labour quickly extends to sexual availability. Trishna works to earn money for her family, including her bed-bound father, and she also has to care for her bed-bound aunt. Meeting Jay means that she takes up a job as a domestic servant in a hotel, swapping unpaid domestic labour for paid domestic work, but in her relationship with Jay she transcends this subservient role only briefly. This is made insultingly clear in a scene towards the end of the film when she is working again as a servant at the hotel Jay manages: when Trishna comes to serve his meal and have sex with him (the two roles having become synonymous), Jay observes that it is stated in the *Kama Sutra* that 'there are three different kinds of heroine that you're allowed to make love to: You've got a maid, a single lady and a courtesan. So which one are you?' When she replies that she doesn't know, he suggests that she is all three. This is not obviously intended by Jay as a

Complacency and entitlement – Jay reads the *Kama Sutra* while waiting for Trishna to serve him

vindictive insult, but it is an accurate summary of the only role available to this character: all Trishna can hope for in a misogynistic society and the suffocating web of inter-personal relations is an intolerable combination of domestic drudgery, isolation, sexual exploitation and objectification.

Winterbottom's films deal with intimacy and love within couples and families, and also the pain of separation and barriers to intimate communication with particular regard to masculinity. To varying extents they also deal with broader social relations exploring the historically intricate ways in which class, race, regional and national identity shape an individual's experience but also the way that these categories structure and obstruct international relations. Viewed as a body of work-in-progress Winterbottom's films and television programmes comprise an extraordinarily rich, expanding, and ever-more complex account of the horrors, atrocities, pleasures, triumphs, banalities, solitariness and companionship, confusion and misunderstandings that characterise life in this world.

Of course, formal play, ambiguity or transgression is not intrinsically demystificatory or challenging. It does not follow that an art-work that refuses certain aesthetic conventions (such as continuity editing, or narrative linearity), is also explicitly critical of the social formations and power relations of the social context from which it emerges. As Dana Polan observes, for example, in an essay on the politics of self-reflexive cinema, Chuck Jones' famously self-referential, circular cartoon, 'DUCK AMUCK closes in on itself, fiction leads to and springs from fiction, the text becomes a loop which effaces social analysis. This is the project of all nonpolitical art, realist or modernist' (Polan 1974). By contrast, many of Winterbottom's films adopt disjointed or self-reflexive structures and styles as an effective means of representing disjointed or alienated social experience. Polan goes on to suggest that where:

> an art does not connect its formal subversion to an analysis of social situations, such art becomes little more than a further example of the disturbances that go on as we live through a day. And a work of art which defeats formal expectations does not lead to protest against a culture that deals continually in the defeating of expectations. (Ibid.)

Looking across the heterogeneity of Winterbottom's body of work, however, what is perceptible is the search for an adequate means of expressing or narrating inequality, injustice and violence (in a broad sense). In the consistent preoccupation of his films and

TV dramas with desire, sexuality, class, ethnicity, national and international politics, formal play or 'subversion' is motivated by a concern with the challenge of exploring these issues in the affective context of popular cinema and television. Winterbottom's cinema constitutes a notable and important form of political cinema for our times. Reading these films politically allows us to attend to the tensions, contradictions and border-crossing strategies of these films in a way that does not close down or limit their significance and affective power by fixing them within the borders they resist.

FILMOGRAPHY

1988

Ingmar Bergman: The Director
Television documentary
Length: 60 mins
UK TX date: 24/5/88
Director: Michael Winterbottom
Editing: Dan Carter
Producer: Alan Horrox
Production company: Thames Television

Ingmar Bergman: The Magic Lantern
Television documentary
Length: 60 mins
UK TX date: 24/5/88
Director: Michael Winterbottom
Editing: Dan Carter
Producer: Alan Horrox
Production company: Thames Television

1989

'Rosie the Great'
Episode 7 from season 7 of children's
   TV series *Dramarama* (1983–89)
UK TX date: 24/7/89
Director: Michael Winterbottom
Screenplay: David Stafford
Cinematography: Ray Orton
Editing: Richard Bradley
Music: Edward Williams

Production design: Stephen Jackson,
   Christine Kinder
Costume design: Jackie Fitt, Jilly
   Staniforth
Executive producer: Alan Horrox
Producer: Richard Staniforth
Leading cast: Julia Wallace (Mrs Peterson),
   Bill Wallis (Graham Lane), Susan
   Jameson (Mrs Preece), Steffan Morris
   (Robert Preece)
Production company: Teliesyn

1991

Shrinks
Fifth episode from a seven-part TV series
   (1991)
Length: 60 mins
UK TX date: 11/3/91
Director: Michael Winterbottom
Screenplay: Richard O'Keefe, Jonathan
   Rich
Editing: Michael John Bateman, Graham
   Walker
Leading cast: Pauline Black (Lexie),
   Yvonne Braceland (Magda Myers),
   Simon Jones (Jack Cavendish), Bill
   Paterson (Matt Henessey), Diane Bull
   (Kate Hennessey), Elizabeth Garvie
   (Beth Myers)
Production company: Euston Films

Time Riders
Four-part children's TV series
Individual episode length: 25 mins
UK TX dates: 16/10/91–6/11/91
Director: Michael Winterbottom
Screenplay: Jim Eldridge
Cinematography: Paul Wheeler
Editing: Olivia Hetreed
Music: Debbie Wiseman
Production design: Hayden Pearce
Costume design: Maxine Brown
Producer: Alan Horrox
Line producer: Julie Baines
Leading cast: Haydn Gwynne (Dr B.B.
    Miller), Kenneth Hall (Ben), Ian
    McNeice (Leather Hardbones),
    Kerry Shale (Hepworth)
Production company: Thames Television

'Cab Rank Cowboys'
Episode 9 in season 6 of TV series *Boon*
    (1986–1992)
Length: 60 mins
UK TX date: 19/11/91
Director: Michael Winterbottom
Screenplay: Peter Mann
Cinematography: Don Perrin
Editing: John Hawkins
Producer: Simon Lewis
Leading cast: Michael Elphick (Boon),
    Samantha Morton (Mandy), Neil
    Morrissey (Rocky Cassidy), David
    Daker (Harry Crawford)
Production company: Central Independent
    Television

1992
Forget About Me
Television film
UK TX date: 1/1/92
Director: Michael Winterbottom
Screenplay: Frank Cottrell Boyce
Editing: Olivia Hetreed
Production design: Katalin Kalmár
Costume design: Philip Crichton,
    Eva Zalavari

Executive producer: Alan Horrox
Producer: Richard Handford
Leading cast: Ewen Bremner (Broke),
    Brian McCardie (Bunny), Zsuzsanna
    Várkonyi (Czilla)
Production companies: Magyar Televízío
    Müvelödéso Föszerkesztöség, Thames
    Television

1993
'Death at the Bar'
Episode 4 in season 1 of TV series
    The Inspector Alleyn Mysteries
    (1990–1994)
UK TX date: 9/5/93
Director: Michael Winterbottom
Screenplay: Alfred Shaughnessy
Cinematography: John Walker
Editing: Jackie Powell, Robin Graham
    Scott
Music Ray Russell
Production design: Martin Methven
Costume design: Ken Trew
Producer: George Gallaccio
Associate producer: Diana Kyle
Leading cast: Patrick Malahide (Chief
    Inspector Alleyn), William Simons
    (Inspector Fox), Alan Gilchrist
    (PC Oates)
Production company: BBC

Love Lies Bleeding
Television film
Length: 89 mins
UK TX date: 22/9/93
Screenplay: Ronan Bennett
Cinematography: Eric Gillespie
Editing: David Spiers
Music: John Harle
Production design: Tom McCullagh
Executive producer: George Faber
Producer: Robert Cooper
Leading cast: Mark Rylance (Conn),
    Elisabeth Bourgine (Sophie Allen),
    Brendan Gleeson (Thomas Macken),
    James Nesbitt (Niall)

Production companies: BBC Northern
   Ireland, Télécip

'Mad Woman in the Attic' (Parts 1 and 2)
The pilot episode of the TV series *Cracker*
   (1993–96), broadcast in two parts.
Length: 102 mins
UK TX dates: 27/9/93, 4/10/93
Director: Michael Winterbottom
Screenplay: Jimmy McGovern
Cinematography: Ivan Strasburg
Editing: Trevor Waite
Music: Julian Wastall
Production design: Chris Wilkinson
Costume design: Janty Yates
Leading cast: Robbie Coltrane (Dr Eddie
   'Fitz' Fitzgerald), Christopher Eccleston
   (DCI David Bilborough), Lorcan
   Cranitch (DS Jimmy Beck), Barbara
   Flynn (Judith Fitzgerald), Geraldine
   Somerville (DS Jane Penhaligon)
Production companies: A&E Television
   Networks, Granada Television

1994
Under the Sun
Television film
Length: 77 mins
UK TX date: 24/2/94
Director: Michael Winterbottom
Screenplay: Susan Campbell
Cinematography: Daf Hobson
Costume design: Rachael Fleming
Producer: Alex Horrox
Leading cast: Kate Hardie (Ellie),
   Caroline Catz (Linda)
Production company: Thames Television

Family
A four-part TV mini-series that was also
   edited into a truncated feature film for
   international theatrical release; the four
   episodes are titled 'Charlo', 'John Paul',
   'Nicola', and 'Paula'.
Length: 200 mins (TV series), 118 mins
   (Feature film version)

TX dates (UK and Ireland): 8/5/94–
   25/5/94
Director: Michael Winterbottom
Screenplay: Roddy Doyle
Series cinematography: Daf Hobson
Series editing: Trevor Waite
Series music: John Harle
Series production design: Mark Geraghty
Series producer: Andrew Eaton
Associate producer: David Newcombe
Leading cast: Sean McGinley (Charlo
   Spencer), Ger Ryan (Paula Spencer),
   Neilí Conroy (Nicola Spencer), Barry
   Ward (John Paul Spencer), Gemma
   Butterly (Leanne Spencer), Jake
   Williams (Jack Spencer)
Production companies: BBC, Radio Telefís
   Éireann

1995
Butterfly Kiss
A television film that also received an
   international theatrical release
Length: 88 mins
UK TX date: 18/8/95
Director: Michael Winterbottom
Screenplay: Frank Cottrell Boyce
Cinematography: Seamus McGarvey
Editing: Trevor Waite
Music: John Harle
Production design: Rupert Miles
Costume design: Rachael Fleming
Producers: Julie Baines, Sarah Daniel
Leading cast: Amanda Plummer (Eunice),
   Saskia Reeves (Miriam), Des McAleer
   (Eric McDermott), Ricky Tomlinson
   (Robert)

Go Now
A television film that also received an
   international theatrical release
Length: 81 mins
UK TX date: 16/9/95
Director: Michael Winterbottom
Screenplay: Jimmy McGovern, Paul Henry
   Powell

Cinematography: Daf Hobson
Editing: Trevor Waite
Music: Alastair Gavin
Production design: Hayden Pearce
Costume design: Rachael Fleming
Executive producer: David M. Thompson
Producer: Andrew Eaton
Co-producer: Roxy Spencer
Associate producer: Sheila Fraser Milne
Leading cast: Robert Carlyle (Nick
    Cameron), Juliet Aubrey (Karen
    Walker), James Nesbitt (Tony), Sophie
    Okonedo (Paula)
Production companies: BBC, PolyGram
    Filmed Entertainment, Revolution Films

'Art's Promised Land'
The second episode from a six-part TV
    documentary series, *Cinema Europe:*
    The Other Hollywood
Length: 60 mins
UK TX date: 8/10/95
Director: Michael Winterbottom
Editing: Trevor Aylward
Music: Philip Appleby, Carl Davis
Producers: Kevin Brownlow, David Gill
Associate producer: Patrick Stanbury
Narrator: Kenneth Branagh
Production company: Photoplay
    Productions

1996
Jude
Length: 123 mins
Director: Michael Winterbottom
Screenplay: Hossein Amini
Cinematography: Eduardo Serra
Editing: Trevor Waite
Music: Adrian Johnston
Production design: Joseph Bennett
Costume design; Janty Yates
Executive producers: Mark Shivas, Stewart Till
Producer: Andrew Eaton
Associate producer: Sheila Fraser Milne
Leading cast: Christopher Eccleston (Jude
    Fawley), Kate Winslet (Sue Bridehead),

Liam Cunningham (Phillotson), Rachel
    Griffiths (Arabella), June Whitfield
    (Aunt Drusilla)
Production companies: BBC, PolyGram
    Filmed Entertainment, Revolution Films

1997
Welcome to Sarajevo
Length: 103 mins
Director: Michael Winterbottom
Screenplay: Frank Cottrell Boyce
Cinematography: Daf Hobson
Editing: Trevor Waite
Music: Adrian Johnston
Production design: Mark Geraghty, Kemal
    Hrustanovic
Costume design: Janty Yates
Producers: Ismet Arnautalic (Croatia),
    Graham Broadbent, Damian Jones
Associate producer (Croatia): Ivo Sunjic
Line producers; Paul Sarony, David Ball
Leading cast: Stephen Dillane (Michael
    Henderson), Woody Harrelson (Flynn),
    Kerry Fox (Jane Carson), Marisa Tomei
    (Nina), Emira Nusevic (Emira), Goran
    Visnjic (Risto Bavic), James Nesbitt
    (Gregg), Emily Lloyd (Annie McGee)
Production companies: Miramax Films,
    Channel Four Films, Dragon Pictures

1998
I Want You
Length: 87 mins
Director: Michael Winterbottom
Screenplay: Eoin McNamee
Cinematography: Slawomir Idziak
Editing: Trevor Waite
Music: Adrian Johnston
Production design: David Bowes, David
    Bryan, Mark Tildesley
Costume design: Rachael Fleming
Executive producer: Stewart Till
Producer: Andrew Eaton
Associate producer: Gina Carter
Leading cast: Rachel Weisz (Helen),
    Alessandro Nivola (Martin), Luka

Petrusic (Honda), Labina Mitevska (Smokey), Ben Daniels (Bob)
Production companies: PolyGram Filmed Entertainment, Revolution Films

1999
With or Without You
Length: 93 mins
Director: Michael Winterbottom
Screenplay: John Forte
Cinematography: Benoît Delhomme
Editing: Trevor Waite
Music: Adrian Johnston
Production design: Mark Tildesley
Costume design: Janty Yates
Producer: Andrew Eaton
Co-producer: Gina Carter
Line producer: Sandra Nixon
Leading cast: Christopher Eccleston (Vincent Boyd), Dervla Kirwan (Rosie Boyd), Yvan Attal (Benoit), Julie Graham (Cathy)
Production company: Revolution Films

Wonderland
Length: 108 mins
Director: Michael Winterbottom
Screenplay: Laurence Coriat
Cinematography: Sean Bobbitt
Editing: Trevor Waite
Music: Michael Nyman
Production design: Mark Tildesley
Costume design: Natalie Ward
Executive producers: David M. Thompson, Stewart Till
Co-producers: Michele Camarda, Gina Carter, Andrew Eaton
Line producer: Anita Overland
Leading cast: Gina McKee (Nadia), Shirley Henderson (Debbie), Molly Parker (Molly), Ian Hart (Dan), John Simm (Eddie), Jack Shepherd (Bill)
Production companies: BBC, Kismet Film Company, PolyGram Filmed Entertainment, Revolution Films, Universal Pictures

2000
The Claim
Length: 120 mins
Director: Michael Winterbottom
Screenplay: Frank Cottrell Boyce
Cinematography: Alwin H. Küchler
Editing: Trevor Waite
Music: Michael Nyman
Production design: Ken Rempel, Mark Tildesley
Costume design: Joanne Hansen
Executive producers: Andrea Calderwood, Martin Katz, Alexis Lloyd, Mark Shivas, David M. Thompson
Producer: Andrew Eaton
Co-producer: Douglas Berquist
Line producers: Jean-Yves Asselin, Anita Overland
Leading cast: Peter Mullan (Daniel Dillon), Milla Jovovich (Lucia), Wes Bentley (Donald Dalglish), Nastassja Kinski (Elena Burn), Sarah Polley (Hope Burn), Shirley Henderson (Annie), Julian Richings (Francis Bellanger)
Production companies: Alliance Atlantis Communications, Arts Council of England, BBC, Canal +, DB Entertainment, Grosvenor Park Productions, Pathé Pictures International, Revolution Films

2002
In This World
Length: 88 mins
Director: Michael Winterbottom
Screenplay: Tony Grisoni
Cinematography: Marcel Zyskind
Editing: Peter Christelis
Music: Dario Marianelli
Executive producers: Chris Auty, David M. Thompson
Producers: Andrew Eaton, Anita Overland
Co-producer: Behrooz Hashemian
Associate producer: Fiona Neilson
Leading cast: Jamal Udin Torabi (Jamal), Enayatullah (Enayat)

Production companies: The Film Consortium, BBC, Film Council, The Works, Revolution Films

24 Hour Party People
Length: 117 mins
Director: Michael Winterbottom
Screenplay: Frank Cottrell Boyce
Cinematography: Robby Müller
Editing: Trevor Waite
Production design: Mark Tildesley
Costume design: Stephen Noble, Natalie Ward
Executive producer: Henry Normal
Producer: Andrew Eaton
Co-producer: Gina Carter
Line producer: Robert How
Assistant producer: Fiona Neilson
Leading cast: Steve Coogan (Tony Wilson), Lennie James (Alan Erasmus), Shirley Henderson (Lindsay), Paddy Considine (Rob Gretton), Andy Serkis (Martin Hannett), Sean Harris (Ian Curtis), Danny Cunningham (Shaun Ryder)
Production companies: Revolution Films, Baby Cow Productions, The Film Consortium, Film Council, FilmFour, Wave Pictures, Channel Four Films

2003
Code 46
Length: 93 mins
Director: Michael Winterbottom
Screenplay: Frank Cottrell Boyce
Cinematography: Alwin H. Küchler, Marcel Zyskind
Editing: Peter Christelis
Music: The Free Association
Production design: Mark Tildesley
Costume design: Natalie Ward
Executive producers: Robert Jones, David M. Thompson
Producer: Andrew Eaton
Line producers: Arti Gupta, Rosa Romero
Leading cast: Samantha Morton (Maria Gonzales), Tim Robbins (William

Geld), Om Puri (Bakhland), Nabil Elouahabi (vendor)
Production companies: BBC, Kailash Picture Company, Revolution Films

2004
9 Songs
Length: 71 mins
Director: Michael Winterbottom
Screenplay: Michael Winterbottom
Cinematography: Marcel Zyskind
Editing: Mat Whitecross, Michael Winterbottom
Executive producer: Andrew Eaton
Producers: Andrew Eaton, Michael Winterbottom
Associate producer: Melissa Parmenter
Cast: Kieran O'Brien (Matt), Margo Stilley (Lisa)
Production company: Revolution Films

2005
A Cock and Bull Story
Length: 94 mins
Director: Michael Winterbottom
Screenplay: Frank Cottrell Boyce
Cinematography: Marcel Zyskind
Editing: Peter Christelis
Music: Edward Nogria
Production design: John Paul Kelly
Costume design: Charlotte Walter
Executive producers: Jeff Abberley, Julia Blackman, Henry Normal, Kate Ogborn, Tracey Scofield, David M. Thompson
Producer: Andrew Eaton
Co-producers: Wendy Brazington, Anita Overland
Leading cast: Steve Coogan (Tristram Shandy, Walter Shandy, Steve Coogan), Rob Brydon (Toby Shandy, Rob Brydon), Keeley Hawes (Elizabeth Shandy, Keeley Hawes), Kelly Macdonald (Jenny), Naomie Harris (Jennie), Jeremy Northam (Mark), Shirley Henderson (Susannah)

Production companies: BBC Films, Baby Cow Productions, EM Media, East Midlands Media Initiative, Revolution Films, Scion Films

2006

The Road to Guantánamo

This film was released simultaneously on four platforms: TV broadcast, internet streaming, DVD and in cinemas.

UK TX date: 9/3/06

Length: 95 mins

Directors: Michael Winterbottom, Mat Whitecross

Editing: Michael Winterbottom, Mat Whitecross

Cinematography: Marcel Zyskind

Music: Harry Escott, Molly Nyman

Production design: Mark Digby

Executive producer: Lee Thomas

Producers: Andrew Eaton, Melissa Parmenter, Michael Winterbottom

Line producer (Iran): Michael Elliott

Leading cast: Riz Ahmed (Shafiq Rasul), Farhad Harun (Ruhel Ahmed), Waqar Siddiqui (Monir Ali), Arfan Usman (Asif Iqbal), Shahid Iqbal (Zahid)

Production companies: Film4, Revolution Films, Screen West Midlands

2007

A Mighty Heart

Length: 108 mins

Director: Michael Winterbottom

Screenplay: John Orloff

Cinematography: Marcel Zyskind

Editing: Peter Christelis

Music: Harry Escott, Molly Nyman

Production design: Mark Digby

Costume design: Charlotte Walter

Producers: Andrew Eaton, Dede Gardner, Brad Pitt

Co-producer: Anita Overland

Local producer (India): Arti Gupta

Line producer (Texas): Susan Kirr

Leading cast: Angelina Jolie (Mariane Pearl), Dan Futterman (Daniel Pearl), Archie Panjabi (Asra), Irrfan Khan (Captain), Will Patton (Randall Bennett), Denis O'Hare (John Bussey)

Production companies: Paramount Vantage, Plan B Entertainment, Revolution Films, Kailash Picture Company

2008

Genova

Length: 94 mins

Director: Michael Winterbottom

Screenplay: Laurence Coriat, Michael Winterbottom

Cinematography: Marcel Zyskind

Editing: Paul Monaghan, Michael Winterbottom

Music: Melissa Parmenter

Production design: Mark Digby

Costume design: Celia Yau

Executive producers: Simon Fawcett, Tessa Ross

Producers: Andrew Eaton, Michael Winterbottom

Co-producer: Wendy Brazington

Line producer: Melissa Parmenter

Local line producers: Philip Koch (USA), Eiffel Mattsson (Sweden)

Leading cast: Colin Firth (Joe), Perla Haney-Jardine (Mary), Willa Holland (Kelly), Catherine Keener (Barbara), Hope Davis (Marianne)

Production companies: Revolution Films, Aramid Entertainment Fund, Film4, Moviola Film och Television AB

2009

The Shock Doctrine

Length: 79 mins

UK TX date: 1/9/09

Directors: Michael Winterbottom, Mat Whitecross

Writer: Naomi Klein

Editing: Paul Monaghan, Mat Whitecross, Michael Winterbottom
Producer: Andrew Eaton
Co-producer: Melissa Parmenter
Line producer (Chicago): Philip Koch
Associate producer (Chicago): Sally Marschall
Narrator: Kieran O'Brien
Production companies: Renegade Pictures, Revolution Films

2010

The Trip
A six-part TV series, this was also edited into a truncated feature film for international cinema and DVD release
Length: 172 minutes (TV series), 107 mins (feature film version)
UK TX dates: 6/11/10–6/12/10
Director: Michael Winterbottom
Cinematography: Ben Smithard
Editing: Mags Arnold, Paul Monaghan
Costume design: Celia Yau
Executive producers: Andrew Eaton, Henry Normal, Simon Lupton, Michael Winterbottom
Producers: Andrew Eaton, Melissa Parmenter
Associate producer: Anthony Wilcox
Leading cast: Steve Coogan (Steve Coogan) Rob Brydon (Rob Brydon), Rebecca Johnson (Sally), Margo Stilley (Mischa)
Production companies: Revolution Films, Baby Cow Productions, Arbie, BBC

The Killer Inside Me
Length: 109 mins
Director: Michael Winterbottom
Screenplay: John Curran
Cinematography: Marcel Zyskind
Editing: Mags Arnold
Music: Joel Cadbury, Melissa Parmenter
Production design: Rob Simons, Mark Tildesley
Costume design: Lynette Meyer

Executive producers: Lily Bright, Chad Burris, Jordan Gertner, Alan Liebert, Randy Mendelsohn, Tom Ritchie, Fernando Sulichin
Co-executive producer: Tricia von Klaveren
Producers: Andrew Eaton, Chris Hanley, Bradford L. Schlei
Co-producers Anna Croneman, Tomas Eskilsson, Susan Kirr
Associate producer: Tara Subkoff
Leading cast: Casey Affleck (Lou Ford), Kate Hudson (Amy Stanton), Jessica Alba (Joyce Lakeland), Simon Baker (Howard Hendricks), Ned Beatty (Chester Conway), Tom Bower (Sheriff Bob Maples)
Production companies: Hero Entertainment, Muse Productions, Stone Canyon Entertainment, Revolution Films, Curiously Bright Entertainment, Indion Entertainment Group, BOB Film Sweden AB, Film i Väst

2011

60 Seconds of Solitude in Year Zero
An anthology of one-minute films by sixty directors from around the world, including Winterbottom. The film was screened once on 22/12/11 in Tallinn, Estonia at the Black Nights Film Festival
Length: 60 mins
Directors: Michael Winterbottom et al.
Producer: Birgit Kruloo
Associate producer: Eero Tammi
Music: Ülo Krigul
Cinematography: Kaligna Deshapriya Vithanage
Editing: Saman Alvitigala

Trishna
Length: 117 mins
Director: Michael Winterbottom
Screenplay: Michael Winterbottom
Cinematography: Marcel Zyskind
Editing: Mags Arnold

Music: Amit Trivedi, Shigeru Umebayashi
Production design: David Bryan
Costume Design: Niharika Khan
Executive producers: Andrew Eaton, Phil
    Hunt, Compton Ross, Shail Shah
Producers: Sunil Bohra, Melissa Parmenter,
    Michael Winterbottom
Co-producers: Jessica Ask, Anurag
    Kashyap, Guneet Monga, Anthony
    Wilcox
Associate producers: Elliot Ross, Fenella
    Ross
Line producers: Alice Dawson, Meraj
    Shaikh
Leading Cast: Freida Pinto (Trishna), Riz
    Ahmed (Jay Singh), Roshan Seth (Mr
    Singh)
Production companies: Film i Väst, Head
    Gear Films, Revolution Films

2012
Everyday
Television film
Length: 106 mins
UK TX date: 18/1/13
Director: Michael Winterbottom
Screenplay: Laurence Coriat, Michael
    Winterbottom
Cinematography: Sean Bobbit, James
    Clarke, Anne Marie Lean Vercoe, Simon
    Tindall, Marcel Zyskind
Editing: Mags Arnold, Paul Monaghan
Music: Michael Nyman
Executive producer: Andrew Eaton
Producer: Melissa Parmenter

Associate producer: Josh Hyams
Leading cast: Shirley Henderson (Karen),
    John Simm (Ian), Shaun Kirk (Shaun),
    Robert Kirk (Robert) Katrina Kirk
    (Katrina), Stephanie Kirk (Stephanie)
Production companies: Revolution Films,
    Channel 4 Television Corporation

2013
The Look of Love
Length: 101 mins
Director: Michael Winterbottom
Screenplay: Matt Greenhalgh
Cinematography: Hubert Taczanowski
Editing: Mags Arnold
Music: Antony Glenn, Martin Slattery
Production design: Jacqueline Abrahams
Costume design: Stephanie Collie
Executive producers: Jenny Borgars,
    Katherine Butler, Andrew Eaton,
    Norman Merry, Danny Perkins, Tessa
    Ross, Piers Wenger
Producer: Melissa Parmenter
Co-producers: Alice Dawson, Josh Hyams
Line producer: Amy Jackson
Leading cast: Imogen Poots (Debbie
    Raymond), Steve Coogan (Paul
    Raymond), Tamsin Egerton (Fiona
    Richmond), Anna Friel (Jean
    Raymond), Chris Addison (Tony Power)
Production companies: Revolution Films,
    Baby Cow Films, Film Four, AGM
    Factory (French version), Lipsync
    Productions

BIBLIOGRAPHY

Agamben, Giorgio (1998) *Homo Sacer: Sovereign Power and Bare Life*. trans. Daniel Heller-Roazen. Stanford: Stanford University Press.

Ahmed, Sara (2008) 'Multiculturalism and the Promise of Happiness', *New Formations*, no. 63, 121–37.

____ (2000) *Strange Encounters: Embodied Others in Post-Coloniality*. London and New York: Routledge.

Alleva, Richard (2007) 'All Too Real: *A Mighty Heart*', *Commonweal*, vol. 134, no. 14, 20–1

Allinson, Deborah (2005) 'Michael Winterbottom', *Senses of Cinema*. http://senses ofcinema.com/2005/great-directors/winterbottom (accessed 11 June 2013).

Anon. (2006) 'Blair: Guantánamo is an anomaly', *The Guardian*, 17 February. http://www.guardian.co.uk/guantanamo/story/0,,1712066,00.html (accessed 28 February 2007).

Anon. (2006a) *The Road to Guantánamo* production notes. http://www.roadto guantanamomovie.com (accessed 11 June 2013).

Anon. (2008) 'US-created terrorism documentary shown at Gitmo tribunal; introduced as 'evidence'', 28/7/08. http://www.infowars.com/us-created-terrorism-documentary-introduced-at-gitmo-tribunal-as-evidence (accessed 27 October 2010).

Anzaldúa, Gloria (1987) *Borderlands/La Frontera: The New Mestiza*. San Francisco: Aunt Lute Books.

Arthur, Paul (2006) '*The Road to Guantanamo*', *Film Comment*, vol. 42, no. 3, 71–2.

Astruc, Alexandre (1968) 'The Birth of a New Avant-Garde: La Camera-Stylo', in Peter Graham (ed.) *The New Wave: Critical Landmarks*. New York: Doubleday, 17–23.

Atkinson, Michael (1998) 'Michael Winterbottom: Cinema as Heart Attack', *Film Comment*, vol. 34, no. 1, 44–7.

Augé, Marc (1995) *Non-Places: Introduction to an Anthropology of Supermodernity*. London: Verso.

Banita, Georgiana (2008) 'Decency, Torture and the Words that Tell Us Nothing', *Peace Review*, vol. 20, no. 1, 58–66.

Baraitser, Lisa (2009) *Maternal Encounters: The Ethics of Interruption*. London and New York: Routledge.

Bardan, Alice (2008) 'Welcome to Dreamland: The Realist Impulse in Pawel Pawlikowski's *Last Resort*', *New Cinemas: Journal of Contemporary Film*, vol. 6, no. 1, 47–63.

Barthes, Roland (1977) *Image – Music – Text*. trans. Stephen Heath. Glasgow: Fontana.

Baudrillard, Jean (1995) *The Gulf War Did Not Take Place*. trans. Paul Patton, Sydney: Power Publications.

Baxter, John (1998) *Stanley Kubrick: A Biography*. London: HarperCollins.

Bazin, André (1971 [1948]) 'An Aesthetic of Reality: Cinematic Realism and the Italian School of the Liberation', in *What is Cinema? Volume II*. trans. Hugh Gray, Berkeley: University of California Press, 16–40.

____ (1985) 'On the *politique des auteurs*', in Jim Hillier (ed.) *Cahiers du Cinéma: The 1950s: Neo-Realism, Hollywood, New Wave*. Cambridge, MA: Harvard University Press, 248–59.

Beckett, Samuel (1983) *Worstward Ho!* London: John Calder.

Bedell, Geraldine (2004) 'A Winterbottom's Tale', *The Observer*, 1 February. http://www.guardian.co.uk/film/2004/feb/01/features.review (accessed 6 February 2012).

Behar, Ruth (1993) *Translated Woman: Crossing the Border with Esperanza's Story*. Boston: Beacon Press.

Bennett, Bruce (2007) 'Towards a General Economics of Cinema', in Susan Bruce and Valeria Wagner (eds) *Fiction and Economy*. London and New York: Palgrave Macmillan, 167–86.

____ (2010) 'Framing Terror: Cinema, Docudrama and the "War on Terror"', *Studies in Documentary Film*, vol. 4, no. 3, 209–26.

Bennett, Bruce and Imogen Tyler (2007) 'Screening Unlivable Lives: The New Cinema of Borders', in Aniko Imre, Katarzyna Marciniak and Aine O'Healy (eds) *Transnational Feminism in Film and Media: Visibility, Representation and Sexual Differences*. London and New York: Palgrave Macmillan, 21–36.

Berlant, Lauren (ed.) (2000) *Intimacy*. Chicago: University of Chicago Press.

Bordwell, David (2003) 'Authorship and narration in art cinema', in Virginia Wright Wexman (ed.) *Film and Authorship*. New Brunswick, NJ: Rutgers University Press, 42–9.

____ (2007) *The Poetics of Cinema*. London and New York: Routledge.

Bordwell, David and Kristin Thompson (1993) *Film Art: An Introduction*. Madison, WI: McGraw-Hill.

Bordwell, David, Janet Staiger and Kristin Thompson (1988) *The Classical Hollywood Cinema: Film Style and Mode of Production to 1960*. Routledge: London.

Boyce, Frank Cottrell (1997) *Welcome to Sarajevo*. London: Faber and Faber.

Broadbent, Sabrina, (2004) *Descent*. London: Chatto and Windus.

Brooks, B. (2005) 'Clooney speaks out about journalism and filmmaking as NYFF opens', *indieWIRE*, 22 September 2005. http://www.indiewire.com/ots/2005/09/george_clooney.html (accessed 11 October 2007.

Brown, James (2004) 'Lights, camera, explicit action', *The Independent*, 13 May, 6–7.

Brown, Mark (2010) 'Ken Loach: TV is the Enemy of Creativity'. *The Guardian*, 15 October 2010. http://www.guardian.co.uk/tv-and-radio/2010/oct/15/ken-loach-london-film-festival (accessed 3 July 2013).

Brunsdon, Charlotte (2004) 'The Poignancy of Place: London and the Cinema', *Visual Culture in Britain*, vol. 5, no. 1, 59–73.

Buckland, Warren (1998) 'A Close Encounter with *Raiders of the Lost Ark*: Notes on Narrative Aspects of the New Hollywood Blockbuster', in Steve Neale and Murray Smith (eds) *Contemporary Hollywood Cinema*. London: Routledge, 166–77.

____ (2006) *Directed by Steven Spielberg: Poetics of the Contemporary Hollywood Blockbuster*. New York and London: Continuum.

Buñuel, Luis (1991) 'Cinema, Instrument of Poetry', in Philip Hammond (ed.) *The Shadow and Its Shadow: Surrealist Writing on the Cinema.* Edinburgh: Polygon, 117–21.

Burdeau, E. (2008) 'En Ligne avec Brian De Palma' [On-line with Brian De Palma], *Cahiers du Cinéma*, no. 631, 12–16.

Butler, Judith (1993) *Bodies that Matter: On the Discursive Limits of Sex.* New York and London: Routledge.

____ (2004) *Precarious Life: The Powers of Mourning and Violence.* London and New York: Verso.

____ (2009) *Frames of War: When is Life Grievable?* London and New York: Verso.

Camino, Mercedes Maroto (2005) '"The war is so young": Masculinity and War Correspondence in Welcome to Sarajevo and Territorio Comanche', *Studies in European Cinema*, vol. 2, no. 2, 115–24.

Castillo, Debra A. and Maria Socorro Tabuenca Córdoba (2002) *Border Women: Writing from La Frontera.* Minneapolis: University of Minnesota Press.

Chang, Kimberly, and L. H. Ling (2000) 'Globalization and Its Intimate Other: Filipina Domestic Workers in Hong Kong', in Marianne H. Marchand and Anne S. Runyan (eds) *Gender and Global Restructuring: Sightings, Sites and Resistances.* New York: Routledge, 27–43.

Ciment, Michel and Yann Tobin (1996) 'Michael Winterbottom', *Positif*, no. 12, 23

Cocteau, Jean (1991) 'Profile of Orson Welles', in André Bazin, *Orson Welles: A Critical View.* trans. Jonathan Rosenbaum. Los Angeles: Acrobat Books, 29–32.

Cook, Pam (ed.) (1985) *The Cinema Book.* London: British Film Istitute.

Cooke, Rachel (2010) 'Michael Winterbottom on The Killer Inside Me', *The Observer*, 23 May 2010. http://www.guardian.co.uk/film/2010/may/23/michael-winterbottom-killer-inside-me (accessed 14 April 2011).

Corner, John (1996) *The Art of Record: A Critical Introduction to Documentary.* Manchester and New York: Manchester University Press.

Cowie, Elizabeth (1999) 'The Spectacle of Actuality', in Jane M. Gaines and Michael Renov (eds.) *Collecting Visible Evidence.* Minneapolis and London: University of Minnesota Press, 19–45.

Craig, Cairns (1991) 'Rooms without a view', *Sight and Sound*, vol. 1, no. 6, 10–13.

Cronin, Paul (ed.) (2002) *Herzog on Herzog.* London: Faber and Faber.

Damico, James (1978) 'Film noir: a modest proposal', *Film Reader*, no. 3, 48–57.

Davies, E. and K. Withers (2006) *Public Innovation: Intellectual Property in a Digital Age.* London: Institute for Public Policy Research.

Dawtrey, Adam (2007) '"Seven Days" to take five years: Winterbottom starts prison drama', *Variety online*, May 20, 2007. http://www.variety.com/article/VR1117965396.html?categoryid=13&cs=1 (accessed 19 December 2008).

Deleuze, Gilles (1992) 'Postscript on the societies of control', *October*, vol. 59, 3–7.

Dix, Andrew (2009) '"Do you want this world left on?": Global Imaginaries in the films of Michael Winterbottom', *Style*, vol. 43, no. 1, 3–25.

Doane, Mary Anne (1992) 'Film and the Masquerade: Theorising the Female Spectator', in Gerald Mast, Marshall Cohen and Leo Braudy (eds) *Film Theory and Criticism: Introductory Readings* (fourth edition). Oxford: Oxford University Press, 758–72.

Drake, Philip (2003) 'Low Blows: Theorizing performance in post-classical comedian comedy', in Frank Krutnik (ed.) *Hollywood Comedians: The Film Reader.* London and New York: Routledge.

Durgnat, Raymond (1996) 'Paint it Black: The Family Tree of Film Noir', in Alain Silver, James Ursini (eds) *Film Noir Reader*. Pompton Plains, NJ: Limelight, 37–51.

Dyer, Richard (2004) 'Feeling English', *Sight and Sound*, vol. 4, no. 3, 16–19.

Ebrahimian, Babak (2004) *The Cinematic Theater*. Lanham, MD: Scarecrow Press.

Ellis, John (1990) *Visible Fictions: Cinema, Television, Video*. London: Routledge.

Elsaesser, Thomas (1987) 'Tales of Sound and Fury', in Christine Gledhill (ed.) *Home is Where the Heart Is: Studies in Melodrama and The Woman's Film*. London: British Film Institute.

Farndale, Nigel (2007) 'Michael Winterbottom: I try not to crack the whip', *Daily Telegraph*, 16 September 2007, http://www.telegraph.co.uk/culture/3667957/Michael-Winterbottom-I-try-not-to-crack-the-whip.html (accessed 6 February 2012).

Fisher, Mark (2009) *Capitalist Realism: Is There No Alternative?* Winchester: Zero Books.

Foucault, Michel (1967) 'Of Other Spaces', trans. J. Miskowiec, http://foucault.info/documents/heteroTopia/foucault.heteroTopia.en.html (accessed 11 September 2007).

_____ (1977) 'What is an author?', in *Language, Counter-Memory, Practice: Selected Essays and Interviews by Michel Foucault*, ed. Donald F. Bouchard. Ithaca, NY: Cornell Universti Press, 113–38.

Frankel, David (2010) 'A Lawman Gone Wrong', *American Cinematographer*, vol. 91, no. 7, 22–4.

Freud, Sigmund (1976) *The Interpretation of Dreams*. trans. James Strachey. London: Penguin.

_____ (1986) *The Essentials of Psychoanalysis*. ed. Anna Freud, trans. James Strachey. London: Penguin.

Gaut, Berys (1997) 'Film Authorship and Collaboration', in Richard Allen and Murray Smith (eds) *Film Theory and Philosophy*. Oxford: Oxford University Press, 149–72.

Getino, Octavio and Fernando Solanas (1976) 'Towards a Third Cinema', in Bill Nichols (ed.) *Movies and Methods, Volume 1*. Berkeley: University of California Press, 44–4.

Gilbey, Ryan (2004) 'Open Mike', *Sight and Sound*, vol. 14, no. 10, 30–4.

Goss, Brian Michael (2009) *Global Auteurs: Politics in the Films of Almodóvar, von Trier, and Winterbottom*. New York: Peter Lang.

Goudal, Jean (1991) 'Surrealism and Cinema', in Philip Hammond (ed.) *The Shadow and Its Shadow: Surrealist Writing on the Cinema.* Edinburgh: Polygon, 91–102.

Grewal, Inderpal and Caren Kaplan (eds) (1994) *Scattered Hegemonies: Postmodernity and Transnational Feminist Practices*. Minneapolis: University of Minnesota Press.

Grimmer, M. (2006) 'Guantanamo Stars Detained in Luton', http://www.thelip.org/?p=129 (accessed 28 February 2007).

Gunning, Tom (2000) 'The Cinema of Attraction: Early Film, Its Spectator, and the Avant-Garde', in Robert Stam and Toby Miller (eds) *Film and Theory: An Anthology*. Oxford: Blackwell, 229–35.

Hayward, Susan (2000) 'Framing National Cinemas', in Mette Hjort and Scott Mackenzie (eds) *Cinema and Nation*. London and New York: Routledge, 88–102.

Higson, Andrew (1995) *Waving the Flag: Constructing a National Cinema in Britain*. Oxford: Clarendon Press.

Hollinger, Karen (1996) '*Film Noir*, Voice-over, and the Femme Fatale', in Alain Silver and James Ursini (eds) *Film Noir Reader*. Pompton Plains, NJ: Limelight. 243–60.

Houellebecq, Michel (2003) *Platform*, trans. Frank Wynne. London: Vintage.

Ignatieff, Michael (2004) 'Terrorist as Auteur', *New York Times*, 14 November 2004, http://www.nytimes.com/2004/11/14/movies/14TERROR.html (accessed 28 September 2009).

Iordanova, Dina (2001) *Cinema of Flames: Balkan Film, Culture and the Media.* London: British Film Institute.

Jaafar, Ali (2007) 'A world without pity', *Sight and Sound*, vol. 17, no. 10, 24–6.

Jacobson, Harlan (2007) '*A Mighty Heart*: Review', *Film Comment*, vol. 43, no. 4, 70–1.

Jameson, Fredric (2004) 'Thoughts on Balkan cinema', in Atom Egoyan and Ian Balfour (eds) *Subtitles: On the Foreignness of Film.* Cambridge, MA and London: MIT Press, 231–57.

Johnson, B. D. (2007) 'A triumph of acting over stardom', *Maclean's*, vol. 120, no. 5, 53.

Johnston, Sheila (2009) 'Michael Winterbottom interview: on his film, *Genova*', *Daily Telegraph*, 31 Mar 2009. http://www.telegraph.co.uk/culture/film/filmmakersonfilm/5060994/Michael-Winterbottom-interview-on-his-film-Genova.html (accessed 30 March 2012).

Kaplan, E. Ann (1978) *Women in Film Noir.* London: British Film Institute.

Kellner, Douglas (2010) *Cinema Wars: Hollywood Film and Politics in the Bush-Cheney Era.* Chichester: Wiley-Blackwell.

Klein, Naomi (2007) *The Shock Doctrine: The Rise of Disaster Capitalism.* London: Penguin.

____ (2009) 'Clarification on "Shock Doctrine" Documentary', August 30, 2009, Available from: http://www.naomiklein.org/articles/2009/08/clarification-shock-doctrine-documentary (accessed 7 June 2011).

Krämer, Peter (1998) 'Post-classical Hollywood', in John Hill and Pamela Church Gibson (eds) *The Oxford Guide to Film Studies.* Oxford: Oxford University Press, 289–309.

Lang, Robert (1997) '*My Own Private Idaho* and the New Queer Road Movies', in Steven Cohan and Ina Rae Hark (eds) *The Road Movie Book.* Routledge: London and New York, 330–48.

Lentini, P. and Bakshmar, M. (2007) 'Jihadist beheading: A Convergence of Technology, Theology, and Teleology?', *Studies in Conflict and Terrorism*, vol. 30, no. 4, 303–25.

Loshitzky, Yosefa (2006) 'Journeys of Hope to Fortress Europe', *Third Text*, vol. 20, no. 6, 745–54.

____ (2010) *Screening Strangers: Migration and Diaspora in Contemporary European Cinema.* Bloomington, IN: Indiana University Press.

Lovell, Alan (2001) 'The British Cinema: The Known Cinema?', in Robert Murphy (ed.) *The British Cinema Book,* London: British Film Institute, 200–5.

McBride, Ian (2005) 'Where Are We Going, and How and Why?', in Alan Rosenthal and John Corner (eds) *New Challenges for Documentary* (second edition). Manchester: Manchester University Press, 485–92.

McLoone, Martin (2001) 'Internal Decolonisation? British Cinema in the Celtic Fringe', in Robert Murphy (ed) *The British Cinema Book.* London: British Film Institute, 184–90.

Marks, Peter (2008) 'Surveillance Screens and Screening in *Code 46*', *Scan: Journal of Media Arts Culture*, vol. 5, no. 1, May 2008. http://scan.net.au/scan/journal/display.php?journal_id=108 (accessed 11 April 2011).

Metz, Christian (2000) 'The Imaginary Signifier', in Robert Stam and Toby Miller (eds) *Film and Theory: An Anthology.* Oxford: Blackwell, 408–36.

Miller, Jacques-Alain (2008) 'Extimity', *The Symptom*, no. 9, June 20, http://www.lacan.com/symptom/?p=36 (accessed 12 June 2013).

Mills, T. (2008) 'Evan Kohlmann: The Doogie Howser of Terrorism', *Spinwatch: Monitoring PR and Spin* website, 29 April 2008. http://www.spinwatch.org.uk/-articles-by-category-mainmenu-8/74-terror-spin/4850-evan-kohlmann-the-doogie-howser-of-terrorism (accessed 27 October 2010).

Mohanty, Chandra Talpade (1991) 'Under Western Eyes: Feminist Scholarship and Colonial Discourses', in Chandra Talpade Mohanty, Anna Russo and Lourdes Torres (eds) *Third World Women and the Politics of Feminism.* Bloomington, IN: Indiana University Press, 51–81.

____ (2003) '"Under Western Eyes" Revisited: Feminist Solidarity through Anticapitalist Struggles', *Signs*, vol. 28, no. 2, 499–535.

Molloy, Patricia (2000) 'Theatrical Release: Catharsis and Spectacle in *Welcome to Sarajevo*', *Alternatives: Global, Local, Political*, vol. 25, no. 1, 75–91.

Monk, Claire (2001) 'Sexuality and heritage', in Ginette Vincendeau (ed.) *Film/Literature/Heritage: A Sight and Sound Reader.* London: British Film Institute, 6–11.

____ (2002) 'The British heritage-film debate revisited', in Claire Monk and Amy Sargeant (eds) *British Historical Cinema: The History, Heritage and Costume Film.* London and New York: Routledge, 176–98.

Mulvey, Laura (1992) 'Visual Pleasure and Narrative Cinema', in Gerald Mast, Marshall Cohen and Leo Braudy (eds) *Film Theory and Criticism: Introductory Readings, Fourth Edition.* Oxford: Oxford University Press, 746–57.

Murray, Craig (2007) *Murder in Samarkand.* Edinburgh: Mainstream.

Naficy, Hamid (2001) *An Accented Cinema: Exilic and Diasporic Filmmaking.* Princeton, NJ: Princeton University Press.

Neale, Steve (1987) *Genre.* London: British Film Institute.

Nichols, Bill (1991) *Representing Reality: Issues and Concepts in Documentary.* Bloomington, IN: Indiana University Press.

Nicholson, Michael (1994) *Natasha's Story.* London: Pan.

O'Connell, John (2010) 'True Stories: The Shock Doctrine', in Damon Smith (ed.) *Michael Winterbottom: Interviews.* Jackson, MI: University Press of Mississippi, 131–4.

Oppenheimer, Jean (2001) 'Production Slate: Mining for Drama, *American Cinematographer*, vol. 82, no. 3, 22–32.

Orr, Deborah (2006) 'A tantalising glimpse of truth can be found on the road to Guantanamo', *The Independent,* 11 March 2006, http://comment.independent.co.uk/commentators/deborah_orr/article350590.ece (accessed 2 October 2007).

Paget, Derek (1998) *No Other Way to Tell It: Dramadoc/docudrama on Television.* Manchester: Manchester University Press.

Paglen, Trevor and A. C. Thompson (2007) *Torture Taxi: On the Trail of the CIA's Rendition Flights.* Cambridge: Icon Books.

Pearl, Judah (2007) 'Mixed Message: Daniel Pearl's father on *A Mighty Heart*', *New Republic*, vol. 237, no. 2, 18–19.

Pearl, Mariane (2003) *A Mighty Heart: The Brave Life and Death of My Husband, Danny Pearl.* New York: James Bennett.

Pidduck, Julianne (2004) *Contemporary Costume Film: Space, Place and the Past.* London: British Film Institute.

Place, Janey (1978) 'Women in film noir', in E. Ann Kaplan (ed.) *Women in Film Noir.* London: British Film Institute, 35–67.

Polan, Dana B. (1974) 'Brecht and the politics of self-reflexive cinema'. *Jump Cut*, no. 1, 1974. http://www.ejumpcut.org/archive/onlinessays/JC17folder/BrechtPolan.html (accessed 6 February 2012).

Power, Nina (2009) *One-Dimensional Woman*. Winchester: Zero Books.

Rajadhyaksha, Ashish (1997) 'India: Filming the Nation', in Geoffrey Nowell-Smith (ed.) *The Oxford History of World Cinema*. Oxford: Oxford University Press. 678–89.

_____ (2008) 'Hindi Cinema', in Pam Cook (ed.) *The Cinema Book* (third edition). London: British Film Institute, 217–21.

Rancière, Jacques (2010) *Chronicles of Consensual Times*. trans. Steven Corcoran, London: Continuum.

Renov, Michael (1999) 'Documentary Horizons: An Afterword', in Jane M. Gaines and Michael Renov (eds) *Collecting Visible Evidence*. Minneapolis: University of Minnesota Press, 313–25.

_____ (2004) *The Subject of Documentary*. Minneapolis: University of Minnesota Press.

Roberts, Shari (1997) 'Western Meets Eastwood: Genre and Gender on the Road', in Steven Cohan and Ina Rae Hark (eds) *The Road Movie Book*. Routledge: London and New York, 45–69.

Root, Jane (1985) 'Film noir' in Pam Cook (ed.) *The Cinema Book*. London: British Film Institute, 93–8.

Rouch, Jean (1981) 'Filming Reality, and the Documentary Vision of the Imaginary', http://www.diplomatie. gouv.fr/en/france-priorities_1/ documentary_2312/non-commercial-distribution_2313/dvd-collection_2314/ grand-ecran-big-screen_4428/tribute-to-jean-rouch_3220/filming-reality-and-the-documentary-vision-of-the-imaginary_3222/by-jean-rouch_3786. html?var_recherche=filmmaking (accessed 2 March 2007).

Sanders, Jonathan (1995) *Another Fine Dress: Role-Play in the Films of Laurel and Hardy*. London and New York: Cassell.

Sarris, Andrew (1992) 'Notes on the Auteur Theory in 1962', in Gerald Mast,

Marshall Cohen and Leo Braudy (eds) *Film Theory and Criticism: Introductory Readings, Fourth Edition*. Oxford: Oxford University Press, 585–8.

Scott, A. O. (2006) '"The Road to Guantánamo" Offers Grim Chronicles that Anger and Stir', *New York Times*, 23 June 2006. http://www.nytimes. com/2006/06/23/movies/23guan. html?_r=1&oref=slogin (accessed 30 June 2008).

Self, Robert T. (2002) *Robert Altman's Subliminal Reality*. Minneapolis: University of Minnesota Press.

Seltzer, Mark (1998) *Serial Killers: Death and Life in America's Wound Culture*. New York and London: Routledge.

Shapiro, Michael (2007) 'The New Violent Cartography', *Security Dialogue*, vol. 38, no. 3, 291–313.

Shaviro, Steven (2010) *Post-Cinematic Affect*. Winchester: Zero Books.

Shohat, Ella and Robert Stam (1994) *Unthinking Eurocentrism: Multiculturalism and the Media*. New York and London: Routledge.

Sobchack, Vivian (2004) *Carnal Thoughts: Embodiment and Moving Image Culture*. Berkeley: University of California Press.

Solnit, Rebecca (2004) *Motion Studies: Time, Space and Eadweard Muybridge*. London: Bloomsbury.

Stacey, Jackie (2010) *The Cinematic Life of the Gene*. Durham, NC: Duke University Press.

Stam, Robert (2000) *Film Theory: An Introduction*. Oxford: Blackwell.

Stanfield, Peter (2011) *Maximum Movies – Pulp Fictions: Film Culture and the Worlds of Sam Fuller, Mickey Spillane and Jim Thompson*. New Brunswick, NJ: Rutgers University Press.

Stringer, Julian (1997) 'Exposing Intimacy in Russ Meyer's *Motorpsycho* and *Faster Pussycat! Kill! Kill!*', in Ina Rae Hark (ed.) *The Road Movie Book*. London: Routledge, 165–78.

Studlar, Gaylyn (1985) 'Visual Pleasure and the Masochistic Aesthetic', *Journal of Film and Video*, vol. 37, no. 2, 5–26.

Szeman, Imre (2002) 'Remote Sensing: An Interview with Ursula Biemann' *The Review of Education, Pedagogy, and Cultural Studies*, vol. 24, no. 1/2, 91–109.

Truffaut, François (1986) *Hitchcock*. London: Paladin.

Tyler, Imogen (2006) '"Welcome to Britain": The Cultural Politics of Asylum', *European Journal of Cultural Studies*, vol. 9, no. 2, 185–202.

Urry, John and Jonas Larsen (2011) *The Tourist Gaze 3.0*. Los Angeles: Sage.

Vajpeyi, Ananya (2007) 'Through Western Eyes', *New Statesman*, 13 September, 38–9.

Virilio, Paul (1992) *War and Cinema: The Logistics of Perception*. London: Verso.

Warner, Michael (2002) *Publics and Counter-Publics*. New York: Zone Books.

Whatling, Clare (1997) *Screen Dreams: Fantasising Lesbians in Film*. Manchester: Manchester University Press.

Wilkinson, Tracy (1998) 'Horror of "Sarajevo" Not Exactly Welcome', *Los Angeles Times*, 9 February, http://articles.latimes.com/1998/feb/09/entertainment/ca-17088 (accessed 3 July 2013).

Williams, Linda (1989) *Hard Core: Power, Pleasure and the "Frenzy of the Visible"*. Berkeley: University of California Press.

_____ (1998) 'Mirrors without Memories: Truth, History, and *The Thin Blue Line*', in Barry Keith Grant and Jeannette Sloniowski (eds) *Documenting the Documentary: Close Readings of Documentary Film and Video*. Detroit: Wayne State University Press, 379–96.

_____ (2003) 'Film Bodies: Gender, Genre and Excess', in Barry Keith Grant (ed.) *Film Genre Reader III*. Austin: University of Texas Press, 141–59.

Williams, Melanie (2006) '*9 Songs*', *Film Quarterly*, vol. 59, no. 3, 59–63.

Williams, Raymond (1975) *Television: Technology and Cultural Form*. London: Fontana.

_____ (1975a) *The Long Revolution*. Westport, CT: Greenwood Press.

Wilson, Emma (2003) *Cinema's Missing Children*. London and New York: Wallflower Press.

Wilson, Tony (2002) *24 Hour Party People: What the Sleeve Notes Never Tell You*. Basingstoke and Oxford: Channel 4 Books.

Winterbottom, Michael (2003) 'Little Boy Lost', *The Guardian*, February 28, http://film.guardian.co.uk/features/featurepages/0,,904358,00.html (accessed: 11 June 2013).

_____ (2006) *The Road to Guantánamo* production notes. http://www.roadtoguantanamomovie.com (accessed 11 June 2013).

Wollen, Peter (1985) 'Godard and Counter-Cinema: *Vent d'Est*', in Bill Nichols (ed.) *Movies and Methods, vol. 2*. Berkeley: University of California Press, 500–9.

_____ (1992) 'The Auteur Theory', in Gerald Mast, Marshall Cohen and Leo Braudy (eds) *Film Theory and Criticism: Introductory Readings*. Oxford: Oxford University Press, 589–605.

Wright, Will (1982) 'The Empire Bites the Dust', *Social Text*, vol. 1 no. 6, 120–5.

Zavarzadeh, Mas'ud (1991) *Seeing Films Politically*. New York: State University of New York Press.

Žižek, Slavoj (1991) *Looking Awry: An Introduction to Jacques Lacan through Popular Culture*. Cambridge, MA and London: MIT Press.

INDEX